THE DOCTRINE OF RECOGNITION

SUNY series in Tantric Studies

Paul Muller-Ortega, editor

K Ṣ E M A R Ā J A

THE DOCTRINE OF RECOGNITION

A Translation of Pratyabhijñāhṛdayam

with an Introduction and Notes by
JAIDEVA SINGH

Foreword by
Paul Muller-Ortega

STATE UNIVERSITY OF NEW YORK PRESS

Published by
State University of New York Press, Albany

Printed in the United States
Published in India by Motilal Banarsidass, Delhi, 1980

Editing and design by Sushila Blackman
For information, address State University of New York Press, State University Plaza, Albany, NY 12246

Library of Congress Cataloging-in Publication Data
Kṣemarāja, 11th cent.
[Pratyabhijñāhṛdaya. English]
The doctrine of recognition: a translation of Pratyabhijñāhṛdayam Kṣemarāja: with an introduction and notes by Jaideva Singh, translator.
p. cm.
Translation of: Pratyabhijñāhṛdaya.
Includes Index.
ISBN 0-7914-0150-2. —ISBN 0-7914-0151-0 (pbk.)
1. Kashmir Śaivism—Doctrines—Early works to 1800. I. Singh, Jaideva. II. Title.
BL1281.1545.K7413 1990
294.5′95—dc19 89—4426
CIP

Dedicated
with profound respect to
Swami Lakṣmaṇa Joo, to whom
alone I owe whatever little I know of
Pratyabhijña philosophy

CONTENTS

viii *Foreword*

1 *Preface*

3 *Introduction*

31 *Analysis of Content*

40 *Contents for Sūtras*

41 *The Doctrine of Recognition*

99 *End Notes*

113 *Glossary*

124 *Sanskrit Index*

128 *English Index*

133 *Appendix*

FOREWORD

It is a great pleasure to introduce this book as part of the ongoing program of publication by SUNY Press in the Tantric Studies series. This book contains a translation of a text about enlightenment written in Kashmir in the tenth century. Its author, Kṣemarāja, was the brilliant disciple and interpreter of one the greatest sages India has produced, the tantric Shaiva guru, Abhinavagupta. Perhaps because of this provenance, its subtle and profound teachings about the Goddess of Consciousness, the power of consciousness or *citi-śakti,* remain as fascinating and compelling for us today as they were a millenium ago. Moreover, Kṣemarāja composed his concise Sanskrit *sūtras* about enlightenment specifically for those who were not trained in logic and philosophy, but who nevertheless had received the enlightening grace of Śiva and were desirous of understanding its nature in more detail. As such, the *Pratyabhijñāhṛdayam (PHṛ)* remains one of the best introductions to the tantric Shaivism of Kashmir. We now know that Kashmir Shaivism is one of the most sophisticated and elegant varieties of Tantric Hinduism. In the following pages the reader will gain access to a rare vision of esoteric Hindu spirituality.

We are fortunate that in 1963 Thakur Jaideva Singh undertook to publish a translation of this text in order that a wider audience could profit from its wisdom. The popularity of Singh's translation of the *Pratyabhijñāhṛdayam* led to a second revised edition in 1977, and now, because of the importance of this book, it is being republished in the present SUNY edition with the title *The Doctrine of Recognition*. This book represents a completely new recasting of the book that was first published in India some twenty-six years ago.

Jaideva Singh presented the *Pratyabhijñāhṛdayam* to the public as the first of what would eventually be five important books, which translate and annotate crucial texts of the Kashmir Shaiva tradition.

As part of his intense interest in this tradition, Singh published in subsequent years translations of the *Vijñānabhairava* (1979), the *Spanda Kārikā*s (1980), the *Śiva-Sūtra*s (1979), and, as the culminating labor of his life, the *Parātriṃśika-vivaraṇa* (1988). Unfortunately, this last book appeared posthumously, as Singh died at the age of 93 on May 27, 1986.

These publications may be credited with greatly contributing to the current vogue in Kashmir Shaiva and Tantric studies. Singh devoted himself tirelessly to translating and accurately interpreting the philosophical worldview of Kashmir Shaivism. He was deeply committed to making the vision of reality contained in these texts accessible to the modern reader. Singh did not undertake his journeys of interpretation into this very esoteric tradition entirely unaided. He studied for many years with Gopinath Kaviraj, one of India's foremost scholars as well as practitioners of the Hindu Tantra. In addition, he sought the help of the sole, living representative of the Kashmir Shaiva tradition, Swami Lakshman Joo. He was convinced, as he said shortly before his death, that, "Kashmir Shaivism is the culmination of Indian thought and spirituality." His labor of love constitutes a legacy that will bring joy and illumination to many.

In the following pages, the reader will find a book that opens up a new universe of spiritual inquiry. In a careful rendering of the Sanskrit text that adheres very closely to the original, the book allows us entry into Kṣemarāja's vision of the nature of consciousness. In the short compass of the text, Kṣemarāja presents the journey of consciousness from the level of the Supreme down into embodiment, transmigration, and bondage, and then up again, to enlightenment and liberation. This journey is explicated in the context of the philosophy and practice of *Pratyabhijñā,* the process of recognition. *The Doctrine of Recognition* is at once a work of profound scholarship and an expression of a vital and powerful spiritual search. Since its composition almost a thousand years ago, the text here translated from the Sanskirt has served as the basic, introductory handbook to the abstruse philosophical system of Recognition.

The tradition of Kashmir Shaivism harks back textually to a series of aphorisms said to have been inscribed on a rock by Śiva, and known as the *Śiva-Sūtras.* This foundational text was revealed to a sage by the name of Vasugupta in about the middle of the ninth century. Vasugupta had two disciples: Kallaṭa, to whom are attributed the *Spanda Kārikās,* and Somānanda, author of a text known as the *Śivadṛṣṭi.* It is Somānanda who is usually credited with being the founder of the philosophy of Recognition, the *Pratyabhijñā* branch of Kashmir Shaivism. However, it was Utpalācārya, a disciple of Somānanda, who systematized this philosophy in his *Īśvara pratyabhijiñā-kārikā*s *(ĪPK).* This great work was commented on twice by Abhinavagupta, Kṣemarāja's teacher, to form the complex and abstruse philosophical system of Recognition. Kṣemarāja composed his *PHṛ* especially for those desirous of understanding the process of recognition but who were unable to master the intricacies of this philosophy as it had been devised by Utpaladeva and Abhinavagupta. In the *PHṛ*, Kṣemarāja explores the notion of recognition in terms of the process of meditative absorption catalyzed by the power of the grace-filled *guru.*

Abhinavagupta, Kṣemarāja's guru, is rightly famous for the creative and authoritative manner in which he forged an unprecedented synthesis of āgamic and tantric Shaivism. As a student at the feet of this polymathic teacher, Kṣemarāja had absorbed the brilliant synthesis of Tantrism, Shaivism, alchemy, yoga, and esoteric ritual which comes to form the Trika-Kaula teachings. Kṣemarāja's forte was his capacity to systematically apply Abhinavagupta's Trika-Kaula to the writing of long commentaries on the fundamental texts of the Kashmir Shaiva tradition. Kṣemarāja was a prolific author, and he is credited with a number of works among which may be mentioned commentaries on the *Svacchanda-tantra,* the *Vijñānabhairava,* the *Spanda Kārikās,* the *Śiva-Sūtras,* as well as many others.

By contrast, the *PHṛ* is a relatively short composition of twenty concise *sūtras* with an autocommentary. It was designed to bring a knowledge of the teachings of Recognition to those who were unprepared for the study of Utpaladeva's massive and dense philosophical treatise on the topic, the *IPK,* as well as Abhinavagupta's own commentaries on this text, the *Laghvī* and the *Bṛhatī.* These closely argued treatises represent the core of what could be called Kashmir Shaiva "philosophy." In the *PHṛ*, Kṣemarāja tried to bring the essence of this philosophy to a wider audience of readers.

Moreover, it is clear that the motive for the composition of the *PHṛ* transcends the purely philosophical and is frankly soteriological. The notion of recognition stands at the very heart of the entire Kashmir Shaiva conception of enlightenment. In order to understand it, we must appreciate the philosophical superstructure which upholds Kashmir Shaiva ideas about the nature of reality and the dilemma of transmigration. This superstructure forms the technical horizon within which Kṣemarāja coalesces his vision of the journey of the *citi-śakti,* the power of consciousness.

Curiously, despite the title of the work, it is the *citi-śakti* and *not* recognition which forms the central focus of Kṣemarāja's exposition. *Pratyabhijñā* is not mentioned directly in the *sūtras* and appears only once or twice in the commentary. Nevertheless, the title of the text is still quite apt, because at the end of his exposition, Kṣemarāja has laid out the fundamental elements of the teachings of Recognition. In fact, the title of the text, here rendered as the *Doctrine* of Recognition, could perhaps be more literally rendered as the *Heart* of Recognition. The symbol of the *hṛdaya* employed by Kṣemarāja in the title of his work alludes to Abhinavagupta's Trika-Kaula teachings about the Heart of Śiva and the process of tantric *sādhana.* Thus, the *PHṛ* stands at the intersection of the philosophical and practical–experiential dimensions of Kashmir Shaivism, and works to unite and interconnect them. It is in the Heart that recognition takes place. The Heart is the concealed and supremely secret presence of infinity within the finite, of Śiva within the transmigrating individual. Thus, Kṣemarāja reveals to us in this text the secret of the doctrine of recognition, and that secret resides in the innermost Heart.

Recognition arises out of an internal knowing, which precedes and anticipates a perceptual re-matching. In some sense, memory plays a fundamental role in ordinary recognition. We know about someone, we remember them, and when we see them walking down the street, we match our memory and our previous knowledge of the person with the physical presence of the person, and we recognize them.

In the spiritual process of recognition, because what we recognize is our Self, we re-cognize, re-member, what we already have always known. We remember *that* we remember. A cosmic amnesia lifts, a veil is removed, a miasmic fog drifts away, and there takes place a fundamental shift in our perception of ourselves and of the universe. This shift, which radically restructures our self-experience, is more than memory, however. It is a synthetic activity of consciousness which creates a new and liberating gestalt of wholeness, in which reality is seen as it really is. The fundamental bases of self-knowledge shift in a hitherto unsuspected fashion to reveal the eternal co-presence of the divine and unconstrained consciousness within the finite and limited awareness of the individual. What is recognized is the Self, is ourselves. The nature of that Self is divinity, is Śiva, is blissfulness, and its recognition constitutes an end to all dilemmas, all limitations, all problems. Thus, in the process of recognition, ordinary awareness comes to encompass its own unbounded source. In the ritual and religious language of the tradition, this leads to the ecstatic cry of recognition, *"I am Śiva—Śivo'ham."*

The *PHṛ* summarizes, in the compass of its twenty *sūtras* and their commentary, a vision of the cosmic process in which the human dilemma arises. How does Śiva come to forget that he is Śiva? Why is recognition necessary in the first place? This is a key theological problem of the Kashmir Shaiva tradition, and it is articulated in terms of a paradox. Śiva is the field of unconstricted light and consciousness, and as such displays unlimited freedom and power. Thus, paradoxically, it is only Śiva who has sufficient power to forget himself, to fragment himself, to limit, bind, and constrict himself. This process of fragmentation and bondage takes place because Śiva wills it, and it subsequently involves Śiva (or, as the text would have it, the power of consciousness, the *citi-śakti*) in the cosmogonic process, the process of manifestation. This is the grand and complex process which precipitates the appearance of the universe. As the *PHṛ* describes it, manifestation unfolds in terms of the progressive coagulation of consciousness into energy and matter, technically described by the appearance of the thirty-six *tattva*s. Side by side with this process, there occurs the constriction of consciousness by the three impurities (*mala*s) to form the limited, atomic self known as the *aṇu*. The further operation of *māyā* and the five sheaths (*kañcuka*s) results in the formation of the life-monad known as the *puryaṣṭaka*—the eight-fold subtle body—and finally, the embodied transmigrating self, the *jīva,* or as Kṣemarāja calls him, the *saṃsārin*.

Thus, the great unconstricted light of consciousness, of Śiva, structures itself into the forms and shapes of the universe, as well as into the myriad individual, transmigrating souls. This is the game or the sport of Śiva. It is the play of consciousness which gives rise to the realm of embodiment and of karmic entrapment, as well as to the moment of release and liberation which will finally arise as a result of recognition. In the *PHṛ*, Kṣemarāja carefully and systematically sets out the details of this philosophical and religious vision.

Given the centrality, indeed, the crucial and indispensible nature of the process of recognition to the attainment of enlightenment, the question may arise: how precisely does it come about? What triggers the powerful experience of recognition? Most of the time, recognition arises from the liberating *śaktipāta,* the descent of spiritual energy from Śiva. Ordinarily, the *śaktipāta* is mediated to the practitioner through the grace of the *guru,* the enlightened master. *Kṣ*emarāja felt that he had received this grace from his master, Abhinavagupta. The *PHṛ* thus constitutes a technical narrative of the nature and acquisition of enlightenment, made all the more vivid and urgent by Kṣemarāja's own experience of it. The release of the energy of consciousness is capable of enlightening what is shadowed, of making unbounded what is limited, of liberating what is caught in bondage. Nevertheless, recognition is a kind of non-event. Once it occurs, it is accompanied by the realization that one knew all along what has just been recognized. It is this deeply paradoxical nature of the process which generates an ecstatic and blissful astonishment in the practitioner.

These considerations lead Kṣemarāja to the notion of the *jīvanmukta,* the one who is liberated while still alive. The *PHṛ* places emphasis on the structure of manifestation and the construction of the transmigrating entity, spelled out in terms of the thirty-six *tattva*s or principles, precisely because the successive emanation of these principles also creates the corresponding ladder of return back up to the source. Kṣemarāja is thus able to delineate the various levels of spiritual experience—the *pramātṛs*—as the totality of Śiva is gradually approached. The *PHṛ* is an extended meditation in the *citi-śakti,* on the movement of consciousness into limitation and transmigration, and then out of these into recognition and liberation. The parabolic orbit of the path of consciousness reaches its vertex with the experience of recognition and there it begins its journey of return to Śiva. Impelled by the descent of the power of *śakti,* the actualization of this power in the service of a *guru,* and the various initiatory rituals which continue to dispense and intensify the original descent of power, recognition finally arises. As it does so, it consolidates the victorious acquisition of freedom in this very body.

The present edition by Jaideva Singh facilitates the appreciation of this vision of Kashmir Shaivism. In his Introduction, Singh provides the reader with a classic, short statement on the philosophy of Kashmir Shaivism written in a careful and technically precise way.

Singh's introduction will be especially useful to the first time student of the tradition, as it gives an overview of the history of the text, its author, and the meaning of the abundant technical terminology. In addition, readers of the *PHṛ* in Singh's translation are fortunate to be guided at every step of the way by detailed notes that explain, annotate, and define. Each sūtra is presented in the body of the text in transliterated Sanskrit form, and then translated along with its commentary. Sanskritists will be happy to have the entire Sanskrit text, including both sūtras and commentary, given in an Appendix.

The words of a *siddha* transmit the inherent power of his or her own enlightenment. To read them is to be impelled beyond a merely rational understanding. May the following pages give the reader a taste of the nectar of enlightenment.

Paul E. Muller-Ortega
Department of Religious Studies
Michigan State University
October 1989

Preface to the First Edition

Pratyabhijñāhṛdayam serves as the best introduction to the Pratyabhijñā philosophy of Kashmir. I have had the good fortune of studying this work with Swami Lakshman Joo, who is practically the sole surviving exponent of this system in Kashmir. Swamiji not only embodies the tradition of the school, but he has also practiced the yogic disciplines recommended by it. He has helped me not only by explaining the technical words but also in identifying the sources of most of the quotations occurring in the book. I am deeply grateful to him for his kind help.

The Sanskrit text adopted is that of the Kashmir Sanskrit Series. The translation closely follows the original—with a few words here and there in brackets to make the sense clearer. The Devanagari text appears in the Appendix. A person knowing even a little Sanskrit can follow the translation almost word for word. I have tried to make the translation as flawless as possible. Some of the highly technical terms have been placed as they occur in the original, but their connotation has been elaborated upon in the notes.

An introduction containing the chief features of the Pratyabhijñā system has been provided. An analysis of the contents of each *sūtra* has also been given. Notes on difficult words and terms have been added, as well as a glossary of technical terms.

While the book was at the proof stage, I referred my difficulties with some of the *sūtras* to Dr. Gopinath Kaviraja and profited greatly from his illuminating exposition. I have used his suggestions with advantage in some of the notes. I am deeply grateful to him for his kind help. Acharya Pandit Rameshwar Jha helped to clarify some difficult passages of the text. I therefore offer him my heartfelt thanks.

JAIDEVA SINGH

Preface to the Second Edition

In this edition, both the Introduction and Notes have been considerably enlarged. Three new topics have been added to the Introduction; substantial additions have been made as well to the Notes. For the sake of improved clarity, some alterations have been made to the translation of the text.

With these additions and alterations, the book has been greatly improved and will, it is hoped, be of significant value to the readers.

JAIDEVA SINGH

INTRODUCTION

The Śaiva religion is perhaps the most ancient faith of the world. Sir John Marshall says in his *Mohenjodaro and the Indus Civilization* that excavations in Mohenjodaro and Harappa reveal that Śaivism has a history going back to the Chalcolithic Age or earlier and thus takes its place as the most ancient living faith in the world. Its many offshoots have appeared in different forms throughout the world. In India, there are three main forms of this religio-philosophy: the Vīra-Śaiva form in Deccan-Karṇāṭaka, the Śaiva-siddhānta in Tamila Nāḍu, and the Advaita Śaiva form in Kashmir. Some features are common to all three, but important differences exist also. In this volume, we are concerned with the Advaita Śaiva philosophy of Kashmir.

In India, there is no such thing as an armchair philosophy. Philosophy is not only a way of thought, but also a way of life. It is not born of idle curiosity, nor is it a mere intellectual game. Every philosophy is a religion, and every religion has its philosophy. India's philosopher is not a tall, spectacled professor who dictates notes to a class or weaves cobwebs of theories in his study. Rather he is one moved by a deep inner urge to know the secrets of life, one who lives laborious days of spiritual discipline and who sees the light by the transformation of his life. Moved to compassion for his fellow men, he tries to transmit the truth he experiences to the logical faculties of man. Thus arose philosophy in India.

The Advaita Śaiva philosophy of Kashmir was of this type. For centuries it was imparted as a secret doctrine to the aspirant who had to live it and test it in the laboratory of the Self. In the course of time, only the cult and ritual remained; the philosophical background was forgotten. Although a select few perhaps still knew the philosophical doctrine transmitted by oral tradition, the first thinker known to history to reduce the main principles to the written form was

Vasugupta. He is said to have lived toward the end of the eighth or beginning of the ninth century A.D. Philosophical writing then became an active process in Kashmir that continued for nearly four centuries. The accumulated literature on this system today is so extensive that its study would require almost a lifetime. Some works of the system still remain unpublished.

ŚAIVA LITERATURE

The literature of the Śaiva or Trika system may be broadly divided into three parts: *Āgama Śāstra, Spanda Śāstra,* and *Pratyabhijñā Śāstra.*

Āgama Śāstra

These scriptures, believed to be a revelation, have been handed down from teacher to pupil. Some of the works under this heading are: *Mālinīvijaya, Svacchanda, Vijñānabhairava, Mṛgendra, Rudrayāmala,* and the *Śiva-Sūtras.* Commentaries on the *Śiva-Sūtras* include the *Vṛtti*, the *Vārttika* of Bhāskara and Varadarāja, and the *Vimarśinī* by Kṣemarāja. Commentaries also exist on some of the *tantras.*

Spanda Śāstra

These writings lay down the important doctrines of the system. The main works under this heading are:

The *Spanda Sūtras* or the *Spanda Kārikās,* which elaborate the principles of the *Śiva-Sūtras.* The following commentaries exist on these: *Vivṛti* by Rāmakaṇṭha, *Pradīpikā* by Utpala Vaiṣṇava, *Upandasandoha* by Kṣemarāja, and *Spandanirṇaya* by Kṣemarāja. *Upandasandoha* contains a commentary only on the first kārikā.

Pratyabhijñā Śāstra

This śāstra contains arguments and counter-arguments, discussions, and reasonings. It provides a logical interpretation of the main doctrines of the system. Somānanda composed *Śivadṛṣṭi.* His pupil, Utpala, is credited with another important work, *Īśvarapratyabhijñā.* The latter has the following commentaries: *Vṛtti* by the author himself; *Pratyabhijñāvimarśinī* and *Pratyabhijñā-vivṛti-vimarśinī* by Abhinavagupta.

A digest of the Pratyabhijñā Śāstra, named *Pratyabhijñāhṛdayam,* was prepared by Kṣ*emarāja.* Abhinavagupta's twelve volume *Tantrāloka,* along with his *Tantrālokasāra,* give an exhaustive treatment of all the important doctrines and disciplines of the system.*

PRATYABHIJÑĀHṚDAYAM

This digest of the Pratyabhijñā system was prepared by Kṣemarāja. He was the brilliant pupil of Abhinavagupta, a versatile genius who was a peerless master of tantra, yoga, philosophy, poetics, and dramaturgy. According to Dr. K.C. Pandey, Abhinavagupta flourished in the tenth century A.D. Since Kṣemarāja was his pupil, he must have also lived in the tenth century. Kṣemarāja wrote the following works: *Pratyabhijñāhṛdayam, Spandasandoha, Spandanirṇaya, Svacchandoddyota, Netroddyota, Vijñānabhairavoddyota, Śivasūtra-vimarśinī, Stavacintāmaṇiṭīkā, Parāprāveśikā, Tattvasandoha.*

Very little is known of the life and parentage of Kṣemarāja. It has been very rightly said that his book, *Pratyabhijñāhṛdayam,* occupies the same place in Śaiva or Trika literature as *Vedāntasāra* does in Vedānta. Avoiding all polemics it gives, in a very succinct form, the main tenets of the Pratyabhijñā system. He says at the very outset of his work:

> **इह ये सुकुमारमतयोऽकृततीक्ष्णतर्कशास्त्रपरिश्रमाः शक्तिपातोन्मिषित-पारमेश्वरसमावेशाभिलाषिणः कतिचित् भक्तिभाजः तेषामीश्वरप्रत्यभिज्ञोपदेश-तत्त्वं मनाक् उन्मील्यते ।**

> In this world, there are some devoted people who are undeveloped in reflection and have not taken pains in studying difficult works (like Logic and Dialectics), but who nevertheless aspire after *samāveśa* with the Highest Lord, which blossoms forth with the descent of Śakti. For their sake, the truth of the teachings of Īśvarapratyabhijñā is being explained briefly.

Kṣemarāja regarded the *Īśvarapratyabhijñā* of Utpalācārya as a very great work on this system. His *Pratyabhijñāhṛdayam* is a concise manual for those who, as a result of divine grace, want to know the main principles of "pratyabhijñā," but are unable to study the great

*I am indebted to J.C. Chatterji's *Kashmir Shaivism* for this historical account.

work of Utpalācārya because of their lack of training in Logic and Dialectics. He has succeeded remarkably well in condensing all the important principles of Īśvarapratyabhijñā while avoiding its rigoristic logical discussion. This manual is, therefore, of utmost importance for those who want to have an elementary knowledge of "pratyabhijñā." Kṣemarāja both composed the sūtras and wrote the commentary.

The word *pratyabhijñā* means "re-cognition." The individual Self (or *jīva*) is divine, or Śiva, but he has forgotten his real nature and is identified with his psycho-physical mechanism. The teaching is meant to enable him to recognize that his true nature, his real Self, is none other than Śiva, and to suggest to him the spiritual discipline by which he can attain "at-one-ment" with Him.

The details of the teaching will be found in the body of this book. We may review here the main ideas of the system under the following heads: (1) Ultimate Reality (2) The Universe of the World Process (3) Svātantryavāda and Ābhāsavāda (4) Ṣaḍadhvā (5) Comparison and Contrast with Śaṁkara's Advaitavāda (6) The Individual Self (7) Bondage (8) Liberation.

1. Ultimate Reality

Reality in its ultimate aspect is *cit* or Parāsaṁvit. *Cit* or Parāsaṁvit is untranslatable; generally it is referred to as "consciousness." I have so translated it for want of a better word. But it should be clearly understood that *cit* is not exactly consciousness. The word "consciousness" connotes a subject-object relationship, a knower and known. But *cit* is not relational. It is just the changeless principle of all changing experience. It is Parāsaṁvit. It has, so to speak, the immediacy of feeling where neither the "I," nor the "This," is distinguished. It is the "coalescence into undivided unity" of "I" and "This." The word "sciousness" may, to some extent, express the idea contained in *cit* or Parāsaṁvit. To use the verb contained in consciousness, the Ultimate Reality or Supreme Self is the Self "sciring itself." In the words of the Pratyabhijñā Śāstra, it is *prakāśavimarśamaya*. The word *prakāśa* again is untranslatable. Literally, it means light, illumination. In the words of *Kaṭhopaniṣad—Tameva bhāntam anubhāti sarvam, tasya bhāsā sarvamidam vibhāti.* "It shining, everything happens to shine. By its light alone does all this appear." Śāṅkara Vedānta also calls Ultimate Reality "prakāśa;" but the sun is *prakāśa;* even a diamond is *prakāśa*. What is the difference between the two?

The Śaiva philosophy says, "Ultimate Reality is not simply *prakāśa*; it is also *vimarśa.*" What is this *vimarśa?* Ultimate Reality is not only "sciousness" (*prakāśa*), but a "sciousness" that also "scires" itself (*vimarśa*). It is not simply *prakāśa,* lying inert like a diamond, but it surveys itself. This sciring or surveying by the Ultimate Reality is called *vimarśa.* As Kṣemarāja has put it in his *Parāprāveśikā*, it is *"akṛtrimāham iti visphuraṇam;"* it is the non-relational, immediate awareness of "I." What this *akṛtrima-aham* is, we shall see later on. If Ultimate Reality were merely *prakāśa* and not also *vimarśa,* it would be powerless and inert. *Yadi nirvimarśaḥ syāt anīśvaro jaḍaśca prasajyeta* (*Parāprāveśikā,* p. 2): It is this pure I-consciousness or *vimarśa* that is responsible for the manifestation, maintenance, and reabsorption of the universe.

Cit "scires" itself as *Cidrūpiṇī Śakti.* This sciring itself as *Cidrūpiṇī Śakti* is *vimarśa.* Therefore, *vimarśa* has different names, such as *parāśakti, parāvāk, Svātantrya, aiśvarya, kartṛtva, sphurattā, Sāra, hṛdaya, Spanda.* (See *Parāprāveśika,* p. 2).

It will thus be seen that the Ultimate Reality is not only Universal Consciousness but also Universal Psychic Energy or Power. This all-inclusive Universal Consciousness is also called *anuttara*—the Reality beyond which there is nothing higher—the Highest Reality, the Absolute. It is both transcendental (*viśvottīrna*) and immanent (*viśvmaya*).

The Śaiva philosophy has been called Realistic Idealism by some writers. I do not think this is a happy characterization. The approach of the Idealists of the West is entirely different from that of the thinkers of Śaiva philosophy. To characterize it in terms of the Western Idealists is only to create confusion. The word "idea" has played havoc in Western philosophy, and it would not be right to import that havoc into Śaiva philosophy. Ultimate Reality is not a mere "idea," whatever that may mean, but the Self underlying all reality; the Changeless Principle of all manifestation.

2. Manifestation: The Universe or the World Process

Whether we refer to Ultimate Reality as Sciousness or Consciousness, it has infinite powers and contains, in potential form, all that is ever likely to be. It is the *svabhāva,* or nature, of Ultimate Reality to manifest. If Ultimate Reality did not manifest, it would no longer be consciousness or Self, but something like an object or not-Self.

As Abhinavagupta puts it:

अस्थास्यदेकरूपेण वपुषा चेन्महेश्वरः ।
महेश्वरत्त्वं संवित्त्वं तदत्यक्ष्यद् घटादिवत् ॥

—Tantr. III.100

If the Highest Reality did not manifest in infinite variety, but remained cooped up within its solid singleness, it would neither be the Highest Power nor Consciouness, but something like a jar.

We have seen that Ultimate Reality or Parama Śiva is *prakāśa-vimarśamaya*. In such a state, the "I" and the "This" are in a state of undivided unity. The "I" is the *prakāśa* aspect, and the "This" or Its consciousness of It as itself is the *vimarśa* aspect. This *vimarśa* is *svātantrya,* Absolute will, or *Śakti*. This *Śakti* is only another aspect of the Supreme Self. In the Supreme experience, the so-called "This" is nothing but the Self. There is one Self experiencing Itself. This *vimarśa* or *Śakti* is not contentless. It contains all that is to be.

यथा न्यग्रोधबीजस्थः शक्तिरूपो महाद्रुमः ।
तथा हृदयबीजस्थं विश्वमेतच्चराचरम् ॥

—*Parātriṁśikā 24*

As the great banyan tree lies only in the form of *potency* in the seed, even so the entire universe with all the mobile and immobile beings lies as a potency in the heart of the Supreme.

Another image often used is that of the peacock. Just as a peacock with all its variegated plumage lies as a mere potential in the plasma of its egg, so the entire universe lies in the Śakti of the Supreme. The Śakti of the Supreme is called *citi* or *parāśakti* or *parāvāk*.

Parama Śiva has infinite Śakti, but the following five may be considered the main ones:

1. *Cit*—the power of Self-revelation by which the Supreme shines by Himself. In this aspect the Supreme is known as Śiva.
2. *Ānanda*—the aspect of absolute bliss. This is also called *Svātantrya*—absolute Will which is able to do anything without any external aid. (*Svātantryam ānandaśaktiḥ: Tantrasāra-* Āhn. 1). In this aspect, the Supreme is known as Śakti. In a sense, *cit* and *ānanda* are the very *svarūpa* (nature) of the Supreme. The rest may be called His Śaktis.

3. *Icchā*—the Will to do this or that, to create. In this aspect, He is known as Sadāśiva or Sādākhya.

4. *Jñāna*—the power of knowing. In this aspect, He is known as Īśvara.

5. *Kriyā*—the power of assuming any and every form (*Sarvākārayogitvam Kriyāśaktiḥ: Tantrasāra* Āhn.1). In this aspect, He is known as Sadvidyā or Śuddha Vidyā.

The Universe is nothing but an opening out (*unmeṣa*) or expansion (*prasara*) of the Supreme or rather of the Supreme as Śakti.

Tattvas of the Universal Experience (1-5)

We have seen that Parama Śiva has two aspects: transcendental (*viśvottīrṇa*) and immanent or creative (*viśvamaya*).

1. *Śiva tattva* is the creative aspect of Parama Śiva. Again the term tattva is untranslatable; it means the "thatness" of a thing. The nearest English word is "principle."*Śiva tattva* is the initial creative movement (*prathama spanda*) of Parama Śiva. As has been said in the first verse of the *Ṣaṭtriṁśat-tattva-sandoha:*

यदयमनुत्तरमूर्तिर्निजेच्छयाखिलमिदं जगत्स्रष्टुम ।
पस्पन्दे स स्पन्दः प्रथमः शिवतत्त्वमुच्यते तज्ज्ञैः ॥

> When Anuttara, or the Absolute, by His *Svātantrya,* or Absolute Will, feels like letting go of the Universe contained in Him, the first vibration or throb of this Will is known as Śiva.

2. *Śakti tattva* is the energy of Śiva. Śakti, in her *jñāna* aspect, is the principle of negation (*niṣedha-vyāpāra-rūpā*). Śakti, at first, negates the "This" or the objective side of experience in Śiva. The state in which objectivity is negated is called the Void. The *cit* or Parāsaṁvit, the "I" and the "This," are indistinguishably united; in *Śiva tattva,* the "This" is withdrawn through the operation of *Śakti tattva,* so that the "I" side of the experience alone remains. This state is called *Anāśrita-Śiva* by Kṣemarāja, who says:

श्री परमशिवः ··· पूर्वं चिदैक्याख्यातिमयानाश्रितशिवपर्यायशून्यातिशून्यात्मतया प्रकाशाभेदेन प्रकाशमानतया स्फुरति ।

> Śiva, in this state, appears as a mere "I," devoid of any objective content. For Śiva to appear as the Universe, a break in the unitary experience becomes necessary. But this break is only a passing phase. To the subjectivity disengaged from the objective content,

> the Universe is presented again, not as an indistinguishable unity but as an "I-This." In this phase, both are distinguishable but not separable, as they form part of the same Self.

Śakti polarizes Consciousness into *Aham* and *Idam* (I and This)—subject and object.

Śakti, however, is not separate from Śiva, but is Śiva Himself in His creative aspect. She is His *Aham-vimarśa* (I-consciousness), His *unmukhatā* (intentness to create). Maheśvarānanda put it beautifully in his *Mahārthamañjarī* (p. 40, Trivandrum Edition):

> स एव विश्वमेषितुं ज्ञातुं कर्तुं चोन्मुखो भवन् ।
> शक्तिस्वभावः कथितो हृदयत्रिकोणमधुमांसलोल्लासः ॥

> He [Śiva] Himself, full of joy, enhanced by the honey of the three corners of his heart—Icchā or Will, Jñāna or Knowledge, Kriyā or Action—raising up His face to gaze at [His own splendor] is called Śakti.

Maheśvarānanda continues:

> यदा स्वहृदयवर्तिनमुक्तरूपमर्थतत्त्वं बहिःकर्तुमुन्मुखो भवति तदा शक्ति-रिति व्यवह्रियते.

> When He becomes intent to roll out the entire splendor of the Universe that is contained in His heart (in a germinal form), He is designated as Śakti.

Śakti is therefore His intentness to create; the active or kinetic aspect of Consciousness.

An idea parallel to *vimarśa* or *unmukhatā* is found in the *Chāndogyopaniṣad* (6.2. 1-3):

> सदेव सौम्य इदमग्र आसीदेकमेवाद्वितीयम्···तदैक्षत, बहु स्याम्, प्रजायेय इति ।

> At first [logically, not chronologically] there was only "Sat"—all alone without a second. He gazed and thought to Himself "May I be many, may I procreate!"

This *Īkṣitṛtva* or *Īkṣitakarma* is parallel to *vimarśa* or *unmukhatā*, but the implications of this *Īkṣitakarma* have not been developed by Śāṅkara Vedānta.

The Śaiva philosophy does not conceive of the Supreme as a logomachist but as an artist. Just as an artist cannot contain his delight within himself but pours it out into a song, picture, or poem, so the supreme Artist pours out the delightful wonder of His splendor into manifestation or creation. Kṣemarāja gives expression to the same idea in his commentary on Utpaladeva's *Stotrāvalī:*

आनन्दोच्छलिता शक्तिः सृजत्यात्मानमात्मना ।

Śakti, thrown up by delight, lets Herself go forth into manifestation.

All manifestation is, therefore, only a process of experiencing the creative ideation of Śiva. In *Śakti tattva,* the *ānanda* aspect of the Supreme is predominant.

Śiva and Śakti *tattvas* can never be disjoined; they remain forever united whether in creation or dissolution—Śiva as the Experiencing Principle, experiencing Himself as pure "I," and Śakti as profound bliss. Strictly speaking, *Śiva-Śakti tattva* is not an emanation or *ābhāsa,* but the Seed of all emanation.

3. *Sadāśiva* or *Sādākhya Tattva.* The will (Icchā) to affirm the "This" side of the Universal Experience is known as *Sadāśiva Tattva* or *Sādākhya Tattva.* In Sadāśiva, Icchā or Will is predominant. The experience of this stage is I *am.* Since "am" or "being" is affirmed in this stage, it is called *Sādākhya Tattva;* (*sat* meaning "being") but "am" implies "this" (I *am,* but "am" what?—I am "this"). The experience of this stage is therefore "I am this," but the "this" is only a hazy experience (*asphuṭa*). The predominant side is still "I." The Ideal Universe is experienced as an indistinct something in the depth of consciousness. That is why this experience is called *nimeṣa.*

निमेषोऽन्तः सदाशिवः

The "This" (*Idam*) is faintly experienced by "I" (*Aham*) as a part of the One Self; the emphasis is, however, on the "I" side of experience. The "This" (*Idam*), or the universe, at this stage is like a hazy idea of the picture that an artist has at the initial stage of his creation. Rājānaka Ānanda in his *Vivaraṇa* on *Ṣaṭtriṁśat-tattvasandoha* (p. 3) rightly says:

तत्र प्रोन्मीलितमात्रचित्रकल्पतया इदमंशस्य अस्फुटत्वात् इच्छाप्राधान्यम् ।

In that state, the "This" side of the Experience is hazy, like a picture of an artist that is about to be portrayed and hence that is still in an ideal state (in the state of an idea). Hence in this state, Will is predominant.

So Kṣemarāja says in his *Pratyabhijñāhṛdaya:*

सदाशिवतत्त्वेऽहन्ताच्छादितास्फुटेदन्तामयं विश्वम् ।

The Universe in *Sadāśiva tattva* is *asphuṭa* or hazy, dominated by a clear consciousness of "I." *Sadāśiva tattva* is the first manifestation.

For manifestation (*ābhāsa*), there must be a perceiver or knower and perceived or known—that is, a subject and an object. In this universal condition, both are bound to be Consciousness, for there is nothing other than Consciousness. Consciousness in this aspect becomes perceptible to Itself; hence a subject and an object.

4. *Īśvara* or *Aiśvarya Tattva.* In the next stage of the Divine experience, *Idam*—the "This" side of the total experience—becomes a little more defined (*sphuṭa*). This is known as *Īśvara Tattva.* It is *unmeṣa* or the distinct blossoming of the Universe. At this stage, *jñāna* or knowledge is predominant. There now exists a clear idea of what is to be created. Rājānaka Ānanda says in his *Vivaraṇa*:

अत्र वेद्यजातस्य स्फुटावभासनात् ज्ञानशक्त्युद्रेकः ।

At this stage the objective side of experience, the "This," or the Universe, is clearly defined; therefore *jñāna-śakti* is predominant.

Just as an artist has at first a hazy idea of the picture he has to produce but later a clearer image begins to emerge in his mind's eye, so at the Sadāśiva stage the Universe is just a hazy idea, but at the Īśvara stage it becomes clearer. The experience of Sadāśiva is "I am this." The experience of Īśvara is "*This* am I."

5. *Sadvidyā* or *Śuddhavidyā Tattva.* In the *Sadvidyā tattva,* the "I" and the "this" side of experience are equally balanced, like the two pans of an evenly held scale (*samadhṛtatulāpuṭanyāyena*). At this stage, Kriyā Śakti is predominant. The "I" and "This" are recognized in this state with such equal clarity that while both "I" and "This" are still identified, they can be clearly distinguished in thought. The experience of this stage may be called diversity-in-unity (*bhedābhedavimarśanātmaka*). While the "This" is clearly distinguished from "I," it is still felt to be a part of the "I" or Self. Both "I" and "This" refer to the same thing (they have *samānādhikaraṇa*).

In *Śiva tattva,* there is the I-experience (*Aham vimarśa*); in Sadāśiva, there is the I-This experience (*Aham-idam vimarśa*); in *Īśvara tattva*, there is the This-I experience (*Idamaham vimarśa*). In each of these experiences, the emphasis is on the first term. In *Śuddhavidyā tattva,* there is equal emphasis on both. (*Aham Aham—Idam Idam.* I am I—This is This). Since this experience is an intermediate stage—between the higher (*para*) and lower (*apara*)—in which there is a sense of difference, it is called *parāpara daśā.*

It is called *Sadvidyā* or *Śuddhavidyā,* because at this stage the true relation of things is experienced. Up to this stage, all experience is ideal (in the form of an idea). Hence it is called the perfect or "pure order" (*śuddhādhvan*)—a manifestation in which the *svarūpa* or real nature of the Divine is not yet veiled.

The Tattvas of the Limited Individual Experience
Māyā and the Five Kañcukas (6-11)

At this stage, *Māyā tattva* begins its play. From this stage onward, there is *aśuddhādhvan* or the order in which the real nature of the Divine is concealed. All this happens because of Māyā, and her *kañcukas.* Māyā is derived from the root *mā,* "to measure out." That which makes experience measurable or limited, severs "This" from "I" and "I" from "This," and excludes things from one another, is Māyā. Up to Sadvidyā, the experience was Universal; the "This" meant "All-this"—the total universe. Under the operation of Māyā, "this" means merely "this," as distinguished from everything else. From now on, limitation (*saṅkoca*) starts. Māyā draws a veil (*āvaraṇa*) on the Self, owing to which one forgets one's real nature; thus Māyā generates a sense of difference.

The products of Māyā are the five *kañcukas* or coverings. We may note them briefly:

- *Kalā.* This reduces the universal authorship (*sarvakartṛtva*) of the Universal Consciousness and brings about limitation with respect to authorship or efficacy.
- *Vidyā.* This reduces the omniscience (*sarvajñatva*) of the Universal Consciousness and brings about limitation with respect to knowledge.
- *Rāga.* This reduces the total satisfaction (*pūrṇatva*) of the Universal and brings about desire for this or that.
- *Kāla.* This reduces the eternity (*nityatva*) of the Universal and brings about limitation with respect to time, i.e., division of past, present, and future.
- *Nityati.* This reduces the freedom and pervasiveness (*svatantratā* and *vyāpakatva*) of the Universal and brings about limitation with respect to cause and space.

The Tattvas of the Limited Individual: Subject-Object

12. Puruṣa

Śiva thus subjects Himself to Māyā and, putting on the five *kañcukas* or cloaks, which limit His universal knowledge and power, becomes Puruṣa or the individual subject. Puruṣa does not merely mean a human being, but every sentient being that is so limited.

Puruṣa is also known as *aṇu,* which literally means point. Point here does not mean a spatial point, for being divine in essence, *aṇu* cannot be spatial. Puruṣa is called *aṇu* because of the limitation of the divine perfection:

पूर्णत्वाभावेन परिमितत्वादणुत्वम् ।

13. Prakṛti

While Puruṣa is the subjective manifestation of the "I am this" experience of Sadvidyā, Prakṛti is the objective manifestation. According to Trika, Prakṛti is the objective effect of Kalā—

वेद्यमात्रं स्फुटं भिन्नं प्रधानं सूयते कला ।

—*Tantrāl.,* Āhn. 9

Prakṛti is the barest objectivity in contrast with Puruṣa who is vedaka or subject. The *guṇas* of Prakṛti exist in a state of equilibrium.

Sāṅkhya and Trika differ in their conception of Prakṛti. Sāṅkhya believes that Prakṛti is universal for all the Puruṣas. Trika believes that each Puruṣa has a different Prakṛti. Prakṛti is the root or matrix of objectivity.

Prakṛti has three *guṇas*—threads or constituents: sattva, rajas, and tamas (producing respectvely *sukha, duḥkha,* and *moha*). Prakṛti is the Śāntā Śakti of Śiva and the *guṇas* sattva, rajas, and tamas are the gross forms of His Śaktis—Jñāna, Icchā, and Kriyā respectively.

Puruṣa is the experient (*bhoktā*) and Prakṛti is the experienced (*bhogyā*).

The Tattvas of Mental Operation

Buddhi, Ahaṁkāra, and Manas (14-16)

Prakṛti differentiates into *antaḥkaraṇa* (the psychic apparatus), *indriyas* (senses), and *bhūtas* (matter). First, we will examine *antaḥkaraṇa.* Literally, it means the inner instrument (the psychic apparatus of the individual). It consists of the *tattvas, buddhi, ahaṁkāra,* and *manas,* through which mental operation takes place.

▪ *Buddhi*. The first *tattva* of Prakṛti, *buddhi* is the ascertaining intelligence (*vyavasāyātmikā*). Two kinds of objects are reflected in *buddhi*: (1) external, such as a jar, the reflection of which is received through the eye, and (2) internal—the images built out of the impressions left behind on the mind (*saṁskāras*).

▪ *Ahaṁkāra*. This is the product of *buddhi*. It is the I-consciousness and the power of self-appropriation.

▪ *Manas*. As the product of *ahaṁkāra, manas* cooperates with the senses in building up perceptions; it builds up images and concepts.

The Tattvas of Sensible Experience (17-31)

1. The five powers of sense-perception—Jñānendriyas or Buddhīndriyas—are the products of *ahaṁkāra*. The five powers are:

Smelling (*ghrāṇendriya*)
Tasting (*rasanendriya*)
Seeing (*cakṣurindriya*)
Feeling by touch (*sparśanendriya*)
Hearing (*śravaṇendriya*)

2. The five *karmendriyas* or powers of action are also products of *ahaṁkāra*. These powers are:

Speaking (*vāgindriya*)
Handling (*hastendriya*)
Locomotion (*pādendriya*)
Excreting (*pāyvindriya*)
Sexual action and restfulness (*upasthendriya*)

The *indriyas* are not sense-organs, but powers that operate through the sense-organs.

3. The five *tanmātras,* or primary elements of perception, likewise are products of *ahaṁkāra*. Literally *tanmātra* means "that only." These are the general elements of sense-perception:

Sound-as-such (*śabda-tanmātra*)
Touch-as-such (*sparśa-tanmātra*)
Color-as-such (*rūpa-tanmātra*)
Flavor-as-such (*rasa-tanmātra*)
Odor-as-such (*gandha-tanmātra*)

The Tattvas of Materiality
The Five Bhūtas (32-36)

The five gross elements or the *pañca-Mahābhūtas* are the products of the five *tanmātras*.

Ākāśa (produced from *śabda-tanmātra*)
Vāyu (produced from *sparśa-tanmātra*)
Teja or Agni (produced from *rūpa-tanmātra*)
Āpas (produced from *rasa-tanmātra*)
Pṛthivī (produced from *gandha-tanmātra*).

3. Svātantryavāda and Ābhāsavāda

Svātantryavāda

The Absolute in this system is known as *cit*, Paramaśiva, or Maheśvara. It is called Maheśvara not in the ordinary sense of God as the first cause that is to be inferred from the order and design in Nature. It is called Maheśvara rather because of its absolute sovereignty of Will, *sva-tantratā* or *svātantrya*. This absolute Sovereignty or Free Will is not a blind force but the *svabhāva* (own being) of the Universal Consciousness (*cit*). It is this sovereign Free Will that brings about the objectification of its ideation. It is free inasmuch as it does not depend on anything external to it; it is free and potent to become anything. It is beyond all the categories of time, space, causality, etc.; these owe their origin to it.

चितिः प्रत्यवमर्शात्मा परावाक्स्वरसोदिता ।
स्वातंत्र्यमेतन्मुख्यम् तदैश्वर्यं परमात्मनः ॥

—Īśvara. Pr. I, p. 203-4

The Divine Power is known as citi. Its essence is Self-Consciousness. It is also known as Parā Vāk. It is in itself ever present, eternal. It is *svātantrya*. It is the main power of the Supreme Self.

Parāvāk, vimarśa, aiśvarya are only the synonyms of Svātantrya.

सा स्फुरत्ता महासत्ता देशकालाविशेषिणी ।
सैषा सारतया प्रोक्ता हृदयं परमेष्ठिनः ॥

—Īśvara. Pr. I, p. 207-8

This *citi* or power of Universal Consciousness is the inner, creative flash which, though in itself unchanging, is the source of all apparent change; it is *mahāsattā* or absolute being. Inasmuch as it is free to be anything, it is the source of all that can be said to exist in any way. It is beyond the determinations of space and time. In essence, this Free, Sovereign Will may be said to be the very heart or nucleus of the Divine Being.

Svātantrya or Māheśvarya means Absolute Sovereignty or Freedom of Will. It connotes unimpeded activity of the Divine Will and is an expression of Self-Consciousness.

स्वातंत्र्य च नाम यथेच्छं तत्रेच्छाप्रसरस्य अविघातः ।

> Svātantrya means the Power to do according to one's will; it is the unimpeded, unrestrained flow of expression of the Divine Will.

Svātantryavāda, or the doctrine of the Absolute Sovereignty and Freedom of the Divine Will to express or manifest itself in any way it likes, is beautifully explained in the following words by Abhinavagupta:

तस्मादनपह्नवनीयः प्रकाशविमर्शात्मा संवित्स्वभावः परमशिवो भगवान् स्वातंत्र्यादेव रुद्रादिस्थावरान्तप्रमातृरूपतया नीलसुखादिप्रमेयरूपतया च अनतिरिक्तयापि अतिरिक्तया इव स्वरूपानाच्छादिकया संविद्रूपनान्तरीयिकस्वातंत्र्यमहिम्ना प्रकाशत इति अयं स्वातंत्र्यवादः प्रोन्मीलितः

—Īś. Pr. V.V. Pt. 1, p. 9

> Therefore the Lord, Parama Śiva (the Absolute Reality), whose own being is Consciousness of the nature of Prakāśa and Vimarśa, who, as the undeniable, ever-present Reality, appears as subject (from Rudra down to immovable entities) and as objects (like blue, pleasure, etc. which appear as if separate, though in essence they are not separate) through the glorious might of *Svātantrya* (Free Will), which is inseparable from Saṁvit (Universal Consciousness), and which does not conceal in any way the real nature of the Supreme. This is the exposition of *Svātantrya-vāda* (the doctrine of Svātantrya).

Ābhāsavāda

From the point of view of the creativity of Ultimate Reality, this philosophy is known as *svātantryavāda;* from the point of view of its manifestation, it is known as *ābhāsavāda*.

In the Ultimate Reality, the entire manifestation is in perfect unity, an undifferentiated mass, just as the variegated plumage of the peacock, with its beautiful, rich color, lies as an undifferentiated mass in the plasma of its egg. This is called, in this system, the analogy of the plasma of the peacock's egg (*mayūrāṇḍarasanyāya*).

The underlying principle of all manifestation is *cit* or pure Universal Consciousness. The world of ever-changing appearances is only an expression of *cit* or *Saṁvid*. All that appears in any form, whether as object, subject, knowledge, means of knowledge or senses, all that exists in any way, is only an *ābhāsa*—a manifestation of the Universal Consciousness. *Ābhāsa* is manifestation or appearance in a limited way. Every kind of manifestation has some sort of limitation. Everything in existence is a configuration of *ābhāsas*.

"दर्पणबिम्बे यद्वन् नगरग्रामादिचित्रमविभागि ।
भातिविभागेनैव च परस्परं दर्पणादपि च ॥
विमलतमपरमभैरवबोधात् तद्वत् विभागशून्यमपि ।
अन्योन्यं च ततोऽपि च विभक्तमाभाति जगदेतत् ॥

—Paramārthasāra, 12-13

> Just as in a clear mirror, varied images of city, village, etc., appear as different from one another and from the mirror, though they are non-different from the mirror, so the world, though non-different from the purest consciousness of Parama Śiva, appears as different both with respect to its varied objects and that Universal Consciousness.

Ābhāsas are explained by the analogy of reflection in a mirror. Just as a reflection is not in any way different from the mirror, but appears as something different, so *ābhāsas* are not different from Śiva and yet appear as different. In a mirror, a village or a tree or a river appear different from the mirror, but are, truly speaking, no different from it. Similarly, the world reflected in the Universal Consciousness is not different from it.

Two exceptions have to be noted, however, in the mirror analogy. First, in the case of the mirror an external object is reflected; in the case of Maheśvara or Universal Consciousness, it is its own ideation that is reflected. In the case of the mirror, external light is what makes reflection possible; Universal Consciousness, however, is its own light; it is the Light of all lights and does not require any external light.

Second, the mirror being non-conscious does not know the reflections within itself, but the Universal Consciousness knows its own ideation, which appears in itself. *Ābhāsas* are nothing but the ideation of the Universal Consciousness appearing as external to the empirical subject.

अन्तर्विभाति सकलं जगदात्मनीह
यद्वद् विचित्ररचना मकुरान्तराले ।

बोधः पुनर्निजविमर्शनसारयुक्त्या
विश्वं परामृशति नो मकुरस्तथा ॥

—quoted by Yogarāja in Paramārthasāra, p. 39

> Just as various objects appear within a mirror, so the entire universe appears within Consciousness or the Self. Consciousness, however, owing to its power of *vimarśa* or Self-consciousness, knows the world; not so the mirror its objects.

All *ābhāsas* rise, like waves in the sea of the Universal Consciousness. Just as there is neither loss nor gain to the sea with the rise and disappearance of the waves, so there is neither loss nor gain to the Universal Consciousness because of the appearance and disappearance of the *ābhāsas.* They appear and disappear but the underlying Consciousness is unchanging. The *ābhāsas* are nothing but the external projection of the ideation of the Divine.

चिदात्मैव हि देवोऽन्तःस्थितमिच्छावशाद्बहिः ।
योगीव निरुपादानमर्थजातं प्रकाशयेत् ॥

—Īś. Pr I. 5.7

> The Divine Being, whose essence is cit (Universal Consciousness), makes the collection of objects that are internally contained appear outside by His Will without any external material, as a Yogi [makes his mental objects appear outside by his mere will].

The Divine Being does not create like a pot-maker, shaping clay into pots. *Sṛṣṭi* simply means to manifest outside what is contained within. The Divine does not require any external material for this; it is accomplished by His mere Will power.

Things that are identical with the Divine Being's knowledge or *jñāna* appear by His Will as *jñeya* or objects; things that are identical with His Self or "I" appear as "this," or the universe. To the empirical subjects, they appear as something external.

It is the Universal Consciousness itself that appears in the form of subjects and objects. Therefore, this appearance cannot be called false. This appearance makes no difference to the fullness or perfection of the Universal Consciousness.

In this philosophy, *Svātantryavāda* stands in contradistinction to *vivartavāda* and *ābhāsavāda* to *pariṇāmavāda*.

4. Ṣaḍadhvā

From another point of view, that of *parāśakti,* manifestation or creative descent is described in the following way:

There is an unbounded potency or basic continuum of power, which is known as *nāda.* This potency condenses itself into a dynamic point or center, called *bindu.* The condensation is not a process in time or space; it is the source of all manifestation. In the highest stage of manifestation, *vācaka* and *vācya* (the indicator and the indicated, the word and object) are one. Six paths or steps of creative descent (*adhvās*) follow; these are known as Ṣaḍadhvā. First of all, there is the polarity of *varṇa* and *kalā.* Primarily, *kalā* is the aspect by which Reality manifests itself as power for evolving universes. The transcendent aspect of Reality, or Parama Śiva, is known as *niṣkala*, for it transcends *kalā* or creativity. The immanent aspect of Śiva is *sakala*; for it is concerned with creativity.

But in the present context, coming after *nāda-bindu, kalā* means a phase, an aspect of creativity. It is here that things begin to differentiate from an integrated whole. *Vācaka* and *vācya* (index and object), which were one at the *parāvāk* stage, begin to differentiate. The first *adhvā* or step of this differentiation is the polarity of *varṇa* and *kalā.* As Swāmī Pratyagātmānanda Saraswatī puts it, *varṇa* in this context does not mean letter or color or class, but a "function-form" of the object projected from *bindu. Varṇa,* therefore, connotes "the characteristic measure-index of the function-form associated with the object." *Varṇa* is the "function-form," *kalā* is the "predicable."

The next stage in the subtle plane is that of *mantra* and *tattva. Mantra* is the "appropriate function-form" or basic formula of the next creative descent—*tattva. Tattva* is the inherent principle; the source and origin of subtle structural forms.

The third and final polarity is that of *pada* and *bhuvana. Bhuvana* is the universe as it appears to apprehending entities like ourselves. *Pada* is the actual formulation of that universe by mind reaction and speech.

The Ṣaḍadhvā may be briefly indicated in the following table:

Vācaka or *śabda*	*Vācya* or *artha*
varṇa	kalā
mantra	tattva
pada	bhuvana

The *trika* or triad on the *vācaka* side is known as *kālādhvā;* the *trika* or triad on the *vācya* side is known as *deśādhvā.*

Varṇādhvā is of the nature of *pramā*. It is the resting place of *prameya* (object), *prāmāṇa* (means of knowledge), and *pramātā* (experient). *Varṇa* is of two kinds: *non-māyīya* and *māyīya*. The *māyīya varṇas* arise out of the *non-māyīya*. The *non-māyīya varṇas* are pure, natural, without limitation, and innumerable. The Vācaka Śakti (indicative power) of *non-māyīya varṇas* is inherent in the *māyīya varṇas,* just as power of heating is inherent in fire.

The *kalās* are five in number: (1) *nivṛtti kalā,* (2) *pratiṣṭhā kalā,* (3) *vidyā kalā,* (4) *śāntā* or *śānti kalā,* and (5) *śāntyatītā kalā.*

As for the *tattvas* and *bhuvanas* contained in each *kalā,* see the Diagram on page 97. According to Abhinavagupta, there are 118 *bhuvanas;* others claim there are 224.

5. Comparison and Contrast with Śaṁkara's Advaitavāda

Śaṁkara's philosophy is known as *Śānta brahmavāda, Kevalādvaitavāda,* or sometimes, as *Māyā-Vedānta-vāda.* The Śaiva philosophy of Kashmir is known as *Īśvarādvayavāda* or *Pratyabhijñā* or *Trika.* Since Śaṁkara believes that *brahman* has no activity, his philosophy is mostly characterized as *Śāntabrahmavāda,* or the philosophy of inactive *brahman,* by the Śaiva philosophers.

The first salient difference between *Śāntabrahmavāda* and *Īśvarādvayavāda* is that, according to the former, the characteristic of *cit* or *brahman* is only *prakāśa* or *jñāna,* whereas according to the latter, it is both *prakāśa* and *vimarśa*. In other words, according to Śaṁkara, the characteristic of *brahman* is only *jñāna* (knowledge); according to *Īśvarādvayavāda,* it is both *jñātṛtva* (or knowledge) and *kartṛtva* (activity). Śaṁkara thinks that *kriyā* or activity belongs only to the *jīva* or the empirical subject and not to *brahman*. He takes *kriyā* in a very narrow sense. Śaiva philosophy takes *kartṛtva* (the power to act) in a broad sense. According to it, even *jñāna* is an activity of the Divine. Without activity, *cit* or the Divine being would be inert and incapable of bringing about anything. Since Parama Śiva is *svatantra* (has sovereign Free Will), therefore he is a *kartā* (doer). As Pāṇini puts it **स्वतन्त्रः कर्ता** "only a free-willed being is a doer." *Svātantrya* (Free Will) and *kartṛtva* (the power to act) are practically the same thing.

In *Śāntabrahmavāda, brahman* is entirely inactive. When *brahman* is associated with *avidyā,* it becomes Īśvara and is endowed with the power to act. The real activity belongs to *avidyā*. The activity of Īśvara ceases when he is dissociated from *avidyā*. Śaṁkara says categorically:

तदेवमविद्यात्मकोपाधिपरिच्छेदापेक्षमेवेश्वरस्येश्वरत्वं सर्वंज्ञत्वं सर्वंशक्तित्वं चं, न परमार्थंतो विद्ययापास्तसर्वोपाधिस्वरूपे आत्मनीशित्रीशितव्यसर्वंज्ञत्वादि व्यवहार उपपद्यते

—Br. Sū. 2. 1.14

> Thus the potency of Īśvara, his omniscience and omnipotence, is contingent upon the limitation caused by the condition or association of *avidyā* (primal ignorance). In the highest sense, when all conditions are removed by *vidyā* (spiritual illumination) from the Ātman, its use of potency, omniscience, etc., would become inappropriate.

So all activity in the case of Īśvara is, according to Śaṁkara, due to *avidyā*.

On the other hand, *jñātṛtva* and *kartṛīva* (knowledge and activity) are, according to Īśvarādvayavāda, the very nature of the Supreme. The Supreme can never be thought of without His activity. In this philosophy, activity is not an adjunct of Īśvara as in Śaṁkara, but His very specific nature. In general, His activity may be summarized in the five-fold act of emanation or projection (*sṛṣṭi*), maintenance (*sthiti*), withdrawal (*saṁhāra*), concealment of the real nature (*vilaya*), and grace (*anugraha*). He performs these five acts eternally, even when he assumes the form of an empirical ego (*jīva*). According to Īśvarādvayavāda, Śiva is *pañcakṛtyakārī* (always performing the five-fold act). According to Śaṁkara, *brahman* is *niṣkriya* (without any activity). Maheśvarānanda says that an inactive *brahman* is as good as unreal.

तथाहि परमेश्वरस्य ह्ययमेवासाधारणस्वभावो यत् सर्वंदा सृष्ट्यादि-पञ्चकृत्यकारित्वम् । एतदनङ्गीकाराद्धि मायावेदान्तादिनिर्णीतस्यात्मनः स्व-स्फुरणामोदमान्द्यलक्षणमसत्कल्पत्वापतितम् ।

—Mahārthamañjarī, p. 52

> This is the specific nature of Parameśvara [Highest Lord]—that He always performs the five-fold act. If this [activity] is not accepted, Ātmā, as defined by Māyā-Vedānta, etc., characterized by the want of the slightest trace of stir or activity, would be as good as unreal.

Īśvarādvayavāda also accepts *avidyā* or *māyā,* but not as something that affects Īśvara; it is rather Īśvara's own voluntarily imposed limitation of Himself by His own *śakti* (power). In sum, according to Īśvarādvayavāda, activity belongs to Īśvara; *māyā* derives its activity from Him.

The second difference between the two philosophies is as follows: *māyā* according to Śāntabrahmavāda, is *anirvacanīya* (indefinable); according to Īśvarādvayavāda, *māyā,* being the *śakti* of Īśvara or Śiva, is real and brings about multiplicity and a sense of difference.

According to Śāntabrahmavāda, *viśva* or the universe is unreal *(mithyā).* Īśvarādvayavāda sees the universe as perfectly real; it is simply a display of Īśvara's power. Since *śakti* is real, the universe which has been brought about by *śakti* is also real. Since Śaṁkara considers *māyā* as neither real nor unreal, his non-dualism is exclusive, but the non-dual Saiva philosophy considers *māyā* as *śivamayī* (an aspect of Śiva). Therefore, the Śaiva non-dualism is integral, all-inclusive. If *brahman* is real and *māyā* is some indeterminate force—neither real nor unreal, as Śaṁkara maintains—then there would be a tinge of dualism in Śaṁkara's philosophy.

Again, according to Īśvarādvayavāda, even in the state of the empirical ego or the *jīva*, the five-fold act of Śiva continues; according to Śāntabrahmavāda, *ātmā* (the self), even in the state of the empirical ego, is *niṣkriya* or inactive, Whatever activity there is belongs to *buddhi.*

According to Śaṁkara's *vivartavāda,* all manifestation is only name and form (*nāma-rūpa*) and cannot be regarded as real in the true sense of the word. According to Īśvarādvayavāda, the *ābhāsas* are real in that they are aspects of the ultimately real or Parama Śiva. Though they do not exist in Parama Śiva in the same way in which limited beings experience them, they exist in Parama Śiva as His experience or ideation. So the *ābhāsas* are, in essence, real. What constitutes the ideation of the Real cannot itself be unreal.

Finally, according to Śaṁkara, in liberation (*mukti*) the world is annulled; in Saiva philosophy, it appears as a gleam of Śiva-consciousness, or an expression of the wondrous delight of Self-consciousness.

We may summarize the views of these two systems as follows:

Śāntabrahmavāda

1. *Cit* or *brahman* is only *prakāśa* (light) or *jñāna* (knowledge). It is *niṣkriya* (inactive).

2. Activity belongs only to *māyā* or *avidyā*. Īśvara assumes activity only when He is affected by *avidyā* or *māyā*.

3. Māyā is *anirvacanīya* (indefinable).

4. Māyā, being indefinable, is loosely associated with Īśvara and

is, in the last analysis, unreal. Māyā seems to play the role of a separate principle. Śaṁkara's non-dualism is, therefore, exclusive.

5. In the case of the empirical ego or *jīva* as well, the *ātman* is inactive. All activity belongs to *buddhi,* the product of *prakṛti.*

6. The universe is *mithyā* or unreal. Manifestation is only *nāma-rūpa* and cannot be regarded as real in the true sense. Śaṁkara's non-dualism is exclusive of the universe.

7. In liberation, the universe is annulled.

8. According to Śaṁkara Vedānta, *avidyā* is removed by *vidyā,* and when this happens, there is *mukti* or liberation; *vidyā* is the result of *śravaṇa, manana,* and *nididhyāsana.*

Īśvarādvayavāda

1. Cit is both *prakāśa* and *vimarśa* (light and activity). Therefore it has both *jñātṛiva* (knowledge) and *kartṛtva* (doership). Generally speaking, it has the five-fold activity.

2. Maheśvara has *svātantrya.* Therefore activity belongs to Him. Māyā is not something that affects Maheśvara or Śiva. Māyā is His own *śakti* by which He brings about multiplicity and sense of difference.

3. Māyā, being the *śakti* of the Divine, is perfectly real.

4. Māyā is *Śiva-mayī* or *cinmayī* and is thus Śiva's own *śakti.* It is not a separate principle. Therefore, Śaiva non-dualism is inclusive and integral.

5. Even in the case of *jīva,* the five-fold activity of Śiva never ceases.

6. The universe is *śiva-rūpa* and therefore real. It is a display of the glory of the Divine. Ābhāsas, being the ideation of Śiva, cannot be false. Śaiva philosophy is thus inclusive of the universe and real non-dualism.

7. In liberation, the universe appears as a form of Śiva-consciousness or real I-consciousness.

8. According to non-dualistic Śaiva philosophy, there are two kinds of *ajñāna: pauruṣa ajñāna,* which is inherent in the *puruṣa* or *aṇu,* and *bauddha ajñāna,* which is intellectual. By *vidyā,* only *bauddha ajñāna* can be removed; *pauruṣa ajñāna* will still remain. Such a person will be rooted only in blank abstractions, he will not realize *Śivatva* or divinization. *Pauruṣa ajñāna* also has to be removed. This can be done only by *śaktipāta,* which comes about either by the *dīkṣā* (initiation) imparted by a self-realized Guru (spiritual director) or by direct divine grace.

6. The Individual Self or Jīva

The individual, according to the Pratyabhijñā system, is much more than simply a psycho-physical being. His physical aspect consists of the five *mahābhūtas,* or highly organized gross elements. This is known as his *sthūlaśarira.* He also has the psychic apparatus known as *antaḥkaraṇa* (the inner instrument) consisting of *manas, buddhi,* and *ahaṁkāra.*

Manas, buddhi, and *ahaṁkāra,* together with the five *tanmātras,* form a group of eight known as *puryaṣṭaka.* This forms the *sūkṣmaśarīra,* in which the soul leaves the body at the time of death.

Prāṇa śakti also works in the *jīva.* This is the divine *śakti* working both in the universe and the individual. By this *prāṇa śakti,* everything is sustained and maintained.

There is also *kuṇḍalinī* that is a form or expression of *śakti.* This lies dormant in the normal human being.

Finally there is *caitanya* or Śiva, his very Self, in the center of his being. Though intrinsically the Self of man is Śiva, he becomes an *aṇu* or limited individual because of *āṇava mala.*

7. Bondage

The bondage of the individual is due to innate ignorance, which is known as *āṇava mala.* It is the primary limiting condition, which reduces the universal consciousness to an *aṇu* or a limited aspect. It comes about by the limitation of the *Icchā Śakti* of the Supreme. Due to *āṇava mala,* the *jīva* considers himself a separate entity, cut off from the universal stream of consciousness. It is consciousness of self-limitation.

Coming in association with the categories of the *aśuddha adhvā,* or the order of the extrinsic manifestation, he becomes further limited by *māyīya mala* and *kārma mala. Māyīya mala* is the limiting condition brought about by *māyā.* It is *bhinna-vedya-prathā*—that which brings about the consciousness of difference, owing to the various limiting adjuncts of the body, etc. This comes about by the limitation of the *jñāna śakti* of the Supreme.

It is by these *malas* that the individual is in bondage and whirls about from one form of existence to another.

8. Liberation

Liberation, according to this system, means the re-cognition (*pratyabhijñā*) of one's true nature. This means, in other words, the attainment of *akṛtrima-aham-vimarśa*—the original, innate, pure I-consciousness. The following verse of Utpaladeva gives an idea of pure I-consciousness.

अहं प्रत्यवमर्शो यो विमर्शात्मापि वाग्वपुः ।
नासौ विकल्पः, स ह्युक्तो द्वयापेक्षी विनिश्चयः ॥

—Īś. Pr. I. 6.1

The pure I-consciousness is not of the nature of *vikalpa,* for *vikalpa* requires a second (all *vikalpa* is relational). The normal psychological I-consciousness is relational (the Self-Consciousness in contrast with the not-Self).

The pure I-consciousness is not of this relational type. It is *immediate awareness.* When one has this consciousness, one knows one's real nature. This is what is meant by liberation. As Abhinavagupta puts it:

मोक्षो हि नाम नैवान्यः स्वरूपप्रथनं हि तत् ।

—Tantrāloka. I. p. 192

Mokṣa (liberation) is nothing but the awareness of one's true nature.

By this real I-consciousness, one attains Cidānanda—the bliss of the *cit* or Universal Consciousness. The *citta* or the individual mind is now transformed into *cit* or Universal consciousness (see Sūtra 13 of Pr. Hṛ.). The attainment of this pure I-consciousness is also the attainment of Śiva-Consciousness in which the entire universe appears as I or Śiva.

According to this system, the highest form of *ānanda* or bliss is *jagadānanda*—the bliss of the world—in which the whole world appears to the liberated soul as *cit* or Śiva.

Liberation cannot be achieved by mere intellectual gymnastics. It comes by *śaktipāta* (the descent of Divine *Śakti*) or *anugraha*—Divine grace.

Śaktipāta or Anugraha

Those who, owing to the *samskaras* of previous births, are very advanced souls receive *tīvra* or intense *śaktipāta.* They are liberated without much *sādhanā* or *praxis.*

Those who are less qualified receive *madhyama śaktipāta.* This induces them to seek a Guru or spiritual preceptor to get initiation and to practice yoga. In due course, they get liberation.

Those who are still less qualified receive *manda* (moderate) *śaktipāta*. This creates in them genuine eagerness for spiritual knowledge and meditation. They will also get liberation in due course of time.

Upāyas

But grace is not the outcome of caprice. It has to be earned by moral and spiritual discipline. The means of earning grace have been divided into four categories: Āṇavopāya, Śāktopāya, Śāmbhavopāya, and Anupāya. These *upāyas* are recommended to get rid of the *malas,* enabling one to become fit for receiving grace.

Āṇavopāya is the means by which the individual utilizes his own *karaṇas* or instruments as means for his transformation, for Self-realization. It includes disciplines such as the regulation of *prāṇa,* rituals, concentration on one's chosen deity. Ultimately, it brings about Self-realization by the unfolding of *madhya-dhāma* or *suṣumnā.* It is also known as *kriyopāya,* because *kriyās*—such as repetition of a mantra and the practice of rituals—play an important part in it. This is also known as *bhedopāya*, because this discipline starts with a sense of *bheda* or difference.

Śaktopāya is concerned with those psychological practices that transform the inner forces and bring about *samāveśa* or immersion of the individual consciousness in the divine. In this *upāya, mantra śakti* comes into play. With it, the individual acquires *prātibha jñāna* or true knowledge; gradually his feeling of duality lessens and his consciousness merges in *parā-saṁvid*. In this discipline, one's meditation is something like: "I am Śiva," "The whole universe is only an expansion of my true Self."

In *āṇavopāya,* the senses, *prāṇa,* and *manas* are pressed into service; in *śāktopāya, manas* functions actively. It is also known as *jñānopāya,* (because of the important role mental activities play in it) and as *bhedābheda-upāya* (because it is based both on difference and identity). By this *upāya*, the *kuṇḍalinī* rises from the *mūlādhāra* without much effort, for the control of *prāṇa,* and brings about Self-realization.

Śāmbhavopāya is meant for advanced aspirants who, by meditating on *Śivatattva,* attain to His consciousness. This is the path of "constant awareness." One starts with the analysis of *pañca-kṛtya, sādhanā* of *vikalpa-kṣaya,* and the conscious practice of seeing the universe as only a reflection of *cit;* later even these practices have to be renounced. This leads easily to pure I-consciousness.

Anupāya can hardly be called an *upāya*. It depends entirely on *anugraha* or grace. This grace may come through one word of the Guru (spiritual director); light may dawn upon the aspiriant and thus he may acquire an experience of the real self in a flash, or divine grace may be showered on him directly and he may instantly realize the Self. The prefix "an" in *anupāya* has been explained by some in the sense of *iṣat*, or "very little." In this sense, *anupāya* means very little or nominal effort on the part of the aspirant. Whether it comes directly or through a spiritual master, *anupāya* connotes realization through very intense grace (*tīvratama śaktipāta*) alone. Sometimes by the very sight of a person who has acquired Self-realization, an aspirant receives illumination and is transformed. *Anupāya* is generally designated as *ānandopāya*.

Kṣemarāja says that by the development of the *madhya* or center, one attains *cidānanda* or bliss of the Supreme consciousness. This *madhya* is distinct from the point of view of the three *upāyas* above. From the point of view of *āṇavopāya, "madhya"* is the *suṣumnā nāḍi* between the *iḍā* and *piṅgalā,* which has to be unfolded. From the point of view of *śaktopāya, "madhya"* is the *parāsaṁvid,* which has to be reached. From the point of view of *śāmbhavopāya, akṛtrima aham,* or the pure I-consciousness, is the *madhya* or center of everything. The *madhya* must be attained by one of the above means.

For the unfoldment of *madhya,* Kṣemarāja recommends *vikalpa-kṣaya, śakti-saṅkoca, śakti-vikāsa, vāha-ccheda,* and the practice of *ādyanta-koṭi* (for details, see Sūtra 18).

Of these, *vikalpa-kṣaya* is *śāmbhavopāya; śaktisaṅkoca* and *vikāsa* are *śāktopāya;* and *vāha-ccheda* and *ādyanta-koṭinibhālana* are *āṇavopāya.*

Pratyabhijñā stresses meditation on *pañca-kṛtya* and the practice of *vikalpa-kṣaya.* The former maintains that the fivefold act of Śiva (*sṛṣṭi, sthiti, saṁhāra, vilaya* and *anugraha*) is going on constantly, even in the individual. The aspirant should constantly dwell on the esoteric meaning of this fivefold act, in order to rise to higher consciousness. The mental perception of the individual, with reference to a particular place and time, is the *sṛṣṭi* in him; the retention and enjoyment of what he perceives is the *sthiti* or preservation. During the delight of I-consciousness, it is absorbed in consciousness; this is *saṁhāra.* When, even after being withdrawn, its impression is about to rise into consciousness again, it corresponds to *vilaya.* When completely absorbed into *cit* or the true Self by the process of *haṭha-pāka,* it is *anugraha.* (See Sūtra 11 for details.) This practice qualifies the aspirant for pure *cidānanda.*

The mind is the happy hunting-ground for all kinds of ideas that arise, one after another like waves on the sea. We get involved in these ideas and are unable to get behind them to experience the stillness of the Self. The practice of *vikalpa-kṣaya* is recommended for getting rid of *kṣobha* or mental agitation and recapturing the underlying consciousness, on the surface of which the *vikalpas* have their play. This cannot be done by force, for that creates resistance. This can be achieved only by *alert passivity,* by relaxing the *citta* or mind, by not thinking of anything in particular, and yet not losing awareness.

By these practices, one acquires *samāveśa* or immersion in the divine consciousness. For this *samāveśa* to be a full, perfect, and enduring experience, one has to practice *Krama-mudrā* (see Sūtra 19). By Krama-mudrā, the experience of identification of the individual consciousness with the Universal Consciousness has to be carried out into the experience of the outer world. This system believes that the *samāveśa* that lasts only as long as *samādhi* (contemplation) lasts is incomplete. In complete or perfect *samāveśa,* even after getting up from contemplation the state continues; the world no longer appears as mere earth, but as "clothed in celestial light," as a play of the Universal Consciousness. The aspirant also feels himself to be nothing but that consciousness. Then the world is no longer something to be shunned, but rather an eternal delight (*jagadānanda*). Then one truly acquires *akṛtrima-aham-vimarśa*—pure I-consciousness in which the world does not stand against the I, in opposition, but is instead the very expression of that I.

This is the conception of *jīvanmukti* in the Pratyabhijñā system. The world-process starts from the pure I-consciousness of Śiva. At the level of man, that I-consciousness gets identified with its physical and psychic coverings, and the world stands over against it as something different *toto caelo.* The task of man is to recapture that pure I-consciousness, in which it and the universe are one.

Surely such a stage cannot be reached all at once. The system visualizes a hierarchy of experients who rise gradually in the evolutionary process to the pure I-consciousness of Śiva.

The normal individual is known as *sakala*. He has all the three *malas—kārma, māyiya* and *āṇava*. After many lifetimes as the plaything of Nature, both physical and psychic—he is seized with psychic fever and tries to know the whence and the whither of this life. This is the first expression of the *anugraha* of Śiva.

If he is not very cautious and indulges in lower kinds of yoga, he may become a *pralayākala*. He is free from *kārma mala* and has only *māyīya* and *āṇava mala,* but he has neither *jñāna* nor *kriyā*. This is not a desirable state. At the time of *pralaya* or withdrawal of the universe, every *sakala* becomes a *pralayākala*.

Vijñānakala is an experient of a higher stage. He has risen above *māyā* but is still below *Śuddha Vidyā*. He is free from the *kārma* and *māyīya malas,* but he has still *āṇava mala*. He has *jñāna* and *icchā,* but no *kriyā*.

Above the *vijnānākala* are the experients in successive ascent known as Mantra, Mantreśvara, Mantra-maheśvara, and Śiva-pramātā. These are free from all the three *malas,* but their experiences of unity consciousness vary (see Chart on page 96 for details).

It is only to the Śiva-pramātā that everything appears as Śiva.

Pure I-consciousness is the *fons et origo* of the entire world process. Involution starts from the pure I-consciousness of Śiva. Evolution gets back to the same pure consciousness, but the pilgrim goes back to his home, enriched with the experience of the splendor of Śiva he has had on the way. Veil after veil lifts, and he is now poised in the heart of Reality. He may now well exclaim in the words of Abhinavagupta:

स्वतंत्रः स्वच्छात्मा स्फुरति सततं चेतसि शिवः
पराशक्तिश्चेयं करणसरणिप्रान्तमुदिता ।
तदा भोगैकात्मा स्फुरति च समस्तं जगदिदम्
न जाने कुत्रायं ध्वनिरनुपतेत् संसृतिरिति ॥

—quoted in Mahārthamañjarī, p. 25

It is Śiva Himself, of unimpeded Will and pellucid consciousness, who is ever sparkling in my heart. It is His highest Śakti Herself that is ever playing on the edge of my senses. The entire world gleams as the wondrous delight of pure I-consciousness. Indeed I know not to what the sound "world" is supposed to refer.

ANALYSIS OF CONTENT

Sūtra 1 ■ *The absolute citi (Consciousness), out of its own free will, is the cause of the siddhi of the universe.*

Universe in this context means everything from Sadāśiva down to the earth. *Siddhi* means bringing into manifestation, maintenance, and withdrawal. *Citi*—the absolute consciousness—alone is the power that brings about manifestation. Māyā, Prakṛti, is not the cause of manifestation. Inasmuch as it [*citi*] is the source of both subject, object, and *pramāṇa* (means of proof), no means of proof can prove it [it is its own source].

Siddhi may be taken in another sense also. It may mean *bhoga* (experience) and *mokṣa* (liberation). The absolute freedom of the ultimate divine consciousness is the cause of these also.

The word *hetu* in this sūtra means not only cause, as interpreted above; it also means *means*. So *citi* is also the means by which the individual ascends to the highest consciousness, where he becomes identified with the divine.

Citi has been used in the singular to show that it is unlimited by space, time, etc. It has been called *svatantra* (of free will) to show that by itself it is powerful enough to bring about the universe, without the aid of Māyā. *Citi* is, therefore, the cause of manifestation, the means of rising to Śiva, and also the highest end. This sūtra strikes the keynote of the entire book.

Sūtra 2 ■ *By the power of her own free will, she [citi] unfolds the universe on her own screen.*

She brings about the universe by the power of her own free will, and not by any extraneous cause. The universe is already contained in her implicitly, and she makes it explicit.

Sūtra 3 ■ *This [the Universe] is manifold because of the differentiation of reciprocally adapted objects and subjects.*

The universe appears to be different and manifold because of the differentiation of experients and the objects experienced. These may be summarized as follows:

1. At the level of *Sadāśiva-tattva,* the I-consciousness is more prominent; the experience of the universe is in an incipient stage. An individual experient who rises to such a level of consciousness is known as Mantra-maheśvara and is directed by Sadāśiva. He has realized *Sadāśiva-tattva* and his experience is—"I am this." The consciousness [of the universe] is not fully distinguished from the "I" at this level.

2. At the level of *Iśvara-tattva,* the consciousness of both "I" and "this" is equally distinct. An individual experient who rises to this level is known as Mantreśvara. The universe is clearly distinct at this stage, but it is identified with the Self. Mantreśvara is directed by Īśvara.

3. At the level of *Vidyā-tattva,* the universe appears as different from "I." There is an experience of diversity, though it is diversity-in-unity. Individual experients of this stage are known as Mantras. They are directed by Ananta-bhaṭṭāraka. They have an experience of diversity all around, of the universe as being distinct from the Self [though it may still belong to the Self].

4. The stage of the experient below *Śuddha vidyā,* but above *Māyā,* is that of *Vijñānākala.* His field of experience consists of *sakalas* and *pralayākalas.* He feels a sense of identity with them.

5. At the stage of Māyā, the experient is known as *pralaya-kevalin.* He has neither a clear consciousness of "I," nor of "this," and so his consciousness is practically that of the void.

6. From Māyā down to the earth, the experient is the *sakala* who experiences diversity all around. The average human being belongs to this level.

Śiva transcends all manifestation. His experience is that of permanent bliss and identity with everything from Sadāśiva down to earth. Actually it is Śiva who flashes forth in various forms of manifestation.

Sūtra 4 ■ *The individual [experient], in whom citi or consciousness is contracted, has the universe [as his body] in a contracted form.*

Śiva or *cit,* by assuming contraction, becomes both the universe and the experient of the universe. Knowledge of this constitutes liberation.

Sūtra 5 ■ *Citi [universal consciousness] itself, descending from [the stage of] cetana, becomes citta [individual consciousness], inasmuch as it becomes contracted in conformity with the object of consciousness.*

The universal consciousness itself becomes, by limitation, the individual consciousness. By the process of limitation, the universal consciousness has either predominance of *cit* or predominance of limitation. In the former, there is the stage of Vijñānākala when *prakāśa* is predominant, or Śuddha-vidyā-pramātā, when both *prakāśa* and *vimarśa* are predominant, or Īśa, Sadāśiva, Anāśrita-Śiva. In the latter case, there is the stage of Śūnya-pramātā, etc.

The universal consciousness itself, by assuming limitation, becomes individual consciousness. Jñāna, Kriyā, and Māyā of the universal consciousness becomes *sattva, rajas,* and *tamas* in the case of the individual.

Sūtra 6 ■ *The māyā-pramātā consists of it [citta].*

The *māyā-pramātā* also is only *citta.*

Sūtra 7 ■ *And [though] he is one, he becomes of twofold, threefold, fourfold form, and of the nature of seven pentads.*

The *cit* is Śiva Himself. Consciousness cannot be split apart by space and time.

Since, by limitation, it assumes the state of the experient and the object experienced, it is also of two forms. As well, it becomes threefold, as it is covered with the *mala* pertaining to *aṇu, māyā,* and *karma.* It is also fourfold, because it assumes the nature of (1) *śūnya,* (2) *prāṇa,* (3) *puryaṣṭaka,* and (4) the gross body. The seven pentads—the thirty-five tattvas that extend from Śiva to the earth—are also its nature. From Śiva down to sakala, he also becomes the sevenfold experient and of the nature of fivefold covering [from Kalā to Niyati].

Sūtra 8 ■ *The positions of the various systems of philosophy are only various roles of that [consciousness or Self].*

The positions of the various systems of philosophy are, so to speak, roles assumed by the Self.

1. The Cārvākas, for instance, maintain that the Self is identical with the *body* characterized by consciousness.

2. The followers of Nyāya practically consider *buddhi* to be the Self in the worldly condition. After liberation, they consider the Self as identical with the void.

3. The Mīmāṁsakas also practically consider *buddhi* to be the Self, inasmuch as they believe the *I-consciousness* to be the Self.

4. The Buddhists also consider only the functions of *buddhi* as the Self.

5. Some Vedāntins regard *prāṇa* as the Self.

6. Some of the Vedāntins and the Mādhyamikas regard *non-being* as the fundamental principle.

7. The followers of Pāñcarātra believe *Vāsudeva* to be the highest cause.

8. The followers of Sāṅkhya practically accept the position of the Vijñānākalas.

9. Some Vedāntins accept *Īśvara* as the highest principle.

10. The Grammarians consider *Paśyantī* or *Sadāśiva* to be the highest reality.

11. The Tāntrikas consider the *Ātman* as transcending the universe to be the highest principle.

12. The Kaulas consider the *Universe* as the Ātman principle.

13. The followers of Trika philosophy maintain that the *Ātman* is both immanent and transcendent.

This sūtra may be interpreted in another way: the experience of external things [such as color] and internal things [such as the experience of pleasure] becomes a means for the essential nature of Śiva or the highest reality to manifest.

Sūtra 9 ■ *Due to its limitation of Śakti, Reality, which is all consciousness, becomes the mala-covered saṁsārin.*

The Will-power being limited, there arises the *āṇava mala*—the *mala* by which the *jīva* considers himself to be imperfect.

Omniscience being limited, there arises knowledge of a few things only. Thus comes into being *māyīya mala,* which consists of the apprehension of all objects as different.

Omnipotence being limited, the *jīva* acquires *kārma mala*.

Thus due to limitation, *sarva-kartṛtva* (omnipotence) becomes *kalā* (limited agency); *sarvajñatva* (omniscience) becomes *vidyā* (limitation with respect to knowledge); *pūrṇatva* (fulfillment) becomes *rāga* (limitation with respect to desire); *nityatva* (eternity) becomes *kāla* (limitation with respect to time); *vyāpakatva* (omnipresence) becomes *niyati* (limitation with respect to space and cause). *Jīva* (the individual soul) is this limited self. When his Śakti is unfolded, he becomes Śiva Himself.

Sūtra 10 ■ *Even in this condition [of the empirical self], he [the individual soul] does the five kṛtyas, like Him [Śiva].*

Just as Śiva performs the fivefold act in mundane manifestation, as an unfoldment of His real nature, so does He do it in the limited condition of a *jīva*.

The appearance of objects in a definite space and time is tantamount to *sraṣṭṛtā* (emanation); their appearance in another space and time, and thus their disappearance to the individual soul, constitutes *saṁhartṛtā* (withdrawal); continuity in the appearance of objects constitutes *sthāpakatā* (maintenance). Because of the appearance of difference, there is *vilaya* (concealment).

When the object is identical with the light of consciousness, it is *anugraha* (grace).

Sūtra 11 ■ *He also does the fivefold act of manifesting, relishing, thinking out, setting of the seed, and dissolution. [This is so from the esoteric standpoint of the yogin.]*

Whatever is perceived is *ābhāsana* or *sṛṣṭi*. The perception is relished for some time. This is *rakti* or *sthiti*. It is withdrawn at the time of knowledge. This is *saṁhāra*.

If the object of experience generates impressions of doubt, etc., it becomes the germinal cause of transmigratory existence. This is *bījāvasthāpana* or *vilaya*. If the object of experience is identified with consciousness, it is the state of *vilāpana* or *anugraha*.

Sūtra 12 ■ *To be a samsārin means to be deluded by one's own powers because of the ignorance of that [authorship of the fivefold act].*

In the absence of the knowledge of the fivefold act, one becomes deluded by one's own powers and thus transmigrates eternally.

While talking of *śakti*, we would do well to realize that the highest Vāk śakti has the knowledge of the perfect "I." She is the great mantra, inclusive of the letters "a" to "ksa" and reveals the empirical experient. At this stage, she conceals the pure distinctionless consciousness and throws up ever-new forms, each different from one another.

The empirical experient, deluded by the various powers, considers the body, *prāṇa,* etc. as the Self. Brāhmī and other *śaktis* bring about emanation and maintenance of difference, and withdrawal of identity in the empirical subject (*paśu-daśā*).

At the stage of *pati* they do the reverse; they bring about the emanation and maintenance of identity, and withdrawal of difference. Gradually they bring about the state of *avikalpa.* This is known as pure Vikalpa power.

The above technique of establishing unity-consciousness is known as *Śāmbhavopāya.*

In the *Śāktopaya* or the *Śākta* technique of unity consciousness, *Cit-śakti* is known as *Vāmeśvarī.* Her subspecies are *khecarī, gocarī, dikcarī,* and *bhūcarī.* These bring about objectification of the Universal Consciousness. By *khecarī śakti,* the universal consciousness becomes an individual subject; by *gocarī śakti,* he becomes endowed with an inner psychic apparatus; by *dikcarī śakti,* he is endowed with outer senses; by *bhucarī,* he is confined to external objects. By yogic practice, *khecarī* brings about consciousness of perfect agency; *gocarī* brings about consciousness of non-difference, *dikcarī* brings about a sense of non-difference in perception, *bhucarī* brings about a consciousness of all obejcts as parts of one Self.

There is a third technique known as *āṇavopāya.* When the *aiśvarya śakti* of the Lord conceals her real nature, in the case of the individual, and deludes him by *prāṇa,* by the various states of waking, dreaming, etc., and by both the gross and subtle body, he becomes a *saṁsārin.* When, in the yogic process, she unfolds the *udāna śakti,* and the *vyāna śakti,* the individual comes to acquire the experience of *turya* and *turyātita* states and becomes liberated while living.

Sūtra 13 ■ *Acquiring full knowledge of it [of the fivefold act of the Self], citta itself becomes citi by rising to the status of cetana.*

When the knowledge of the fivefold act of the Self dawns upon the individual, ignorance is removed. The *citta* (individual consciousness) is no longer deluded by its own limiting powers; it recaptures its original freedom, and, by acquiring a knowledge of its real nature, rises to the status of *citi* (universal consciousness).

Sūtra 14 ■ *The fire of citi, even when it descends to the [lower] stage, though covered [by māyā], partly burns the fuel of the known [the objects].*

If *citi* intrinsically is non-differentiating consciousness, how can it be characterized by a sense of difference at the level of the individual?

The answer is that even at the level of the individual, *citi* cannot completely lose its nature of non-differentiation; all the known multifarious objects are assimilated into *citi* itself [in the knowledge-situation], and the objects become a part and parcel of *citi*. As fire reduces to itself everything thrown into it, so *citi* assimilates to itself all the objects of knowledge. Being covered by *Māyā, citi* does not reduce objects of knowledge to itself completely; these objects appear again due to previous impressions (*saṁskāras*).

Sūtra 15 ■ *In the reassertion of its [inherent] power, it makes the universe its own.*

Bala or power means the emergence of the real nature of *citi*. Then *citi* manifests the whole universe as identical with itself. This is not the temporary play of *citi,* but is rather its permanent nature. It is always inclusive; without this inclusive nature of *citi,* even the body and other objects would not be known. Therefore, the practice recommended for acquiring the power of *citi* is meant only for the removal of the false identification of oneself.

Sūtra 16 ■ *When the bliss of cit is attained, consciousness becomes stabilized in cit as one's only Self. Even the body is experienced as identical with cit.*

The steady experience of identity with *cit* means *jīvanmukti* (liberation even in this physical body). This comes about by the dissolution of ignorance upon recognition of one's true nature.

Sūtra 17 ■ *With the development of the madhya (center), one acquires the bliss of consciousness.*

By the development of the center, the bliss of the spirit can be obtained. *Saṁvit,* or the power of consciousness, is called the center because it is the support or ground of everything in the world. In the individual, it is symbolized by the central *nāḍī,* (*suṣumnā*). When the central consciousness in man develops or when the *suṣumnā nāḍī* develops, then the bliss of universal consciousness exists.

Sūtra 18 ■ *The means [for the development of the center] are: dissolution of vikalpa; saṅkoca-vikāsa of śakti; cutting of the vāhas; the practice [of the contemplation] of the koṭi (point) of the beginning and the end.*

The first method is *vikalpakṣaya.* One should concentrate on the heart and not allow any *vikalpa* to arise. By thus reducing the mind to an *avikalpa* condition and holding the Self as the real experient in the focus of consciousness, one develops the *madhya* or consciousness of central reality and enters the *turya* and *turyātīta* condition. This is the main method of Pratyabhijñā for *madhya-vikāsa.*

The other methods, *saṅkoca* and *vikāsa* of *śakti,* do not belong to Pratyabhijñā but are recommended for their utility. *Saṅkoca* of *śakti* means withdrawing the consciousness that rushes out through the gates of the senses and turning it inward, towards the Self. *Vikāsa* of *śakti* means holding the consciousness steadily within, while the senses are allowed to perceive their objects. Another way of acquiring *saṅkoca* and *vikāsa* of *śakti* is with the practice of *prasara* and *viśrānti* in the stage of *ūrdhva kuṇḍalinī.* Emergence from *samādhi,* while retaining its experience, is *prasara* or *vikāsa;* merging back into *samādhi* and resting in that condition is *viśrānti* or *saṅkoca.*

The third method is *vāha-ccheda*—cessation of *prāṇa* and *apāna* by repeating inwardly the letters "ka," "ha," etc. without the vowels and tracing the mantras back to their source, where they are unuttered.

A fourth method is *ādyanta-koṭi-nibhālana*—the practice of fixing the mind, at the time of the arising of *prāṇa* and its coming to an end, between the *ādi* (the first, or heart) and the *anta* (the distance of twelve fingers from the heart).

Sūtra 19 ■ *In vyutthāna, which is full of the after-effects of samādhi, one finds the attainment of permanent samādhi, by dwelling on one's identity with cit (Universal Consciousness) over and over again.*

Even on the occasion of *vyutthāna,* the yogin sees the entire universe dissolve in *cit* by the process of *nimīlana-samādhi.* Thus he acquires permanent samādhi by *Kramamudrā.*

Sūtra 20 ■ *Then [on the attainment of Kramamudrā], as a result of entering into the perfect I-consciousness or the Self—which is in essence cit and ānanda (consciousness and bliss) and of the nature of the great mantra-power—one attains lordship over the group of deities of consciousness that brings about all emanation and reabsorption of the universe. All this is the nature of Śiva.*

When one masters *kramamudrā,* one enters into the real, perfect I-consciousness or Self and acquires mastery or lordship over the group of consciousness-deities that bring about emanation and absorption of the universe. The perfect I-consciousness is full of light and bliss. No longer is the individual deluded into considering his body [gross or subtle], *prāṇa,* or the senses as the "I;" he now considers the divine light within as the real "I." This real "I" is the *saṃvit, Sadāśiva,* and *Maheśvara.* This I-consciousness means the resting of all objective experience within the Self. It is also called *Svātantrya* or sovereignty of Will—the lordship and primary agency of everything. This consciousness of pure "I" is the *fons et origo* of all the mantras, and therefore it is extremely powerful. It is the universal *cit* itself. By acquiring this consciousness, one becomes the master of these *śaktis* that bring about the emanation and absorption of the universe.

CONTENTS

45	*Sūtra 1*
49	*Sūtra 2*
50	*Sūtra 3*
52	*Sūtra 4*
55	*Sūtra 5*
57	*Sūtra 6*
58	*Sūtra 7*
59	*Sūtra 8*
64	*Sūtra 9*
65	*Sūtra 10*
67	*Sūtra 11*
69	*Sūtra 12*
75	*Sūtra 13*
76	*Sūtra 14*
77	*Sūtra 15*
79	*Sūtra 16*
80	*Sūtra 17*
82	*Sūtra 18*
88	*Sūtra 19*
90	*Sūtra 20*

THE DOCTRINE OF RECOGNITION

OṂ—Adoration to one who is the very embodiment of bliss and auspiciousness. Now the PRATYABHIJÑĀHṚDAYA [The Doctrine of Recognition][1]

Adoration to Śiva,[2] who eternally[3] brings about the five processes,[4] who makes manifest the Highest Reality, which is at the same time the Highest Value[5]—His Self[6]—[which is also the Real Self of each

1. See end note 1.
2. See end note 2.
3. *Satatam* (eternally) may be read with *namaḥ* to mean "my eternal adoration to Śiva" or with *pañcakṛtya-vidhāyine* to mean "my adoration to Śiva who eternally brings about the five processes." The latter construction is better, as it indicates that Śiva's activity is incessant.
4. See end note 3.
5. *Paramārtha*. *Parama* means the Highest; *artha* means both "reality" and "goal or value." *Paramārtha* connotes both the Highest Reality and the Highest Value. In Indian thought, the Highest Reality is also the Highest Value of man. The meaning and purpose of human life resides in the realization of the Highest Reality.
6. *Svātma* may mean either one's nature or one's self. In the former case, the meaning would be "the Highest Reality, whose nature is *cidānandaghana*. In the latter case, it would be "the Highest Reality—His Self." There is a double entendre in *svātma:* His Self (the self of Śiva) and the self of each individual. The implication is that His Self is identical with the Real Self of each person. This

individual] that is a mass of consciousness and bliss.[7]

Out of the great ocean [of the Doctrine] of Recognition, which is the quintessence of the secret doctrine[8] concerning Śaṁkara,[9] is drawn the cream [the essential part] by Kṣemarāja to nullify the poison of *saṁsāra*.[10]

In this world, there are some devoted people who are undeveloped in reflection, who have not taken pains to study difficult works like Logic and Dialectics. They nevertheless aspire after *Samāveśa*[11] with the highest Lord, which blossoms forth with the

---

translation is preferable, as it is more in line with the general tenor of this system.

7. *Cidānandaghana* means a mass of consciousness and bliss. In Śāṅkara Vedānta, the expression used is generally "saccidānanda"—*sat* (existence), *cit* (consciousness), and *ānanda* (bliss). Here *sat* has been dropped as superfluous, for in this system *cit* or consciousness alone is *sat* or real. *Cit* and *sat*—consciousness and existence or reality—are synonymous. Nothing outside consciousness may be called existent or real. Śaṅkara also says, *Sat eva bodha, bodha eva sattā*—Existence itself is consciousness, and consciousness itself is existence.

8. *Upaniṣat* means sitting down near or at the feet of another (a teacher) to listen to his words. It, therefore, has come to mean *rahasya* or secret knowledge obtained in this manner. Here the word means secret or esoteric doctrine.

9. *Śaṁ karoti iti Śaṁkaraḥ,* one who brings about happiness and welfare is Śaṁkara. This is another name of Śiva. *Śaṁkaropaniṣat,* therefore, means the esoteric doctrine pertaining to Śaṁkara or Śiva—or Śaiva philosophy.

10. *Saṁsāra—Saṁsarati iti saṁsāraḥ,* "that which is always on the move or is in continuous process." The word "world" can hardly do justice to this idea. Etymologically the word *saṁsāra* also means the "wandering through" (a succession of states) by the *jīva* or individual soul. In this sense, *saṁsāra* is called *viṣa* or poison. It is not the world per se that is poison, but the "wandering through" of the *jīva,* as a being disconnected from Reality, severed from his innermost Center, that is poison. *Viṣa* is derived from the root *viṣ,* in the third conjugation (*veveṣṭi*), meaning "to pervade;" hence anything actively pernicious, like poison. The root *viṣ,* in the fourth conjugation (*viṣṇāti*), means also "to separate, to disjoin." There may be a suggestion here that *saṁsāra* is *viṣa* because it disjoins us, disconnects us from Śiva.

11. *Samāveśa,* the noun form of *sam-ā-viś,* means "to enter into." *Samāveśa,* therefore, means mergence or identification. *Samāveśa* with the Highest Lord means identification of the individual self with the Universal Self. The individual, in this state, feels that he is nothing other than Śiva. *Samāveśa* also means "taking possession of the individual by the Divine." The outcome is the same—identification with Śiva. According to Abhinavagupta, *āveśa* means the subordination or disappearance of the personal nature of the aspirant and his identification with the divine nature of Śiva.

Āveśaśca asvatantrasya svatadrūpanimajjanāt. Paratadrūpatā Śambhorādyācchaktyavibhāginaḥ.

Tantrāloka—I volume I Āhnika, v. 173

descent of Śakti.[12] For their sake, the truth of the teaching of *Īśvara-pratyabhijñā*[13] is being briefly explained.

To explain the universal causality of the divinity that is the Self [of all], its attainability by easy means, and the high reward, it is said:

12. *Śakti* is the energy of Śiva and therefore not different from him. With it, he brings about *pañcakṛtya* or the five cosmic processes. *Śakti-pāta* means the descent of *Śakti*. *Śakti-pāta* upon an individual means the imparting of *anyugraha* or grace to him.
13. This is an excellent work of Pratyabhijñā by Utpalācārya, who flourished in the ninth century.

SŪTRA 1[14]

The absolute[15] citi,[16] of its own free will, is the cause of the Siddhi[17] of the universe.

Citiḥ svatantrā viśva siddhi hetuḥ.

COMMENTARY

"Of the universe" (*viśva*) means from Sadāśiva[18] down to earth. *Siddhi* means "in effectuation," in bringing about *sṛṣṭi* (manifestation), *sthiti* (continued existence), and *saṁhāra* (or resting) in the highest Experient.[19] [In bringing all this about,] the Highest Śakti[20]—the divine consciousness or power, which is absolute and of free will—consists of the highest *vimarśa,*[21] and is not different than

14. Sūtra (lit. thread) has come to mean that which, like a thread, runs through or holds together certain ideas; a rule; a formula; a direction. Compare the Latin, *sutura,* and English, suture. A sūtra must contain the fewest possible words, must be free from ambiguity, must be meaningful and comprehensive, must not contain useless words and pauses, and must be faultless.
15. *Svatantrā* is an adjective qualifying *citi.* This means dependent only on itself and nothing else. It means that it is absolved of all conditions and is free to do anything it likes. The word Svatantra has, therefore, been rendered by two terms: "absolute" and "of its own free will."
16. *Citi* means universal consciousness-power and is feminine in gender. *"Cit"* is generally used for Śiva and *"citi"* for His Śakti. They are distinguished from *citta,* which means "individual consciousness."
17. *Siddhi* means effectuation, which includes: *prakāśana* or *sṛṣṭi,* emanation; *sthiti,* maintenance of what is emanated; and *saṁhāra,* withdrawal or reabsorption.
18. See end note 4.
19. *Parapramātṛ* means the Highest Experient. *Pramātṛ* means measurer or the subject of experience. The highest experient is *Parama-Śiva,* the highest Śiva.
20. *Parāśakti*—the highest Śakti. This is distinguished from the subsidiary *śaktis* that pervade the universe and bring about all kinds of things. They are various aspects of the highest *Śakti. Śakti* means divine consciousness, or conscious energy which is non-distinct from Śiva. It is Śiva himself in his active aspect of manifestation and grace.
21. *Vimarśa* is a highly technical term of this system. (See end note 5)

Śivabhaṭṭārka[22] and is the *hetu* (cause). It is only when *citi,* the ultimate consciousness-power, comes into play that the universe comes forth into being [lit., opens its eyelids] and continues as existent; when it withdraws its movement, the universe also disappears from view [lit., shuts its eyelids]. One's own experience bears witness to this fact. The other things, *Māyā, Prakṛti,* etc., since they are [supposed to be] different from the light of consciousness, can never be sure of anything [lit. anywhere], for not being able to appear, owing to their supposed difference from consciousness-power, they are [as good as] non-existent. But if they appear, they become one with the light [of consciousness] . Hence *citi,* which is that light, alone is the cause. *Māyā* and *Prakṛti* are never the cause. Therefore, space, time, and form, which have been brought into being and are vitalized by it [*citi*], are not capable of penetrating its real nature, because it is all-pervading, eternal [lit., ever-risen],[23] and completely full [in itself]. This is to be understood by the import [of the sūtra].

If all is *cit* or consciousness then it may be objected that the universe itself is non-existent [lit. nothing whatsoever], different as it is from *cit* (consciousness). If it be maintained that the universe is non-different [from *cit*], how can one establish the relation of cause and effect [between *cit* and *jagat*]?[In the highest sense, causal relation does not mean succession, but simultaneous expression. The flutter of *citi* is simultaneous manifestation of the universe.]

The answer is, it is the divine consciousness alone (*cideva bhagavatī*), luminous, absolute, and free-willed as it is, which flashes forth in the form of innumerable worlds. This is what is meant by the causal relation here. It is used in its highest sense.[24] Since this

22. *Śiva-bhaṭṭāraka*—Derived from the root *bhaṭ,* "to nourish," *bhaṭṭāraka, bhaṭṭāra,* and *bhaṭṭa* have the same meaning. Literally they mean "the lord that nourishes or supports." The words *bhaṭṭāra* or *bhaṭṭāraka* mean venerable Lord, a term that has been attached to Śiva to show reverence.

23. *Nityodita* means "eternally risen." In this system, *nitya* (eternal) is generally not the word used for the foundational consciousness, but rather *nityodita*—ever-risen, ever-existent. *Nityodita* is that which never sets, but is always risen; whatever both rises and sets is called "*śāntodita.*" This term is also used because the system wants to emphasize that the eternal consciousness is ever active; there is always *spanda* or vibration in it.

24. In causal relation, the effect is believed to be different from the cause. *Cit* is supposed to be the cause of the universe, but if the universe is non-different from the cause, how can it be its effect (for the effect must be different from the cause)?

[consciousness] alone is the cause of the *siddhi*—manifestation of the universe which consists of *pramātṛ*[25] (subjects or knowers), *pramāṇa*[26] (knowledge and its means), and *prameya*[27] (objects or the known)—knowledge (*pramāṇa*), whose main function is to bring to light new objects, is neither fit nor qualified to prove the [ultimate] consciousness, which is absolute, unlimited, and self-luminous. This is declared in *Trikasāra* [as follows].

> Just as [when] one tries to jump over the shadow of one's head with one's own foot, the head will never be at the place of one's foot, so it is with *baindavī Kalā*.[28]

Since it [consciousness] is the cause of the *siddhi* of the universe—as well as *saṃhāra,* which consists in bringing about *sāsarasya,*[29] or identity with the highest non-dual [consciousness], therefore it is called *svatantrā,*[30] or free-willed. Its free will being recognized, it becomes the cause of the *siddhi* (fruition, perfection, attainment) of the universe. Such a *siddhi* is of the nature of *bhoga* (experience) and *mokṣa*[31] (liberation from the bondage of limited experience). The sūtra should be interpreted in this sense also.

[Here the word *hetu* is taken in the sense of "means."] Again, *viśva* or universe means [external objects like] blue, [inner feelings

25. *Pramātṛ* (lit. measurer), subject of knowledge.
26. *Pramāṇa* (lit. instrument of knowledge) means of knowledge, proof of knowledge.
27. *Prameya* (lit. to be measured) means the known or object of knowledge.
28. *Baindavī Kalā. Baindavī* means "pertaining to *bindu.*" *Kalā* means "śakti." *Baindavī kalā* means the power of knowership of the highest Self of consciousness—the power of Self-consciousness. Here it means that power by which the Self is always the subject, never the object. In this verse, the feet are compared to *pramāṇa* (means of proof); the head is compared to *pramātā,* the knowing Self. Just as it is impossible for one's feet to catch up to the shadow of one's head, so is it impossible to know the knower (*pramātā*) by the various means of knowing, for those means owe their existence to the knower.
29. *Samsarasa*—one having the same feeling or consciousness. *Sāmarasya,* therefore, means identity of consciousness. In *Saṁhāra* or withdrawal, *citi* reduces the universe to sameness with the Highest Reality. The foundational consciousness is both the alpha and the omega of the universe.
30. *Svatantrā*—*Citi,* or the divine consciousness, is called *svatantrā,* because whether engaged in *sṛṣṭi* (manifestation), *sthiti* (maintenance), or *saṁhāra* (withdrawal), she is sovereign; she does not depend upon any extraneous condition.
31. *Viśva-siddhi* may also mean the effectuation of both *bhoga* (enjoyment of the bliss of real I-consciousness) and *mokṣa* (liberation). When the absolute free will of *citi* is recognized, she brings about real enjoyment as well as freedom from limitation. In this sense also, she is the cause of *viśva-siddhi.*

like] pleasure, or [limited experient] body, *prāṇa*, etc. Its [the *Viśva*'s] *siddhi* (fulfillment or establishment) is the *hetu* or means of the awareness of *citi*. This *siddhi* consists of *āveśa* or merging in the Self, which is the nature of *vimarśa*, by gradual mounting, beginning with *pramāṇa* or knowledge[32] [and coming to rest in the *pramātā* or knower]. By "means" is meant here "easy means." As it is said in the excellent *Vijñānabhaṭṭāraka* (*Vijñānabhairava*, v. 106):

> The consciousness of object and subject is common to all the embodied ones. The yogins, however, have the distinction of being mindful of this relationship. [The object is always related to the subject; without this relation to the subject, there is no such thing as an object. The yogī is always conscious of that witnessing awareness, from which the subject arises and into which it finally rests.]

Citi (consciousness) used in the singular [in the sūtra] denotes its non-limitation by space, time, etc., [and thus] shows the unreality of all theories of dualism. The word *svatantra* (absolute, of free will) [in the sūtra] points out that the supreme power is of the essence of *cit*, and thus is distinguished from the doctrine of Brahman[33] [of Śaṅkara Vedānta, where the *cit* is considered non-active]. The word *viśva* declares that it (*cit*) has unlimited power, can bring about everything, is an easy means [for emancipation], and is [itself] the great reward.

But here a question arises. If *citi* is the cause of the universe, it would presuppose material cause [to bring about this apparently different universe] and [thus there would be] non-abandonment of dualism. Apprehending this [question], he [the author] says:

32. *Pramāṇopārohakrameṇa*—by gradual mounting, beginning with knowledge. From the known, or *prameya*, one has to mount to *pramāṇa* or knowledge; from knowledge one has to mount to the *pramātā* or the knower, to the highest Self. All *pramāṇas* rest in the *pramātā*, the knower.

33. *Brahmavāda* (the doctrine of Brahman) refers to Śaṅkara-vedānta, in which Brahman is said to be nonactive.

SŪTRA 2

By the power of her own will [alone], she (citi) unfolds the universe upon her own screen [in herself, as the basis of the universe].

Svecchayā svabhittau viśvam unmīlayati.

COMMENTARY

Svecchayā—by the power of her own will—not by the will of another, as [is maintained by] the Brahman doctrine, and other similar [systems]. Moreover "by the power of her own will" implies [that she brings about the universe] by her power *alone,* not by means of [any extraneous] material cause. In this way [on the presupposition of material cause], if the absolute free will is denied to her [*citi*], her *cit*-ness itself would not be possible [*cit* and free will are inseparable].

Svabhittau means on her own screen [in herself], not anywhere else. She unfolds the previously defined universe [from Sadāśiva down to earth] like a city in a mirror, which though non-different from it, appears as different.[34] *Unmīlana* means only making explicit what is already lying [implicitly in *citi*]. By this is meant the existence of the universe [in *citi*] as identical with the light [of *citi*].

Now, to make clear the nature of the universe by means of analysis, he [the author] says:

34. *Darpaṇe nagaravat*—Just as a city appearing in a mirror is not different from the mirror but appears as different, so the universe appearing in *citi* is not different from it, though it appears as different.

SŪTRA 3

That [the universe] is manifold because of the differentiation of reciprocally adapted (anurūpa) objects (grāhya) and subjects (grāhaka).

Tan nānā anurūpa grāhya grāhaka bhedāt.

COMMENTARY

Tat (that) means the universe; *nānā* means manifold. Why [manifold]? Because of the differentiation (*bheda*) between objects and subjects, which are *anurūpa,* or in a state of reciprocal adaptation.

[The correspondence or reciprocal adaptation of object and subject now follows:]

Just as in the Sadāśiva principle [there is the experience of] the total universe (*Viśva*) as an object (*grāhya*) of the nature of *parā-para*, or both identical and different, [a stage in which the experience is of the form "I am this," in which] the experience is dominated (*āc-chādita*) by the Consciousness of I (*ahantā*), and [in which the experience of] this-ness (*idantā*) is [yet] incipient (*asphuṭa*), so there is the group of experients (*pramātārs*) called *mantramaheśvaras* who are governed by the blessed Lord Sadāśiva,[35] and whose existence in that state is brought about by the will of the highest Lord.

Just as in the *Īśvara tattva* (principle) the entire universe is apprehended (*grāhya*) [in the form, "I am this"] where both the consciousness of "I" (*ahantā*) and that of "this" (*idantā*) are simultaneously distinct (*sphuṭa*), so [*tathāvidha eva*] is [the consciousness of] the group of individual experients, [known as] *mantreśvara,* governed by the venerable Īśvara.[36]

35. See end note 6.

36. *Īśvara tattva* is the next stage of manifestation; in it the consciousness of an "I" and a "this" is equally prominent. The ideal universe, which is involved in the absolute consciousness, becomes clearly defined here as a "this." *Jñāna* is predominant in this *tattva*. Corresponding to this *tattva* is the individual [mystic] experient, known as Mantreśvara, who has realized the *Īśvaratattva,* and whose consciousness is also of the form "I am this." The universe here is

In the stage of Vidyā or Śuddha Vidhyā, just as there are the experients, called Mantras, of different states together with many secondary distinctions, governed by Anantabhaṭṭāraka, so also is there, as an object of knowledge (*prameya*), one universe whose sole essence consists of differentiations.[37]

Above Māyā [and below Śuddha Vidhyā] are the experients, called Vijñānākalas, who are devoid of [the sense of] agency (*kartṛtā*), and who are of the nature of pure awareness (*śuddha-bodhātmānaḥ*). Corresponding to them is their object of knowledge or field of experience (*prameya*), which is identical with them (*tadabhedasāram*), [consisting of] *sakalas* and *pralayākalas* known to them [*paricita*] in their previous states of existence (*pūrvāvasthā*).[38]

At the stage of Māyā [are] the experients of the void (*Śūnya*) or *pralayakevalins.* Their field of experience consists of the insensible, which is quite appropriate to their state.[39]

[After the *pralayākalas*] are stationed the *sakalas* [from Māyā] up to the earth, who are different from everything and limited. Their field of experience is as limited and different as themselves (*tathābhūtam*).[40]

---

identical with the Self. The consciousness of Sadāśiva is *Ahamidam*—"I am this." The consciousness of Īśvara is *Idamaham*—"This am I."

37. *Vidhā* or *Śuddha Vidyā* is the stage where diversity or *bheda* begins, though there is unity in diversity. *Kriyā* is predominant in this *tattva*. Corresponding to this are experients called Mantras, who see diversity, though it is diversity-in-unity. The Lord who rules over these experients is called Anantabhaṭṭāraka. The consciousness of this stage is *Idam ca Aham ca* or *Aham idam ca*—the universe as different but also as belonging to me. Though the "this" appears as distinct from "I," it is only an aspect of "I." It is *distinct* from "I," but not *different*. Hence the consciousness of this stage is known as *Śuddha Vidyā*.

38. *Vijñānākala* is the experient of the stage below *Śuddha Vidyā* but above Māyā. Here the experient is devoid of agency; he is pure awareness. His field of experience consists of *sakalas* and *pralayākalas.* He has a sense of identity with his field of experience (*tadabhedasāram*). He is free from *Māyiya* and *Kārma mala,* but is still subject to *Āṇava mala*.

39. In this state, the experient has neither the clear consciousness of *aham* (I) nor of *idam* (this). His I-consciousness is identical with the void that one experiences in deep sleep. He has the feeling of a vague something, which is practically nothing. The *Pralayākala-pramātā* is identified with the *prakṛti* at the time of dissolution. The yogins who have an experience only of the void are like the *pralayākala-pramātā*. He is free from *Kārma mala* but is subject to *Āṇava* and *Māyiyamala*.

40. The *sakalas* are the *devas* (gods) and *jīvas* (individual selves) who do not have true knowledge of the Self, and whose consciousness is only that of diversity. The average human being belongs to this level. The *sakalas* are subject

Śivabhaṭṭāraka, however, who transcends all these [all the experients from Mantramaheśvara to Sakala], is constituted only of *prakāśa* (light, consciousness).[41] Again in blissful Paramaśiva (highest Śiva), who both transcends the universe and is the universe, who is the highest bliss and consists of a mass of *prakāśa* (light, consciousness), flashes the entire universe from Śiva down to the earth in identity [with Paramaśiva]. Actually [in that state], there is neither any other subject (*grāhaka*) nor object (*grāhya*). Rather, what is practically meant to be stated (*abhihitaprāyam*) is this: in actuality the highest blissful Śiva alone manifests himself in this way, in numerous forms of multiplicity.

As the Lord has the entire universe as his body, so:

SŪTRA 4

The [individual] experient also, in whom citi or consciousness is contracted, has the universe [as his body] in a contracted form.

Citi saṁkocātmā cetano'pi saṁkucita viśvamayaḥ.

COMMENTARY

The magnificent highest Śiva, desiring to manifest the universe, which lies in Him as identical with Himself in the form of Sadāśiva and other appropriate forms, flashes forth (*prakāśamānatayā sphurati*) at first as non-different from the light [of consciousness] (*prakāśābhedena*), but not experiencing the unity of consciousness [in

to all the three *malas*—*Āṇava, Māyīya* and *Kārma*.

41. The suggestion is that in this state *vimarśa* is latent; only *prakāśa* is predominant. (See chart on page 96 for details of Sūtra 3.) From Vijñānākala up to Sakala, there is no presiding deity, because the operation of Mahāmāyā begins from the Vijñānākala stage and because ignorance begins from the Mahāmāyā stage.

which the universe is identified with consciousness; *cidaikya-akhyātimaya*].[42] Known also as *anāśrita-śiva* (*anāśrita-śiva-prayāya*),[43] it is [as yet] more void than the void itself [from the point of view of any objective manifestation].[44] Then He unfolds Himself in the totality of manifestations—principles (*tattvas*), worlds (*bhuvanas*), entities (*bhāvas*) and their respective experients (*pramātāras*)—that are only a solidified form (*āśyānatārūpa*) of cit-essence.[45]

As the Lord is universe-bodied (*bhagavān viśvaśariraḥ*), so the [individual] experient—because of consciousness being contracted—has the body of the entire universe in a contracted form, much like how the *vaṭa* tree resides in a contracted form in its seed. Likewise, the Siddhānta [the settled doctrine of the system] say: "One body and embodied really include all the bodies and the embodied."

Triśiromata[46] also declares that the subject or self becomes the universe in contracted form. It begins by saying:

> The body is of the form of all gods;[47] hear now, concerning it,

42. *Akhyāti* is the state that, for the first time, negates or keeps away from Śiva the consciousness of his full nature (*Śiva svarūpāpohanam).*
43. *Anāśrita-Śiva-paryāya—anāśrita* means unrelated to anything; lit. whose synonym is Śiva, who has no objective content yet. Below Śaktitattva and above Sadāśiva-tattva, *avasthā* refers to a state, not a *tattva*. This refers to that phase of reality where *Śakti* begins temporarily to veil the Self, and thus to isolate the universe from the Self, producing *akhyāti*—ignorance of its real nature. This is why *śakti* is said to be *sva-svarūpāpohanātmākhyātimayi niṣedhavyāpāra-rūpā* (*Paramārthasāra,* p. 10)—Śakti brings about *akhyāti* by negating or isolating the universe from the Self and thus veiling its real nature. The full experience of the Self is that in which the "I" and the "This" (or the Universe) are one. The loss of this whole or full experience of the Self is *saṁsāra;* the regaining of it is *mukti*.
44. *Śūnyātiśūnyatayā*—being as yet more void than the void itself. It is called *śūnya* here from the point of view of absence of objective content or objectivity.
45. *Āśyānatā* means solidification—concrete manifestation of the subtle essence of *cit* (*cit-rasa*). *Rasa* is sap or juice in this context; as juice may be solidified, so *cit* may assume concrete manifestation.
46. *Triśiromate*—the mystical doctrine concerning the three-headed Bhairava. The three heads of god, Bhairava, are the symbolic representation of the three Śaktis of the Divine: Parā, Parāparā, and Aparā. Parā is the supreme state in which there is no distinction or difference whatsoever between Śiva and Śakti. In Parāparā there is identity-in-distinction, while in Aparā there is complete difference.
47. *Sarvadevamoyaḥ kāyaḥ*—the universe is considered to be like a body, constituted by all the gods. The gods here symbolize both the *pramātā* and the *prameya,* all the subjects and objects—the experients and the experienced.

> my dear.[48] It is called earth because of its solidity, and water because of its fluidity.

It ends by saying,

> The three-headed Bhairava[49] is present in person (*sākṣāt vyavasthitaḥ*), pervading the entire universe.

The implication is the experient or subject is identical with Śiva, whose body is the universe, because the light [of consciousness] is his true nature, and because of the reasoning of the Āgamas [just] mentioned. Only because of his [Śiva's] *Māyā-Śakti* does he [the experient] appear as contracted; his real nature is not manifested. Contraction also, on [close] examination, consists of only *cit* (consciousness); contraction is manifested only as of the nature of *cit*, otherwise it becomes mere nothing. Thus every subject is identical with the revered Śiva, whose body is the universe. It has been said by myself [elsewhere]:

> If it be said that *akhyāti* or nescience is that which never appears, [which is never experienced], then appearance or knowledge alone remains. If it be said that *akhyāti* does appear [is experienced in some form], then [obviously], being of the nature of knowledge, knowledge alone remains.[50]

With this intention, the identity of the *jīva* (the individual experient) and Śiva [the universal experient] has been declared in

---

Another reading is *Sarva-tattva-mayaḥ kāyaḥ*—the body of the universe is constituted by all the *tattvas.*

48. *Priye*—Dear one, or My dear. The Āgama literature is generally in the form of a dialogue between Śiva and his consort Pārvati. Hence, "Priye"—O dear one.

49. Bhairava means the terrible one who destroys the weakness of the lower self. This is the name of Śiva. In the hermeneutic interpretation of Bhairava, "*bha*" indicates "*bharaṇa*"—maintenance, "*ra*" indicates "*ravaṇa*"—withdrawal, "*va*" indicates "*vamana*"—ejecting or manifesting of the universe. Thus, Bhairava indicates all the three aspects of the Divine. Bhairava has been called "three-headed;" the three heads symbolically represent either his three śaktis—*parā, parāparā,* and *aparā*—or Nara, Śakti, and Śiva.

50. The source of this verse has not yet been traced. The idea here is expressed as a paradox. But what does "*akhyāti*"—nescience or non-knowledge—mean? Does it appear or not? In other words, is it experienced or not? If *akhyāti* is never experienced, then it is nothing and only *khyāti* or knowledge remains. If *akhyāti* does appear (is experienced), then being *khyāti* or experience, *khyāti* again remains. So *khyāti* or knowledge cannot be eliminated in any case.

Spandaśāstra[51] [in the verse] starting with, "Because the *Jīva* is identical with the whole universe," and ending with [the line] "Hence whether in the word or object or mental apprehension, there is no state that is not Śiva."[52] (*Spandakārikā* of Vasugupta—Niṣyanda, II, v.3-4)

Knowledge of this truth alone constitutes liberation; want of the knowledge of this truth alone constitutes bondage. This will be surely clarified later on [lit., this will come to pass].

An objection might be raised about the subject or experient being of the nature of *vikalpa,*[53] and *vikalpa* being due to *citta.*[54] *Citta* being there [being the nature of the subject], how can he [the subject] be of the nature of Śiva?[55] Apprehending [such an objection] and in order to settle [the connotation of] *citta,* the [author] says:

S Ū T R A 5

Citi (universal consciousness) itself descending from [the state of] cetana (the uncontracted conscious stage) becomes citta (individual consciousness) inasmuch as it becomes contracted (saṅkocinī) in conformity with the objects of consciousness (cetya).

Citireva cetana padādavarūḍhā cetya saṁkocinī cittam.

51. The reference is to *Spandakārikā,* Ch. 11, vv. 3-4.
52. Another reading of the last half of this line is: *na savasthā na yā Śivaḥ.*
53. See end note 7.
54. *Citta* means the individual consciousness.
55. The objector means to say: The subject goes on making all kinds of *vikalpas,* for he does all his thinking by means of *citta,* and the nature of *citta* is to form *vikalpas.* So long as the *citta* lasts, how can the subject be of the nature of Śiva, who is *nirvikalpa*?

COMMENTARY

Truly speaking, *citta* (individual consciousness) is the exalted *citi* (universal consciousness) itself. When *citi,* concealing its real nature, accepts contraction or limitation, then it has only two aspects. Sometimes it flashes forth with the predominance of *cit,* subordinating to itself limitation which has made its appearance; sometimes [it appears] with the predominance of limitation. In the case of *cit* being predominant in its natural state, and there being the predominance of *prakāśa* only [without *vimarśa*], its *pramātṛ,* or experient, is *Vijñānākala.* In the case of both *prakāśa* and *vimarśa* being predominant,[56] the experient is *vidyāpramātā.*[57] Even in this state (*prakāśa-parāmarśa-pradhānatve*), as the contraction [of consciousness] is gradually less, there are the stages of Īśa, Sadāśiva, and Anāśrita-Śiva.[58] In the predominance of *cit,* however, acquired through effort of contemplation [*samādhi*], the knowership of the pure path[59] reaches the highest degree by stages.[60]

Where, however, contraction or limitation [of *cit*] is predominant, there occurs the knowership of the void, etc.[61]

This being the position, *citi* (the universal consciousness) itself—in the form of the limited subject, descending from its stage of *cetana* (universal consciousness), disposed towards comprehending objects, being limited by external and internal objects of consciousness [like blue and pleasure, respectively]—becomes *citta* (individual consciousness). Thus has it been said in the excellent *Pratyabhijñā.*

Jñāna, Kriyā, and the third Śakti, Māyā of the Lord (Śiva), appear as *sattva, rajas* and *tamas* in the case of the *paśu* (individual *jīva*)

56. *Parāmarśa* here is a synonym of *vimarśa.*
57. Vidyāpramātṛtā—the experients of vidyā-tattva—Mantras.
58. Sadāśiva, Īśa, Anāśrita-śiva, see end note 5, and fn. 36 and 43. *Tanutā* here means attenuation, not corporeality.
59. Śiva, Sadāśivā, Īśvara, and Śuddhāvidyā together are known as Śuddhādhvā—the pure or higher path. Mantra, Mantreśvara, Mantra-maheśvara, etc. are Śuddhādhvā experients. Predominance of *cit* is common to both Vidyāpramātāras and Śuddhādhva-pramātāras. But in the former case, it is natural whereas in the latter, it is acquired through the effort of samādhi.
60. The idea is that *cit-pradhānatva* (predominance of *cit*) is either natural (*sahaja*) or acquired through the effort of samādhi (*samādhi-prayatnopārjita*). In the first (natural) type, there may be either predominance of *prakāśa* only—in which case the experient is Vijñānākala—or of both *prakāśa* and *vimarśa*—in which case the experients are the *Vidyāpramātaras.* In the second type, the *Śuddhapramātaras* reach the highest degree by stages.
61. Śūnyapramātṛ, etc. See fn. 39. The word *ādi,* i.e. etc. includes *sakalas* also.

with respect to the objective realities which are like His [Lord's] own limbs.[62] By this and other such statements, [it is clear that] *citi* (universal consciousness), which is of the nature of absolute freedom and which has the powers of *jñāna, kriyā,* and *māyā,* appears, owing to excess of limitation in the state of *paśu* (the individual soul), as *citta* (individual consciousness), which is of the nature of *sattva, rajas,* and *tamas.*[63] This has been stated in *Pratyabhijñā* (i.e. Īśvara-pratyabhijñā of Utpaladeva I.4, 3).

The individual consciousness is, even in the state of Vikalpa,[64] of the nature of the highest Real (Śiva). With a view to pursuing That (*tat*, the Highest Real), it has been said in the excellent *Tattva-garbha-stotra:*

> Therefore in all those who are pursuers of the Highest Truth, the self-luminous character of their innermost nature never disappears [in any condition].

In view of the fact that *citta* alone is the real nature of *Māyā-pramātṛ,* it is said:

S Ū T R A 6

The Māyāpramātṛ[65] *consists of it [citta].*

Tanmayo māyā pramātā.

62. The meaning of the verse is: what is *jñāna* in the case of Śiva appears as *sattva* in the case of *paśu* or *jīva* (the individual); what is *kriyā* in the case of Śiva (the Absolute Consciousness) appears as *rajas* in the individual; what is *māyā* in the case of Śiva appears as *tamas* in the individual.

63. *Sattva, rajas,* and *tamas* are the three *guṇas* that characterize Prakṛti, the root principle of manifestation. This has been elaborately described by Sāṅkhya and accepted by practically all systems of Hindu philosophy. *Guṇa* means strand, a constituent, an aspect of Prakṛti. *Sattva* is the aspect of harmony, goodness, enlightenment, and *sukha* or pleasure. *Rajas* is the aspect of movement, activity, and *duḥkha,* or commotion. *Tamas* is the aspect of inertia, and *moha,* or dullness and indifference.

64. Vikalpa—see end note 7.

65. Māyāpramātā is the experient of the impure path—the sphere of limitation. Māyāpramātā includes *pralayākalas* and *sakalas.* See fns. 40 and 41 and the chart on p. 96.

COMMENTARY

Citta is predominant in the sphere of life and body. The sphere of the void also consists of the *saṁskāras* (impressions) of the *citta,* otherwise one who awakes [from the experience of the void] would not be able to follow one's duties. Therefore, *māyāpramātṛ* consists of *citta* only. With this purport, the *Śivasūtras*, while discussing reality (*vastu-vṛtta-anusāreṇa*), having said that universal consciousness (*caitanyam*) is the Self, say again that "individual consciousness (*cittam*) is the Self," when the occasion for discussing the characteristics of *māyāpramātṛ* arises.

Since *mukti* or liberation is possible only by correct knowledge of the true nature of the Self, and transmigration (*saṁsāra*) is due to incorrect knowledge, it is therefore appropriate to analyze the true nature of it [the Self] bit by bit.

SŪTRA 7

And [though] he is one, he becomes of twofold, threefold, fourfold form, and of the nature of seven pentads.

Sa caiko dvirūpas trimayaś caturātmā sapta pañcaka svabhāvaḥ.

COMMENTARY

From the viewpoint of what has already been stated, exalted Śiva, who is of the nature of *cit,* is the one Atmā and none other, because the light [of consciousness] cannot be divided by space and time, and the merely inert cannot be a subject.[66]

Since consciousness [light of consciousness] itself, through the sovereignty of its free will,[67] assumes the limitation of *prāṇa* and the state of the experient of limited objects, thus it is of twofold form:

66. This means the *jaḍa,* or the merely inert, can only be an object of experience, not a subject of experience.
67. *Svātantrya* is the abstract noun of *Svatantra,* which means "one's own rule," "not conditioned by anything outside oneself," such as *māyā*. It is the absolute,

the manifester [the light of consciousness] and limited manifestation.

Owing to its being covered by the *mala*[68] related to *aṇu, māyā,* and *karma,* it becomes threefold.

It [also] becomes fourfold because of its assuming the nature of *Śūnya,*[69] *prāṇa, puryaṣṭaka,*[70] and the gross body.

The seven pentads—the thirty-five *tattvas* (principles) from Śiva down to the earth—are [also] its nature [or *sapta* and *pañca* here may be taken separately as seven and five]. So from Śiva down to *sakala,* the consciousness consists of a heptad of experients.[71] Though its essential nature is that of *cit* (consciousness), *ānanda* (bliss), *icchā* (will), *jñāna* (knowledge), *kriyā* (action)—a fivefold nature—it assumes the form of another pentad, limited by the coverings of *kalā, vidyā, rāga, kāla,* and *niyati,*[72] owing to *akhyāti* (nescience). Thus only when it is recognized that the one Reality, which is only Śiva, becomes thirty-five principles, seven experients, a pentad of five powers consisting of *cit,* only then does it [consciousness] become a bestower of [spiritual] liberty; otherwise [in the absence of this recognition], it is the cause of *saṁsāra* (passing on from existence to existence).

S Ū T R A 8

The positions of the various systems of philosophy are only various roles of that [Consciousness or Self].

Tad bhūmikāḥ sarva darśana sthitayaḥ.

---

spontaneous, free will of the divine consciousness, outside the causal chain; the free, creative act of the Universal consciousness.

68. See end note 8.

69. Of the nature of *Śūnya—Śūnya pramātā* or *pralaya-kevalī*—whose field of experience is the void.

70. *Puryaṣṭaka*—literally, the city of eight; refers to the subtle body consisting of the five *tanmātras* (the fundamental undifferentiated essence of the five gross elements), *manas, buddhi,* and *ahaṁkāra.* It is also known as *sūkṣmaśarīra* or *liṅga-śarira,* which is the vehicle of the *saṁskāras.*

71. The seven experients are Śiva-pramātā, Mantra-maheśvara, Mantreśvara, Mantra, Vijñānākala, Pralayākala, and Sakala.

72. See end note 4.

COMMENTARY

The positions of all systems of philosophy [*Cārvākas* and others] are, so to speak, this Self's assumed roles, accepted of His own accord, like the roles accepted by an actor.

Thus, the *Cārvākas* (followers of the Cārvāka system) maintain that the Self is identical with the body characterized by consciousness. The followers of Nyāya[73] and Vaiśeśika consider the Self, so long as it is in the worldly condition, as practically identical with *buddhi* (intuitive faculty of certain knowledge), which is the substratum of knowledge, and other qualities. In liberation, when *buddhi* disappears, they regard the Self as almost identical with the void. The followers of Mīmāṁsā are also tied down to *buddhi* in that they think the "I" veiled by the *upādhis,*[74] or the limiting conditions of pleasure and pain, is the Self. The followers of Sugata[75] also stop with only the functions of *buddhi,* maintaining that the fundamental principle is only a continuum of cognitions. Some followers of Sugata also stop with only the functions of *buddhi,* maintaining that the fundamental principle is only a continuum of cognitions. Some followers of Vedānta regard *prāṇa* (the vital principle) as the Self.

The Brahmavādins (advocates of the Veda) consider non-being (*abhāva*) as the fundamental principle on the grounds [of the Upaniṣadic dictum] that "all this was originally nonbeing." They accept the position of the void, and they are [thus] rooted in it. The Mādhyamikas[76] are also in the same position.

The Pāñcarātras[77] [believe] that Lord Vāsudeva is the highest cause (*prakṛti*);[78] the individual souls are like sparks of him, and so,

73. By etc. is meant *Vaiśeśika.*

74. *Upādhi*—lit., something placed near, which affects or limits a thing without entering into it as its constituent.

75. *Sugata* (lit., one who has fared well) is a title of the Buddha. Therefore his followers are known as *Saugatas.*

76. The Mādhyamikas are the followers of the Madhyamaka (the system of the middle way) school of philosophy. They believe in *śūnya* (the void) as the fundamental principle.

77. The *Pāñcarātra* or *Bhāgavata* system is the main philosophy of Vaiṣṇavaism. On the origin of *Pāñcarātra,* see Sir R.G. Bhandarkar's *Vaiṣṇavaism, Śaivism and Minor Religious Systems.* The word *Pāñcarātra* perhaps refers to some religious rites, lasting for five nights. The followers of *Pāñcarātra* are called *Pāñcarātras* here.

78. The word *prakṛti* here does not mean the Prakṛtī or root-matter of the Sāṅkhyas. *Parā prakṛti* here means the highest cause. The followers of the *Pāñcarātra* system consider Vāsudeva both as the material cause and controlling

taking the individual souls to be transformations of the highest cause, they cling to the non-manifest[79] [as the source of everything].

The Sāṅkhyas,[80] and others [of similar views], cling to the stage characterized predominantly by the Vijñānākalas.[81]

Other knowers of Vedānta cling to the Īśvara-principle [as the highest] status, [depending as they do on the Upaniṣadic dictum]— "Being alone was there in the beginning."

The exponents of Vyākaraṇa,[82] considering the Ātman (Self) principle as *śabda-brahman*[83] in the form of *paśyanti,*[84] attribute the highest reality to the status of Śrī Sadāśiva. Likewise other systems may also be inferred [to represent only a part of our system]. This has also been described in the Āgamas[85] [in the following verse]:

> The Buddhists rest content with the Buddhi principle, the Ārhatas[86] with the *guṇas,* the Veda-knowers with the Puruṣa, and the Pāñcarātrikas[87] with *avyakta.*

The Tāntrikas[88] maintain that the *ātman* principle transcends the

---

cause of all manifestation.

79. Kṣemarāja seems to have become confused here. The Pāñcarātras consider Vāsudeva, not "*avyakta*" (non-manifest), as the ultimate source. Śaṅkara puts their position quite correctly in his commentary on Brahmasūtras, in Utpattyasambhavādhikaraṇa:

तत्र यत् तावदुच्यते योऽसौ नारायण. परोऽव्यक्तात् प्रसिद्धः परमात्मा सर्वात्मा स आत्मनात्मानमनेकधा व्यूहावस्थित इति, तन्न निराक्रियते

80. Sāṅkhyas here means "the followers of Sāṅkhya."
81. See fn. 38.
82. The Vaiyākaraṇas were the followers of the Grammar School of Philosophy, which considered grammar a means of spiritual liberation. Their philosophy has been described under the heading "Pāṇini-darśanam" in *Sarva-darśana-saṁgraha* by Mādhava. The reference is obviously to Bhartṛhari's *Vākyapadiya,* which considers *paśyantī* as Śabdabrahma or Reality as Vibration.
83-84. See end note 9.
85. The āgamas (here Śaiva-Āgamas) refer to a body of literature containing the doctrine of the Śaivas. Āgama means tradition, that which is handed down from generation to generation.
86. By Ārhatas (the deserving, dignified) is meant the Jains. They maintain that the universe consists of *paramāṇus* (atoms of matter) which are eternal. They are subject to change or development inasmuch as they assume different *guṇas* (qualities). The Āgama quoted means to suggest that the Jains consider these *guṇas* as the highest reality they have discovered and they are unable to go further than the *guṇas.*
87. *Pāñcarātrikas*—see fn. 77.
88. The followers of Tantra are known as *tāntrikas.* The word "tantra" has been

universe. Those who are wedded to the sacred texts of Kula[89] consider that the *ātman* principle is steeped in the universe [that the universe is only a form of the Ātman]. The knowers of Trika[90] philosophy, however, maintain that the *ātman* principle is both immanent in the universe and transcends it.

Thus, of the one Divine whose essence is consciousness, all these roles are displayed by His Absolute Will, [and] the differences in the roles are due to the degree to which that absolute free will chooses to either reveal or conceal itself. Therefore there is only one Ātman, pervading all these [roles].

Those of limited vision, however, identify themselves with the various [limited] stages of His will. Even when it is clear that the essential reason for the erroneous concepts of the experients lies in their identification with the body, they are unable to comprehend the great pervasion [of the *Ātman*] described above [by *Trika* philosophy]—that the *Ātman* is both immanent and transcendent—unless the Śakti[91] of the Highest descends upon them. As has been said:

> The Vaiṣṇavas and others who are colored [whose minds are colored] by the attachment or color of *Vidya,*[92] do not know the highest God, the omniscient, full of knowledge. Likewise, [it has been said] in *Svacchanda Tantra,* (10th Paṭala, verse 1141):

---

explained in two ways: (1) from the root "tan," to expand; that in which the principles of reality are expanded and elaborately described is tantra. (2) from the root "tantra" to control, to harness; that which teaches how to control and harness the various forces of reality is tantra.

89. *Kula* here means "Śakti" (the divine manifesting power). The reference here is obviously to the Śaktas, the worshipers of Śakti.

90. *Trika*—The *Pratyabhijñā* philosophy is known as Trika inasmuch as it describes Parama Śiva or the Highest Reality as manifesting itself in a group of three (*trika*): Śiva, Śakti, and Nara. From "et cetera" in Trika, may be understood Tripurā or Mahārtha.

91. *Paraśaktipāta*—The grace of the Highest. *Śaktipāta* or grace is of two kinds: *para* (highest) and *apara* (lower). *Paraśaktipāta* connotes the transmutation of the empirical or limited ego into the fullest Divine Consciousness. Such grace can be imparted only by the Divine. In *Apara Śaktipāta* (lower grace), though the ego realizes his identity with the Divine, he is yet unable to realize that the entire universe is only a manifestation of himself and has thus not yet obtained the fullest Divine Consciousness of Śiva. *Apara Śaktipāta* (lower grace) can be imparted by a spiritual director or gods.

92. *Vidyā* (as one of the five *kañcukas*) is impure knowledge (*aśuddha-vidyā*). It is the principle of limitation, which does not allow the individual to have a synoptic view of reality.

> It is only *Māyā* that whirls these [followers of other systems] around, who desire to obtain liberation (*mokṣa*) in non-liberation [in those disciplines and scriptures that are incapable of offering liberation].

[It has been said in the *Netra Tantra*, 8th Paṭala, verse 30]:

> Those who are attached to the limited as the Self [the body as Self, the *buddhi* as Self, etc.] do not reach the highest stage of Śiva.

Also [there is another interpretation of the sūtra: If *darśana* is understood not as a system of philosophy, but merely as knowledge; *sthiti,* not as a stage, but as inward cessation; *bhūmikā,* not as a role, but as means, then the interpretation is as follows]: The *sthitis,* or the inward *cessation* of all *darśanas*, all empirical knowledge—such as the experience of [an external thing as] the color blue, or an [inner] experience like pleasure—becomes a means of manifestation for the essential nature of *tat,* Śiva, who is of the nature of consciousness and a mass of bliss. So, whenever the external form [of consciousness] comes to rest in the essential nature [of the knower], there ensues the cessation of the external thing (*saṁhāra*), rest in a condition of inner peace, and then commencement of a continuous series of various experiences (*saṁvit-santati,*) which will be arising anew (*udeṣyat*). Thus this venerable *turīyā*[93] (fourth) consciousness, whose nature is to hold together emanation, maintenance, and reabsorption, flashes forth ceaselessly—now sending forth diversities of various emanations (created things), and now withdrawing [them]—always [both] emaciated and yet always full and also not undergoing any of these forms.[94] It has been said in *Śri Pratyabhijñā-ṭikā:* "When reabsorbing the objects, she [Śakti] flashes [rises in her nature], and so she is full.[95] This venerable [power] being resorted to more and more makes her devotee her own, step by step.

If *Ātman,* (the Self) as described [above], has [such] greatness,

93. See end note 10.

94. This exhausts all four alternatives. The idea is that through *turīyā, Saṁvid* goes on projecting things out of herself (which shows that she is perfectly full and rich), and reabsorbing them into herself (which shows that she is depleted and must take back things to make up her loss); yet in herself she transcends all these alternatives.

95. *Avaleha* means licking, devouring—reabsorbing the objects. Space, time, and objects are devoured by *turīyā,* in which only I-consciousness remains.

how can it be an *aṇu* (jīva) covered with *mala,*[96] enclosed with *kalā*[97] and other *kañcukas,* a *saṁsārin* (transmigrating from one life to another)? [In answer to this question], the author says:

SŪTRA 9

As a result of its limitation of Śakti, reality, which is all consciousness, becomes the mala-covered samsārin.

Cidvat tacchakti saṁkocāt malāvṛtaḥ saṁsārī.

COMMENTARY

When the highest Lord, whose very essence is consciousness, conceals by His free will pervasion of non-duality and assumes duality all round, then His will and other powers, though essentially non-limited, assume limitation. Then only does this [soul] become a transmigratory being, covered with *mala.* Thus the Will-power [of the Absolute], whose sovereignty is unrestricted, assuming limitation, becomes *āṇava-mala,* which consists in its considering itself imperfect. [In the case of] knowledge-power, owing to its becoming gradually limited in the world of differentiation, its omniscience becomes reduced to knowledge of [only] a few things. By assuming extreme limitation, beginning with the acquisition of an inner organ and organs of perception, it acquires *māyīya-mala,*[98] which consists of the apprehension of all objects as different. [In the case of] action-power, its omnipotence in this world of differentiation becomes reduced to the doership of [only] a few things. Starting with assuming limitation in the form of organs of action, it becomes extremely limited and acquires *kārma-mala,*[99] which consists of doing good or

96. For *aṇu* and *mala,* see end note 8.
97. *Kalā* here means limitation with respect to authorship and efficacy. Regarding *kalā* and the other *kañcukas,* see end note 4.
98. *Māyiya-mala*—see end note 8.
99. *Kārma-mala*—see end note 8.

evil. Thus by accepting limitation, the *śaktis* (powers)—omnipotence, omniscience, perfection, eternity, omnipresence—appear respectively as *kalā* (limited agency), *vidyā* (limitation with respect to knowledge), *rāga* (limitation with respect to desire), *kāla* (limitation with respect to time), and *niyati* (limitation with respect to space and cause).[100] Thus constituted this [*ātman* or Self] is called *saṁsārin* (a transmigratory being), poor in Śakti. With the [full] unfoldment of his *śaktis,* however, he is Śiva himself.

Is there any mark appropriate to the Śiva state, by which the Self, even in the *saṁsārin* stage, may be recognized as Śiva himself? It is declared, "There is," [and so the next sūtra] says:

S Ū T R A 1 0

Even in this condition [of the empirical self], he [the individual] does the five kṛtyas (deeds) like Him [like Śiva].

Tathāpi tadvat pañca kṛtyāni karoti.

C O M M E N T A R Y

Here lies the distinction between the *Īśvarādvaya*[101] philosophy and [that of] the Brahmavādins:[102] that the divine, whose essence is consciousness, always retains his authorship of the fivefold act.[103]

100. *Kalā. . .niyati*—end note 4; see p. 13 for more detail on the limitation of the powers of Śiva.

101. *Īśvarādvaya-darśana* means the system of philosophy that *does not believe in any other principle (advaya)* than Īśvara, the Lord. This is the characterization of the Śaiva philosophy of Kashmir, which maintains that Śiva is the whole and sole reality. There is "no second" (*advaya*), no principle other than Śiva. Īśvara here is a synonym of Śiva. He appears both as the world or the field of experience and the experient; as the knower (*pramātā*), knowledge (*pramāṇa*), and the knowable (*prameya*).

102. Brahmavādins refers to those Vedantists who believe that a principle other than Brahman, called Māyā, is responsible for *sṛṣṭi, sthiti* and *saṁhāra*. Literally, it means advocates of the Brahman doctrine.

103. *Pañca-vidha-kṛtya*—the fivefold act. For details see end note 3. In Sūtra 10, the fivefold act is described epistemologically.

This is in accordance with what has been stated by the grand *Svacchanda* and other disciplines [of Śaiva philosophy], (See *Svacchanda Tantra,* 1st Paṭala, 3rd verse): "[I bow to the] Divine who brings about emanation (*sṛṣṭi*), reabsorption (*saṁhāra*), concealment (*vilaya*), maintenance [of the world] (*sthiti*), who dispenses, grace (*anugraha*), and who destroys the affliction of those who have bowed down [to Him]."

Just as the Exalted One (Śiva), by the process of expansion in the extrinsic course[104] (mundane manifestation), brings about emanation, as an unfoldment of his real nature, so does He carry out the five processes even in the condition of *saṁsāra,* by limiting His consciousness-power. So [it has been said] (in *Īśvarapratyabhijñā,* VI Āhnika, 7th verse).

> This being the position [*tat evam* here means *tat evam sati*], even in the empirical state (*vyavahare'pi*), the Lord entering into the body, etc., causes the objects [lit. collection of objects] to appear outwardly by His Will, though appearing within Himself.

[The fivefold processes in the condition of the world are shown below.]

Thus according to the *Pratyabhijñākārikā,* when the great Lord, who is consciousness [lit. whose form is consciousness], enters into the sphere of the body, *prāṇa*—on the occasion of the attention becoming external—makes objects, like blue, appear in definite space and time. This is His act of emanation (*sraṣṭṛtā*). Objects appearing in another space and time refers to His act of withdrawal or absorption (*saṁhartṛtā*). The actual [continued] appearance of blue, etc. is His act of maintenance (*sthāpakatā*). Its appearance as different refers to His act of concealment[105] (*vilayakāritā*). The appearance of everything as identical with the light [of con-

104. *Śuddhetara-adhvā* (lit., course other than the intrinsic)—*Śuddhādhvā* is the intrinsic or supramundane manifestation; *aśuddhādhvā* is the mundane or extrinsic manifestation. Sadāśiva, Īśvara, and Śuddhavidyā are in the region of *Śuddha-adhvā* or supramundane manifestation. The *tattvas* from *māyā* to the five gross elements are in the region of *aśuddha-adhvā,* the extrinsic course or mundane manifestation. This has been called *aśuddha-addhvā* or impure course, because in this there is a sense of *bheda* or difference. In *Śuddha-adhvā,* or the pure course, there is a sense of *abheda* or non-difference.

105. This is called *vilaya,* because the real nature of the Self is veiled in this state.

sciousness][106] refers to His act of grace (*anugrahītṛtā*). I have demonstrated how the Lord is always the author of the fivefold act extensively in *Spandasandoha*. If this authorship of the fivefold act, which occurs within one's own personal experience, is pursued steadily with firm understanding, it reveals the Lord's greatness to the devotee. Those who always ponder over this [fivefold act of the Lord], knowing the universe as an unfoldment of the essential nature [of consciousness], become liberated in this very life. This is what the [sacred] tradition maintains (*ityāmnātāḥ*). Those who do not ponder this, seeing all objects of experience as essentially different, remain forever bound.

This is not the only mode of the authorship of the fivefold act. Another esoteric mode exists apart from this. So he says:

SŪTRA 11

These [five deeds are] manifesting, relishing, experiencing as self, settling of the seed, dissolution.

Ābhāsana rakti vimarśana bījāvasthāpana vilāpanatastāni.

COMMENTARY

He does these fivefold acts;[107] this is [syntactically] connected with the previous sūtra. From the viewpoint of the highest end (*mahārthadṛṣṭyā*),[108] whatever appears through the successive function-

106. In the matter of knowledge, the object known in a way becomes one with the knowing subject. The actual *pramiti* (knowledge), divested of the accidents, of the *prameya* (the known object), will be found to be one with the *parmātṛ* (the knowing subject).

107. Here the fivefold act is described from the point of view of the esoteric experience of the yogin, in which *ābhāsana* is *sṛṣṭi; rakti* is *sthiti; Vimarśana* is *Saṁhāra; bijāvasthāpana* is *vilaya;* and *vilāpana* is *anugraha.*

108. *Mahārtha* is the esoteric aspect of this system.

ing [lit. expansion] of the goddess of sight and other [perceptual functions] is, [so to speak] emanated (*sṛjyate*) [this is *ābhāsana* or manifesting]. An object being thus emanated (brought forth into appearance), when [the Self], without closing the eye relishes it for some time, is maintained [in experience] by the goddess of maintenance. [This relishing of the experience for some time represents *sthiti* or maintenance.] It is withdrawn at the time of *vimarśa* (*vimarśana-samaye*), also called a sudden flash of delight (*camatkāra*).[109] [This knowledge of the object represents *saṁhāra*.][110] As Rāma has said:

> The mountain of manifoldness that cannot be split by others, even by the thunderbolt of contemplation [*samādhi*, lit. collectedness of consciousness], is experienced as oneself and thus destroyed by those who are endowed with the power that accrues from devotion to you.

However, if during reabsorption or withdrawal [of the experience of manifoldness or differentiation], it [the object of experience] generates various *saṁskāras* (impressions) of doubt inwardly, then it acquires the state of *saṁsāra* in germinal form. This state is bound to spring forth into existence again, and thus it superimposes [on the experient] the state of *vilaya* (concealment of the real nature of the Self). On the other hand, if while it [the world that has been reduced to a germinal form] is being held inwardly, along with anything else being experienced at that time, it is burned to sameness in the fire of consciousness, by the process of *haṭhapāka*[111] and by the device of *alaṁgrāsa*,[112] then he [the yogin], by bringing about perfection, enters the state of grace. This kind of authorship of the fivefold act, though always within reach of everyone, does not becomes manifest

109. *Vimarśana* or *camatkāra* is the experience of "Ah! How wonderful!" It is like the delight of an artistic experience; hence it is called *camatkāra*, which means an intuitive flash of artistic experience.

110. The knowledge of the object is called *saṁhāra* here because the object is withdrawn. The object as an object disappears and only its knowledge remains.

111. *Haṭhapāka*. An object of experience is brought into sameness with the real essence of the experient in two ways: (1) *śānti-praśama* and (2) *haṭhapāka praśama*. *Prásama* means "reducing completely the world of experience to oneness with the experient." This is a slow, gradual process; *haṭhapāka* is an intense, persistent process.

112. *Alaṁgrāsa*. *Alam* means *paripūrṇarūpatayā*, *nis-saṁskāratayā*—fully, perfectly, when no impression or germ of *saṁsāra*, as separate from consciousness, is allowed to remain; *grāsa* is *grasanam* (lit., swallowing). Here it means *svātmasātkaraṇam*—bringing it to sameness with the Self.

without the instruction of a good Guru (spiritual master). One should, therefore, take to the reverential service of a good Guru so that this [the experience of the fivefold act] may become manifest to him.

He, however, who does not acquire the complete knowledge [of the authorship of the fivefold act], owing to the lack of guidance from a good Guru, remains deluded by his own powers (*śaktis*), since the real nature of each [*śakti*] is concealed [from him]. Therefore it is said:

SŪTRA 12

To be a saṁsārin means being deluded by one's own powers, because of the ignorance of that [authorship of the fivefold act].

Tad ṁaparijñāne svaśaktibhir vyāmohitatā saṁsāritvam.

COMMENTARY

Tat or "of that" [in the sūtra] means the authorship of this fivefold act, which is always happening; *aparijñāne* or ignorance means "not flashing forth" due to the absence of the manifestation of one's own power, which becomes effective through the descent of *Śakti*. [The rest of the sūtra means] acquiring the condition of a *saṁsārin* (transmigrant) is due to delusion (*vyāmohitatvam*), [which means] being nailed by various doubts created by the *śāstras* (scriptural text) and worldly opinions.

As stated in the excellent *Sarvavīrabhaṭṭāraka:*

> Through ignorance, people are subject to uncertainty; hence follow birth and death.
> The essence of all mantras[113] consists of letters or sounds, [and] the essence of all letters or sounds is Śiva.

113. In *mantra, man* implies *mananāt* (by pondering), and *tra* implies *trāyate*

Now, the *vākśakti* (power of speech) [known as] *parā*[114] (supreme)—who is identical with the light of consciousness (Śiva), who is of the form of the great mantra that is eternally sounded, who consists of the consciousness of the perfect "I," who contains within herself (who is pregnant with) the whole assemblage of *śaktis* formed by the sound beginning with "a" and ending with "kṣa"[115]—brings into manifestation the sphere of the [limited] subject or experient through the successive phases of *paśyantī,*[116] *madhyamā,* etc. In this state [of the limited experient], she conceals her real form as *parā* and produces in the empirical subject (*māyā-pramātuḥ*) evernew *vikalpa* activity[117] every moment, which brings into view objects that are obscure and particular. She also presents the stage of *avikalpa*[118] as veiled by the [*vikalpa* activity], though [the *avikalpa* state] itself is quite pure. Under these circumstances, and deluded by the peculiar *śaktis* in the form of "*ka*" and other consonants that are presided over by Brāhmī[119] and other deities, the deluded man helplessly considers the limited body, *prāṇas,* etc. as the Self.

Brāhmī and the other deities, in the state of the *paśu* (bound soul)—manifesting emanation and maintenance with respect to dif-

---

(protects, saves). Mantra, therefore, means "that by pondering which protects, or saves." Mantra is a sacred word (or words) which, when properly uttered and meditated upon, becomes efficacious in all sorts of ways; here, in bringing about liberation.

114. Parāvāk. It is *citi* (consciousness-power), which consists of an inner sound born of *non-māyiya* letters. It is ever sounded, ever throbbing. It is the *Svātantrya Śakti,* the free, unfettered, absolute Will-power, the main glorious supreme sovereignty of the Divine. It is called *parā* because it is supreme, perfect. It is called *vak* because it sounds forth, utters forth, the universe by its "I-consciousness." Also see end note 8. (Īśvara pr. vi., p. 253.)

115. *A* to *kṣa* includes all the letters of the Devanāgarī script. These letters, according to the Śaiva philosophy, represent various *śaktis.*

116. See end note 9.

117. See end note 7. The *vikalpa*-activity refers to the *vikṣepa* aspect of *Śakti,* which projects all kinds of differences. The *ācchādana,* or veiling, refers to the *āvaraṇa* aspect of *śakti*. It throws a veil over the real nature of the Self, and thus it conceals the *avikalpa* stage of the Self. In this one sentence, the writer has referred to both the *vikṣepa* and the *āvaraṇa* aspects of *Śakti*.

118. *Avikalpa* is the distinctionless consciousness. It is the opposite of *vikalpa*. It is mere awareness, without a "this" or "that." It is *turyātita avasthā,* a stage of consciousness beyond the *turya*.

119. Brāhmī (lit., pertaining to Brahmā). The class of letter presided over by this deity is *Ka*. The other *śaktis* and their class of letters are: Māheśvari (*Ca*), Kaumārī (*Ṭa*), Vaiṣṇavī (*Ta*), Vārāhī (*Pa*), Indrāṇī (*Ya*), Cāmuṇḍā (*Śa*), and Mahālakṣmī (*A*).

ferences, and withdrawal with respect to non-difference[120]—bring about only limited *vikalpas*. In the *pati* (lord) stage, however, these [deities] manifesting withdrawal with respect to difference and emanation and maintenance with respect to non-difference, gradually, by reducing the *vikalpas*, [ultimately] disclose the great *avikalpa* stage, which enables one to enter into the blissful *bhairava-mudrā*.[121] At this stage, they [the *śaktis*] cause to appear the *pure vikalpa śakti*,[122] which is deeply merged in consciousness and bliss [and which enables one to feel like the following]:

> He who knows that all this glory [of manifestation] is mine [belongs to the spirit], who realizes that the entire cosmos is his Self, possesses *maheśatā*[123] even when the *vikalpas*[124] have their play.
>
> (*Īśvara-pratyabhijñā*,
> Āgamādhikāra II, Āhnika, 12th verse.)

Hence the state of a *saṁsārin* (transmigrant) consists, as explained above, of the delusion brought about by one's own *śaktis*.

[The above is known as *Śāmbhavopāya* or the *Śāmbhava* technique of attaining unity-consciousness. The *Śāktopāya* or the *Śākta* technique follows.]

Further, the exalted consciousness-power (*citi-sakti*) known as Vāmeśvarī,[125] because she emits (projects) the universe and also because she has to do with the contrary course of *saṁsāra*, displays herself wholly in the condition of the bound subject (*paśu*), as the

120. See end note 11.
121. See end note 12.
122. *Śuddha* (pure) *vikalpa*—This is the *vikalpa* in which the Sādhaka feels—*Sarvo mamāyam vibhavaḥ*—all this glory of manifestation is of (my) Self; he identifies himself with Śiva. It is a total consciousness and the means for passing into *nirvikalpa*, or consciousness free from differentiations. This is called *śuddha vikalpa* or pure *vikalpa*, because though it is still *vikalpa* or mental formulation, it is *śuddha* or pure inasmuch as it is a *mental* formulation of the identity of oneself with the Divine.
123. *Maheśatā*— This is an abstract noun form of "Maheśa," which means the great Lord (Śiva). Maheśatā or Māheśvarya, therefore, means the power or status of the great Lord, Śiva. It connotes the state in which the soul is perfected and identified with Maheśa, the great Lord or Śiva.
124. *Vikalpas*—See end note 7.
125. *Vāmeśvarī*—The author here states why this *śakti* is known as *vāmeśvarī*: The word *vāma* is connected with the verb *vam*, which means "to spit out, emit, eject." The Śakti is called Vāmeśvarī because she emits or sends forth the

[empirical] subject in the form of *khecari,*[126] as the inner organ in the form of *gocarī,* as the outer organ in the form of *dikcarī,* and as objective existents in the form of *bhūcarī.* Resting in the stage of the void [concealing the true nature of the Self], she shines forth, having concealed her highest reality as *cid-gagana-carī* through the *khecarī* group. The latter consists of the śakti of *kalā,* of the nature of limited doership, etc. She appears, through the *gocarī* group, in the form of the deity *antaḥ-karaṇa*[127] (the inner psychic apparatus) whose main functions are ascertainment of difference (*bheda-niścaya*); [in its *buddhi* aspect] identification [of the Self] with different things (*bheda-abhimāna*), and ideation of things as different (*bheda-vikalpana*); [in its *manas* aspect] by concealing her real nature, which consists of the ascertainment of non-difference, etc. She also appears through the *dikcarī* group, in the form of the deity of the outer senses whose main function is perception of difference, by concealing her real nature. She appears, through the *bhūcharī* group, in the form of knowable objects that have the nature of differentiated appearances all round, by concealing the real nature of the Universal Self, and by deluding the heart of creatures.[128]

In the *pati* stage, however, the *śakti* manifests herself as *cidgaganacari,* whose essence consists of universal doership; as *gocarī,* whose essence consists of the *ascertainment* of non-difference; as *dikcarī,* whose essence consists of the *perception* of non-difference; as *bhūcarī,* whose essence consists of [revealing] objects as non-different, like one's limbs. All of these open up the heart of the *pati.*

Venerable Dāmodara, who commands unfeigned respect due to his innate *camatkāra* (bliss), also says in the Vimuktakas (independent

universe, out of the Absolute. The word *vāma* also means "left, reverse, contrary, opposite." This *śakti* is called Vāmeśvarī also because while in the Śiva state there is unity-consciousness; in the state of Saṁsāra, the *contrary* or *opposite* condition happens (there is difference-consciousness), and also because everyone considers the body, *prāṇa,* etc., to be his Self. This play on the word *vāma* cannot be retained in the translation.

126. See end note 13.

127. There are three apsects of *antaḥkaraṇa—buddhi, ahaṁkāra* and *manas. Buddhi* ascertains; *ahaṁkāra* brings about identification of the Self with the body, etc., and assimilation of experience with oneself, and *manas* determines a thing as this or that.

128. Though *cakra* means group, assemblage, or wheel, it suggests an array of forces (like an army) that has to be penetrated before the individual can ascend to universal consciousness. It is difficult to bring out this subtle suggestion in translation.

verses): "Vāmeśa (Vāmeśvarī), and other goddesses, having their sphere in the knowing subject [as *khecarī*], in his inner organ [as *gocarī*], in the outer senses [as *dikcarī*], and in objective existences [as *bhūcarī*], bring about liberation by full knowledge (*parijñāna*), thus making him whole (*pūrṇa*) and bondage by ignorance (*ajñāna*), thus making him limited (*avacchinna*). So, being a *saṁsārin* consists of being deluded by one's own *śaktis*.

[The *āṇavopāya*—the āṇava-technique of attaining unity-consciousness—follows.]

Again the highest Lord, whose essential nature is consciousness, has his own unique *aiśvarya-śakti*.[129] His essential nature consists of doership,[130] which is essentially a *sphurattā* or flashing forth[131] of divine light. When she [*aiśvaryaśakti*], by concealing her real nature, causes delusion in the *paśu* state (the state of a bound soul)—by the phases of *prāṇa, apāna,* and *samāna śaktis,*[132] by the states of waking, dream, and deep sleep, and by the *kalās*[133] of the body, *prāṇa,* and *puryaṣṭaka*[134]—then this delusion is the condition of one's being a *saṁsārin* (transmigrating from life to life). When, however, she unfolds the *udāna-śakti*[135] that appears in *madhyadhāma*[136] as of the

129. *Aiśvaryaśakti* is the sovereign power of the Lord. This is also His *Svātantrya-śakti,* His absolute free Will.
130-131. Flashing forth or *sphurattā* is here another name of *prakāśa*. Doership or *kartṛtā* is another name of *vimarśa*. Regarding the distinction between *prakāśa* and *vimarśa,* see end note 5.
132. See end note 14.
133. *Kalās* means organs or phases; here, those phases that bind the soul to the world.
134. *Puryaṣṭaka*. This is synonomous with *sūkṣmaśarīra,* the vehicle of the *saṁskāras,* which is not cast off at death like the *sthūla śārīra* or the physical body. *Puri* means "a city" and *aṣṭakam* means "a group of eight;" *puryaṣṭaka* thus means the city of the group of eight. This group of eight consists of the *five tanmātras, manas, buddhi,* and *ahaṁkāra*.
135. *Udāna śakti* is the *śakti* that appears when *prāṇa* and *apāna* become equally balanced. *Udāna* then becomes active, moves up through the *madhya-dhāma* or *suṣumnā,* and brings about the *turya* or fourth state of consciousness.
136. *Madhya-dhāma* is the middle *nāḍi,* or *suṣumnā*. There are two *nāḍīs* running parallel to the *suṣumnā*. They are not physical but *prāṇic* and are known as *iḍā* and *piṅgalā*. *Prāṇa* flows through the *iḍā* and *apāna* through the *piṅgalā*. *Suṣumnā* is a *prāṇic nāḍī* travelling upward inside the spinal column towards the brain. Normally, just the *prāṇa* and *apāna śaktis* are active. When, however, through the practice of yoga, *prāṇa* and *apāna* currents are equilibrated, the *suṣumnā nāḍī* becomes open and the *udāna* current flows through it, bringing about the *turya* state of consciousness.

nature of *turya*[137] state and *vyānaśakti,*[138] whose essence is to pervade the universe and which appears as of the nature of *turyātīta,*[139] and both of which are a mass of consciousness and bliss, then even in the embodied state one reaches the stage of *pati*[140] and attains liberation while still living.

Thus "being deluded by one's own *śaktis* (powers)" has been interpreted in three ways.

The *cidvat sūtra*[141] (Sūtra 9) states that the light of consciousness, assuming limitation, becomes a *saṁsārin* (an individual migrating from one conditioned existence to another). Here it has been said, from a different angle, that it becomes a *saṁsārin* because it is deluded by its own powers. It may be observed from yet another angle that one with limited powers [an individual soul]—in spite of his having *prāṇa* and other [limitations]—when not deluded by those powers, becomes, according to the thesis of the sacred tradition, the Lord [Himself], with a body. In other words, he can be described as the venerable Śiva Himself. As the Āgama says:

> They are the highest Lord in a veiled form, having entered a human body.

It has also been said in a commentary[142] on the *Pratyabhijñā* that:

137. See end note 15.
138. *Vyāna-śakti*—Macrocosmically, it pervades the entire universe, and microcosmically, when the *kuṇḍalinī* becomes awakened, it pervades the entire body and brings about the *turyātīta* condition.
139. *Turyātīta* means transcending the fourth state. It is a state beyond the *turya*. *Turya* is *turīya* (fourth) in relation to the three states of waking, dream, and deep sleep; but in *turyātīta,* the above three states disappear as separate states. Hence when the three states have disappeared, *turya* can no longer be called *turya*. It is called *turyātīta,* in which the *turya* or fourth state has been transcended. It is a state where pure consciousness is like an ocean without any agitation whatsoever; it is full of bliss. It is the consciousness of Śiva himself or one who has reached that stage in which the entire universe appears as his Self. In *turya, manas* becomes attenuated; in *turyātīta* it is dissolved in *śakti*. When the *turya* state becomes fully developed and reaches perfection, it is transformed into *turyātīta*. In this state, everything appears to the individual as *Śiva* or the Self.
140. *Pati*—This refers to the condition in which the individual soul realizes his identity with the universal Self or Śiva.
141. In Sūtra 9, the *saṁsāritva* has been described from the metaphysical point of view; here it has been described microcosmically, both in the individual's *paśu daśā* (bound state) and *pati daśā* (liberated state).
142. It is not clear which Pratyabhijñā-ṭikā is referred to here. Perhaps it may be the untraced *vivṛti* on the Pratyabhijñā-kārikās by Utpalācārya.

They also attain to perfection who consider the body or even the jar, consisting of the thirty-six *tattvas* (principles), as a form of Śiva.

To reveal the essential truth, the meaning of the above sūtra has been put conversely:

SŪTRA 13

Acquiring the full knowledge of it [the authorship of the fivefold act of the Self], citta[143] *(the individual consciousness) itself, by inward movement, becomes citi*[144] *(universal consciousness) by rising to the status of cetana.*[145]

Tat parijñāne cittam eva antarmukhībhāvena cetana padādhyārohāt cḥitiḥ.

COMMENTARY

From the viewpoint of the knowable object, this sūtra has been already discussed in connection with the explanation given for Sūtra 12. From the viewpoint of wording, however, it is being explained as follows:

After full knowledge of *it* [the self's authorship of the fivefold act]—due to the lack of knowledge being removed, the delusion caused by one's own *śakti* (power) having ceased because of the attainment of *svātantrya*—the *citta* [explained in Sūtra 5] gives up the limiting tendency of extroversion, becomes introverted, and rises to the status of *cetana*. That is, gradually it rises to the status of the knowing subject, whereby dissolving the aspect of limitation, and

143. *Citta* means the limited individual consciousness; the psychological status of the individual.

144. *Citi* means the universal consciousness, consciousness in its initial, unconditioned state. It is also known as *cit*.

145. *Cetana* in this context means the consciousness of the Self.

attaining its real nature, it becomes *citi*. It now enters its highest stage of *cit*.

A question arises here. If the nature of *cit-śakti* in its highest aspect cancels [lit. devours] all differences, it should remain so [retain that nature] even in the *māyā*-sphere [even in its condition of manifestation of the universe]—just as the Sun manifests objects even when it is covered by clouds. [It is the nature of the Sun to manifest objects, and it does so even when it is covered by clouds. Likewise, if it is the nature of *citi* to cancel all difference, it should retain this nature even when it is covered by *māyā*. *Citi* is compared to the Sun, *māyā* is compared to clouds.] Raising this issue, the author replies below:

SŪTRA 14

The fire of citi, even when it descends to the (lower) stage, though covered [by Māyā], partly burns the fuel of the known [objects].

Citivahnir avarohapade channo'pi mātrayā meyendhanaṁ pluṣyati.

COMMENTARY

Citi is [here likened to] fire because it devours [assimilates to itself] the [phenomenal] universe. In its stage of descent in the *māyā-pramātā* [experient conditioned by *māyā*], though covered [by *māyā*], because of its [inherent] freedom, it partly burns, or assimilates into itself, the fuel of the objects of knowledge, such as blue, yellow, etc., This occurs in spite of its true nature being veiled, just as fire burns fuel even though covered by copious ashes.[146] [The sense is that since the objects of knowledge are assimilated by consciousness to itself, their difference is annihilated. As *knowledge,* the objects are simply part and parcel of consciousness itself.] The intention of

146. The ashes here are compared to *māyā; citi* is compared to fire.

using the word *mātrā* [in part, partly] [in the sūtra] is this: Though devouring [the object of knowledge], it consumes it only in part, because it again makes it rise by means of the *saṁskāras* (the impressions of the object left on the mind). That all experients have the power of devouring [assimilating objects of experience to consciousness] is proved by one's own experience. As has been [rightly] said by the revered Utpaladeva[147] in his hymns:

> Since all the creatures, even Brahmā, Indra, and Viṣṇu,[148] go on devouring [assimilating], therefore, O God, I adore the universe that is of your own form.[149]
>
> (*Śiva-stotrāvali* xx.17)

When, however, [the aspirant], by accomplishing the *prasara* or going forth of the [divine] senses, adopts the means of the practice of *sarga* or emanation [of the objective existence] and, by accomplishing the *saṅkoca* or withdrawal [of the senses], adopts the means of the practice of *saṁhāra,* or withdrawal [of the objective existence],[150] then

S Ū T R A 1 5

In acquiring the [inherent] power of citi, the aspirant assimilates the universe to himself.

Balalābhe viśvam ātmasāt karoti.

147. Utpaladeva or Utpalācārya flourished in about 900-950 A.D. This quotation is from his *Stotrāvalī* in praise of Śiva.
148. The traditional trinity consists of Brahmā, Viṣṇu, and Śiva. Since, in this system, Śiva is the term most often used for the Absolute, Indra has been substituted for Śiva in the trinity.
149. The idea is that all conscious beings go on devouring or experiencing objects in various ways—assimilating things into themselves; therefore, "I adore the universe, which is simply yourself inasmuch as you constantly assimilate it to yourself."
150. Here, *prasara* and *saṅkoca* of the senses are connected successively with

C O M M E N T A R Y

Citi, by the submergence of the covering of the body, *prāṇa,* etc., and by bringing into prominence her essential nature, by her emergence, is *bala* or power. As has been said,

> Then having resorted to that power, the mantras[151] [acquire the power and efficiency of the all-knowing, Śiva].

Thus when the power [of consciousness] is gained—when one assumes one's real nature that has now emerged—one makes the universe, from the earth to Sadāśiva, one's own. That is, one makes the universe appear as identical with one's Self. This has been said by the ancient teachers in the *Kramasūtras* in their own characteristic language:

> Just as a fire set ablaze consumes fuel, so should one consume the objects of sense, which act like fetters.

It would not be right to say, "The all-inclusive role of *citi,* when it assimilates to itself the entire universe, is only temporary. How then can it [the inclusive role] be accepted?" [This objection is not valid], for the inclusive nature of *citi* appears as temporary only because of the emergence and immergence of the body, etc. In reality, the temporary appearance of the inclusive nature of *citi* is due to the emergence of the body, etc. which are brought into manifestation by the sovereign will of *citi* herself. This all-inclusive role, however, is continuously manifesting. Otherwise [if *citi* were not continuously manifesting], even the body would not be manifest [would not appear as an object of consciousness]. Therefore the [yogic] practice is recommended to remove the [false] identification of the experient with the body, etc., not for attaining the status of the experiencing consciousness that, by its very nature, is always luminous.

---

sarga and *saṁhāra* of the objective existence. *Saṅkoca* in this context does not mean contraction or limitation, but closing or withdrawing.

151. This is a quotation from the *Spandakārikā* (II, 10) of Vasugupta. The full verse is translated as:

तदाक्रम्य बलं मन्त्राः सर्वज्ञबलशालिनः ।
प्रवर्तन्तेऽधिकाराय करणानीव देहिनाम् ॥

"The mantras, having resorted to that power [of *citi*] alone, acquire the power and efficiency of the all-knowing [Śiva] and then proceed to carry out their specific functions, as the senses of the individual [carry out their specific

This is what the author of the excellent *Pratyabhijñā* means. And thus:

SŪTRA 16

When the bliss of cit is attained, one is stable in the consciousness of identity with cit, even while the body, etc., are being experienced. This state is called jīvanmukti (liberation even while one is alive).

Cidānanda lābhe dehādiṣu cetyamāneṣvapi. Cidaikātmya pratipatti dārḍhyaṁ jīvamuktiḥ.

COMMENTARY

When, on the attainment of the bliss of consciousness—on the attainment of *samāveśa*[152] or the contemplative experience of unity consciousness in which the entire universe is experienced as identical with the Self, even in *vyutthāna,*[153] in which the body, *prāṇa,* blue, pleasure, etc.[154] are experienced like so many coverings—there is firmness in the consciousness of identity with *cit*. That is, there is a lasting experience of unity consciousness with *cit*. This is due to the force of the [residual] impressions of unity-consciousness [produced] during contemplation, which are strengthened by the various means to be propounded. That firmness of consciousness, of identity with *cit,* is *jīvanmukti*—liberation of one who is still alive, who still retains

functions by the power of the individual, not by themselves]."

152. *Samāveśa* means *samādhi* in which there is unity-experience—in which the entire universe appears as the Self, in which the consciousness of the empirical Self is completely subordinated and becomes identified with the consciousness of Śiva.

153. *Vyutthāna* means literally "rising up"—rising up from the condition of contemplation to everyday normal experience.

154. *Deha-prāṇa-nīla-sukhādiṣu. Deha* and *prāṇa* are examples of the "subject" in whom *deha* is relatively outer and *prāṇa,* inner; *nīlasukhādiṣu* are examples of the "object" of which again *nīla* is outer experience, and *sukha* is inner experience.

his vital breaths. In that condition, the fetters [of ignorance] completely dissolve and one recognizes one's true nature.

As has been said in the *Spandaśāstra:*

> He who knows thus [the universe is identical with the Self] and regards the whole world as a play [of the Divine], being ever united [with the universal consciousness] is without doubt, liberated even while alive.
>
> (*Spandakārikā,* Niṣyanda II, v. 5)

How is the bliss of *cit* acquired? In this regard, the *sūtrakāra* (composer of the sūtras) says:

SUTRA 17

With the development of the madhya (center) comes the acquisition of the bliss of consciousness.

Madhya vikāsāc cidānanda lābhaḥ.

COMMENTARY

The exalted *saṁvit* (universal consciousness) is itself the center, as it is present as the innermost [reality] of all, and inasmuch as the form or nature of anything is not possible without its being attached to it as the ground or support. In spite of this [of its being the innermost reality and ground of every possible thing], according to the dictum "at first *samvit* is transformed into *prāṇa,*" it conceals its real nature in the stage of *Māyā.* Accepting the role of *prāṇa-śakti*[155]—resting in the planes of *buddhi,* body, etc., in descending order—it has followed the course of the thousand *nāḍis.* Even there [at the stage of the individual embodiment] it remains principally in the form of the *madhyama-*

155. *Prāṇa-śakti* here means the primal energy, not *prāṇavāyu* or the breath of that name. The transformation of consciousness into *prāṇa* is a step towards its progressive materialization. This *prāṇa* is also known as *mahāprāṇa.*

nāḍī,[156] whose substratum is Brahman in the form of *prāṇa-śakti,* right from *brahmarandhra*[157] down to *adho vaktra,*[158] like the central rib of a *palāśa*[159] leaf. [It is called *madhyama-nāḍī or central nāḍi*] because it is the source and the resting place of all functions. Even with such a construction, its nature remains hidden to the *paśus* (the ignorant *jīvas*). When, however, the exalted *samvit* (consciousness) being the innermost reality of all forms, the center (*madhya*), develops by the means described above [the practice[160] of *pañcakṛtya*] or when the central *brahma-nāḍi*[161] develops[162] as is to be described, then, because of that development, there comes the attainment of the bliss of *cit* (the universal consciousness). Then comes liberation while one is alive, as described earlier.

Regarding the method that brings about the development of the center, it is said:

156. See end note 16.
157. *Brahmarandhra.* According to Tantra, there are *cakras* or centers of *prāṇa* located in the *praṇā-maya-kośa.* These are called *cakras* because they are like a wheel in appearance. They absorb and distribute *prāṇa* or vitality to the *prāṇamaya-kośa,* and through it, to the physical body.

When the higher *cakras* are fully activated, they impart to the individual certain subtle and occult experiences. Their names, together with the nearest physical organs, are: Mūlādhāra (below the genitals), Svādhiṣṭhāna (above the genitals), Maṇipūra (navel), Anāhata (heart), Viśuddha (throat), Ájñā (third eye), Sahasrāra or Brahmarandhra (crown).
158. *Adho-vaktra* (lit., the lower organ) is the *meḍhra-kanda,* which is situated below the *mūlādhāra* at the root of the rectum.
159. Palāśa is the *butea frondosa* or the Dhāka tree, as it is otherwise called. *Suṣumnā* is compared to the midrib of the *palāśa* leaf, and *nāḍīs* springing from it are compared to the small fine veins joined to the midrib of the *palāśa.*
160. "When, however, the exalted *samvit. . .* above." This refers to the development from the Śāmbhavopāya and Śāktopāya points of view.
161. *Brahmanādi* is the same as the *madhya-nāḍi* or *suṣumnā.*
162. "When the central *brahmanāḍi* develops." This refers to the development from the *āṇavopāya* point of view.

SŪTRA 18

The means [for the development of the madhya] are dissolution of vikalpa, saṅkoca and vikāsa of śakti, cutting of the vāhas, the practice [of the contemplation] of the koṭi (point, extremity) of the beginning and the end.

Vikalpa kṣaya śakti saṁkoca vikāsa vāhacchedādyanta koṭi nibhālanādaya ihopāyāḥ.

COMMENTARY

In the unfolding of the central *śakti,* the dissolution of *vikalpa,* etc. is the means. It has already been explained that the unfoldment of *samvid,* which forms the center of all, is achieved by following the authorship of the fivefold process. However, another means is also being mentioned. There is an easy means by which one can dispense with all the fetters of rigorous disciplines like *prāṇāyāma,*[163] *mudrā,*[164] *bandha,*[165] etc. When [an aspirant] keeps his *citta* (individual consciousness) concentrated on the *samvid* or *cit* [lit. heart],[166] restraining, by the method alluded to, the *vikalpas*[167] that obstruct staying in one's real nature, by not thinking of anything whatsoever, and thus by laying hold of the *avikalpa* state, he becomes used to regarding his *cit* as the [real] knower, untarnished by body, etc. So

163. *Prāṇāyāma* means breath control. Various methods of breath control can be found in books on yoga.

164. *Mudrā* literally means "seal," or "mark." In yoga, it means certain finger positions practiced in yogic discipline. In a wider sense, it means control of certain organs and senses that help in concentration; also it means concentration—Bhairavī-mudrā. See *Gheraṇḍasaṁhitā,* Upadeśa 3.

165. *Bandha*—This is a yogic practice in which certain organs of the body are contracted or locked.

166. *Hṛdaya* here does not mean the physical heart, but the deepest consciousness. It has been called *hṛdaya* because it is the center of reality. It is the light of consciousness, in which the entire consciousness is rooted. In the individudal, it is the spiritual center.

167. See end note 7.

within a short time, he attains absorption into *turya*[168] and the state transcending *turya* (*turyātīta*).[169]

As has been stated in the *Īśvara-pratyabhijñā,* (IV A.I. Ā., kā, 11):

> By giving up *vikalpa,* and by one-pointedness [of mind], one gradually reaches the stage of Īśvara-ship.

The excellent *Spanda* also states:

> When [mental] agitation would dissolve, then would ensue the highest stage.
>
> (*Spandakārika,* Ni. I, kā. 9)

So also in the *Jñānagarbha:*

> When, O mother, men renounce all mental activities and are poised in a pure state, being free from the bondage of the pursuit of sense-activities, then by thy grace is that supreme state realized at once, which rains down the nectar of undiminished and unparalleled happiness.

This means has been described first because it is the highest and because it has been taught in the *Pratyabhijñā* doctrine. The *saṅkoca* of Śakti, etc., though not taught in the *Pratyabhijñā* doctrine, have been mentioned nevertheless, as they belong to the sacred tradition or are incidentally connected with it. If many means are described, someone may enter [the state of *samāveśa*] through any one of them. The *saṅkoca* of Śakti means the turning in toward the Self, by the process of withdrawal of that consciousness that is spreading out through the gates of the senses [towards the objects]. As stated in the first mantra of Chapter 4 of Kaṭhavallī, belonging to the *Atharvaupaniṣads.*[170]

> The self-existent one pierced the openings [of the senses]
> outward,
> Hence one looks outward, not within one's Self.
> Some wise man, wishing to taste immortality
> With reverted eyes (introspectively)
> beholds [lit. beheld] the immanent Self.

168. *Turya* (lit., fourth) is the same as *turīya.* See end notes 9 and 14. It is the state in which there is pure consciousness of *ātman,* and the sense of difference disappears. In this *Udāna* śakti is active.
169. *Turyātita* is the state higher than *turya.* Unity consciousness that began in *turya* is consummated in *turyātita,* in which the whole universe appears as the Self. See *Īśvarapratya-bhijñā-vimarśini,* Vol. II, pp. 246–47. In *turyātita, vyāna śakti* is active. See fn. 139.
170. *Kaṭha Upaniṣad* really belongs to the black Yajurveda. The original read-

Or [the *saṅkoca* of the *śakti* may be] the [sudden] turning back from all sides of the externally spread *śakti,* like the contraction of the limbs of the tortoise, and its withdrawal into the interior when afraid. As has been said, "It being reverted there is resting in the ever-present [ātman].[171] The *vikāsa* of *Śakti* hidden within results from the simultaneous opening of all the sense organs.

> The object [of one's aspiration] is to be seen within, while the external sight may be kept steady without closing and opening of the eyelids.

This technique of inner absorption with external expansion of the senses is known as *bhairavīmudrā.*

As has been said in *Kakṣyāstotra:*

> Throwing, by will, all the powers, like seeing, etc., simultaneously and on all sides, into their respective objects and remaining [unmoved] *within* like a golden pillar, you [O Śiva] alone appears as the foundation of the universe.

Kallaṭa, the great scholar, has also said: "That [the development or *vikāsa* of *madhya śakti*] is accomplished by transformation [by viewing the inward- and outward-going consciousness as the same], even in the presence of forms. As far as *saṅkoca* and *vikāsa* of Śakti are concerned, *vikāsa* connotes the practice of the condition of expansion and resting of *śakti* in the stage of the *ūrdhva-kuṇḍalinī.*[172] This is gradually brought about by restraining the *prāṇa* between the eyebrows by means of the power of the subtle *prāṇa,* which develops gradually though the regulation of the vibrations in the cavities of the nose.

---

ing is *icchan* (wishing; seeking); the reading here adopted is *aśnan* (eating, tasting). In this context *aśnan* means "wishing to taste."

171. There are two states of clear Self-consciousness: *śāntodita* and *nityodita.* In the first, there may be diminution of the clarity of Self-consciousness sometimes, but in the second, Self-consciousness is complete and permanent.

172. *Ūrdhva-Kuṇḍalinī* is the condition where the *prāṇa* and *apāna* enter the *suṣumnā* and the *kuṇḍalinī* rises. *Kuṇḍalinī* is a distinct *śakti* that lies folded up in three and a half *valayas* or folds in the *mūlādhāra.* When she rises from one three-fourths of the folds, goes up through the *suṣumnā,* crosses Lambikā, and pierces Brahmarandhra, she is known as *Ūrdhva-kuṇḍalinī;* this pervasion of hers is known as *vikāsa* or *viṣa.* Lambikā is the *prāṇic* crossroad of four *prāṇic* channels, near the palate. The first two channels are for the flow of *prāṇa* for all the *jīvas.* The third channel is the one through which the yogin rises from the *mūlādhāra,* by means of *ūrdhva-kuṇḍalinī,* to Brahmarandhra. The fourth channel is for

In the state of *adhaḥ kuṇḍalini*,[173] whose location is indicated by the sixth organ of *meḍhrakanda*[174] after strengthening the *prāṇa śakti*, there is entrance or absorption in its root, tip, and middle. As has been said in the Vijñāna-bhaṭṭāraka:

> One should throw [concentrate] the delightful *citta* in the middle of *vahni* and *viṣa*,[175] whether by itself or permeated by *vāyu* (prāṇic breath); one would then be joined to the bliss of sexual union (*smarānanda*).[176]
>
> (*Vijñānabhairava*, 68)

Here *vahni* represents the stage of *saṅkoca* by the process of the entrance of *prāṇa* [in *meḍhra-kanda*]. The *viṣa* locus represents the stage of *vikāsa*, by the technique of *prasara* in accordance with the etymological explanation of the root "to pervade."

By "both *vālas*" is to be understood *prāṇa* and *apāna*. One [*apāna*] is concerned with the left, and the other [*prāṇa*] is concerned with the right [*nāḍi* or channel of *vāyu*]; *cheda* means cessation or pause by the sounding of *anacka* sounds,[177] like *ka, ha*, etc., inwardly, before which, however, they should be stopped in the heart. As has been said in *Jñāna-garbha:*

> In the heart lotus of one whose mind has been controlled, whose two *nāḍis* (the channels of *vāyu*) [whose flow of *vāyu* in the two *nāḍis*] extending on both sides have been stilled by the restraint brought about by sounding voweless "K" and whose blinding

---

those accomplished yogins whose *prāṇavāyu* rises directly to Brahmarandhra without having to pass through *mūlādhāra*.

173. The field of *Adhaḥ-kuṇḍalinī* is from Lambikā down to one three-fourths of the folds of *kuṇḍalinī* lying folded in the *mūlādhāra*. *Prāṇa* goes down in *adhaḥ-kuṇḍalinī* from Lambikā towards the *mūlādhāra*. This is known as *saṅkoca* or *vahni*.

174. *Saṣṭha-vaktra*. The ears, eyes, nose, mouth, and the anus are, in this system, known as *pañca-vaktra* or five organs; *meḍhra-kanda*, near the root of the rectum below the *mūlādhāra*, is the *ṣaṣṭha-vaktra*, the sixth organ.

175. See end notes 17 and 18.

176. *Smarānanda* (bliss of sexual union). When the *citta* can be restrained between the *adhaḥ* and *ūrdhva kuṇḍalinī* in this way, then one has the joy of sexual union. This is "inverted" kāma. Sexual union is external; this union is internal.

177. *Anacka*. *Aca* means a, i, u, ṛ, ḷ, e, o, ai, au—all the vowels; *anacka* is sounding ka, ha, etc, without the vowel. The real meaning of the yogic practice of *anacka* sounding is to concentrate on any mantra back to the source, where it is unuttered.

darkness has been dispelled, arises that sprout of your knowledge,
This, O [world mother], is adequate to produce *parameśa-ship*
even in the *paśu*.[178]

The first point is the heart. The last point is the measure of twelve [a measure of twelve fingers].[179] *Nibhālana* means exercise or practice by fixing the mind at the time of the rising of *prāṇa* and its coming to an end between these two[180] [between *hṛdaya* and *dvādaśānta*]. As has been said in *Vijñānabhairava* (v. 49):

He whose senses are merged (*nilīnākṣaḥ*) in the ether of the heart, who has entered mentally into the center of the heart lotus, who excludes everything else from consciousness [who is one-pointed], attains supreme happiness, O Beautiful One.[181]

It has also been said in the *Vijñānabhairava* (v. 51):

If one turns one's mind to *dvādaśānta,* howsoever and wheresoever, the fluctuation of his mind will diminish every moment, and in a few days, he will acquire an extraordinary status.

The word *ādi,* "et cetera," refers to the practice of the *unmeṣa* condition. As has been said in the *Spanda* (*Spandakārikā* N. 3, Kā. 9): "That is to be known as *unmeṣa;*[182] one may see it for oneself."

178. The following points have to be noted. This is in praise of *jagadambā*—the world mother: *tava* (your) refers to *"jagadambā." Anackaka...cchido; vidhṛtacetasaḥ* and *dāritāndḥamasaḥ* are compounds qualifying *"hṛdaya-paṅkajasya." Vidyāṅkuro* is connected with *"tava,"* or *dāritāndha-tamasaḥ* may be taken as qualifying *"tava."*

179. *Dvādaśāntaḥ* means a measure of twelve fingers; literally, it means the end of twelve fingers.

180. The *prāṇa* starts at the point of *hṛdaya (prāṇollāsa),* which here means the center of the diaphram, and ends (*viśrānti*) at *dvādaśānta*—a distance of twelve fingers from it. *Apāna* (*vāyu*) starts from *dvādaśānta* (distance of twelve fingers) and ceases at *hṛdaya* (the center of the diaphram). *Nibhālana* means fixing the *citta* or mind at the start of *prāṇa* at the heart, and at its cessation at a distance of twelve fingers from the heart, and at the start of *apāna* from *dvādaśānta* and its cessation at *hṛdaya.* This is known as *Śakti-dvādaśānta,* or *kauṇḍalinī;* it is like the *prāṇāpāna smṛti* (*pāṇāpāna sati*) of Buddhist yoga. There is another *dvādaśānta,* over the crown of the head, which is known as *Śiva dvādaśānta* or *prakriyānta.*

181. "Beautiful one" refers to the *devī* (the goddess). This is addressed to the *devī.* Most of the mystic teachings in this system are in the form of a dialogue between Śiva and the Devī (goddess).

182. *Unmeṣa* (lit., unfolding) is a technical term of this yoga. Only half of the verse has been quoted in the text. The full verse is, *Eka-cintā prasaktasya yataḥ syād aparodayaḥ, unmeṣaḥ sa tu vijñeyaḥ svayam tam upalakṣayet.* This means while one is engaged in one thought, and another arises, the mental resting at the

Under this concept are also summed up the tasting, etc., of pleasant objects. As it is said in the excellent *Vijñānabhairava,* (v. 72, 73, and 74):

> When one experiences the expansion of the joy of savor arising from the pleasure of eating and drinking, one should meditate on the perfect condition of this joy, and then one would become full of great bliss.
>
> When a yogin mentally becomes one with the incomparable joy of song and other objects, then of such a concentrated yogin, there is identity with that [with the incomparable joy], because he becomes one with it.
>
> Wherever the *manas* (the individual mind) finds its satisfaction, let it be concentrated on that. In every such case, the true nature of the highest bliss will shine forth.[183]

Similarly, any other *bhāvanā* [meditation] on the Self full of bliss may be inferred. The words "et cetera" in the sūtra refer to methods such as these for the development of the *madhya* (center).

From the development of the *madhya* results the attainment of the bliss of the spirit. This indeed is the *samādhi* [at-one-ment] of the highest yogin, also known as *Samāveśa,*[184] *samāpatti,* and other such synonymous terms. For bringing about its permanence [the permanence of *samādhi*], the [following] method has been mentioned.

---

junction point between the two is known as *unmeṣa*. The nature of the mind is to pass successively from thought to thought; but if one rests mentally immediately after one thought, just before another arises, one develops the quality of *unmeṣa*. It means resting in the *spanda* between two thoughts or images—resting in the consciousness that is the background of both the thought or images. It is the unfoldment of the creative nature of the Supreme. This is the explanation according to *Śāktopāya*.

According to *Śāmbhavopāya,* the emergence of the *pāramārthika bhāva* or the highest Reality, while one is engaged in meditating on the object of one's devotion, is known as *unmeṣa*.

183. Three methods have been recommended here for rising to the highest bliss by concentrating on aesthetic enjoyment: (1) *āsvāda-dhāraṇā,* concentrating on the savor of eating and drinking, (2) *śabda-dhāraṇā,* concentrating on the aesthetic enjoyment of music, and (3) *manastuṣṭi-dhāraṇā,* concentrating on whatever pleases the mind .

184. See end note 19.

SŪTRA 19

In vyutthāna, which is full of the after-effects of samādhi, one finds the attainment of permanent samādhi by dwelling on one's identity with cit (the universal, supreme consciousness) over and over again.

Samādhi saṃskāravati vyutthāne bhūyo bhūyaś cidaikyāmarśān-nityodita samādhi lāhhaḥ.

COMMENTARY

A great yogin who has attain *Samāveśa* is still full of the *samādhi* state, even during what is considered to be *vyutthāna.*[185] In the condition of *vyutthāna,* he beholds the [entire] mass of entities to be dissolving in the *cit-sky,* like a bit of cloud in autumn,[186] reeling joyfully from the savor of *samādhi,* like one intoxicated, resorting to introversion again and again, and meditating on his identity with *cit* by the process of *nimīlana-samādhi.*[187]

As stated in the *Krama-sūtras,*

> The *sādhaka* (the aspirant practicing yogic discipline), [even] while gazing outward remains in *samāveśa* by *Kramā mudrā,*[188] which is characterized by inwardness. Owing to the force of *āveśa,* there takes place in this first an entrance of consciousness from the external into the internal, and [then] from the internal into the external. Thus this *mudrā-krama* is of the nature of both the external and internal.

185. *Vyutthāna*—Literally "rising." In yoga, it means coming to normal consciousness after contemplation.
186. This state appears when *dehātma-bhāva* or the delusion of identity with the body disappears.
187. *Nimīlana-samādhi* is the inward meditation with closed eyes in which the individual consciousness is absorbed in the universal consciousness. In this, even the trace of object as object disappears, and becomes one with *cit.* This is real introversion, or *antarmukhatā,* and leads to full I-consciousness or *pūrṇāhantā.*
188. *Krama-mudrā* or *Mudrā-Krama.* This is defined in the text itself by the Krama-sūtra. In this, the mind swings alternately between the internal and the

The meaning of this quotation is as follows: *Krama-mudrayā,* by *krama-mudrā; Krama* means the succession of the cyclic consciousness of emanation (*sṛṣṭi*), maintenance (*sthiti*), and reabsorption (*saṁhṛti*). *Mudrā* means *mudrayati*—the *turiyā* (fourth) power of consciousness [consciously] makes one's own the world-process that [already] rests in the [highest] Self. *Antaḥ-svarūpayā* means by the essential nature of the full or perfect "I." [The entire sentence means: The *sādhaka* or aspirant, the yogin of the highest type, becomes *samāviṣṭa*—one who has realized the unfolding of the highest *Śakti*—even while extroverted, even while he is busying himself with sense-objects. [This he is able to do] by *Krama-mudrā,* which is of the nature of full consciousness of the perfect self. In this process there occurs—through the assimilation [lit., devouring] of the totality of the external sense-objects into the internal, into the highest *citi* plane [the plane of highest or universal consciousness]—penetration into the inner, or *samāveśa,* by the very process of assimilation. Again there occurs, through the internal—through the realization of the nature of *citiśakti* by the power of *samāveśa*—a penetration or entrance into the external or the totality of externalization (*vamana*). This [*praveśa,* penetration or entrance] is [also] a *samāveśa* of the nature of the manifestation of the solidification of the essence of *cit* (universal consciousness).

His eternally active (*nityodita*) *samāveśa,* which is external and internal at the same time, is of the nature of *mudrā,*[189] because (1) it distributes *muda*—joy—on acount of its being of the nature of the highest bliss; (2) it dissolves (*drāvaṇāt*) all fetters; (3) it seals up the universe into the being of the inner *turīya* (the fourth or highest consciousness).

It is also called Krama (succession, cycle) because (1) it causes emanation, etc., to appear in succession (*krama*) (2) it itself consists of their successive appearance (*krama*).

Now he describes the fruit of the attainment of this *samādhi.*

---

external. The internal appears as the universal consciousness, and the external no longer appears as merely the world, but as the form of Śiva or universal consciousness. *Mudrā* here is not used in its ordinary sense of certain finger postures. The sense in which it is used here is given further on in the text itself.

189. *Mudrā* is etymologically derived in three ways: *mudam rāti (dadāti),* that which gives *mud* or joy; *mum drāvayati,* that which dissolves *mu* (bondage); *mudrayati iti,* that which seals up [the universe in *turīya*].

SŪTRA 20

Then [on the attainment of krama-mudrā], as a result of entering into the perfect I-consciousness or Self, which is in essence cit and ānanda (consciousness and bliss) and of the nature of the power of great mantra, there accrues the attainment of lordship over one's group of the deities of consciousness that brings about all emanation and reabsorption of the universe. All this is the nature of Śiva.

Tadā prakāśānanda sāra mahāmantra vīryātmaka pūrṇāhantā veśāt sadā sarva sarga saṁhāra kāri nija saṁvid devatā cakreśvaratā prāptir bhavatīti śivam.

COMMENTARY

On attaining lasting *samādhi,* there accrues lordship over the group of the deities of consciousness.[190] The group (*cakra*) always brings about every kind of emanation and reabsorption of the universe—beginning with *Kālāgni*[191] and ending with the last *Kalā* (phase) [known as *śāntā kalā*]—by entering into the natural *camatkāra* or bliss of Self-consciousness. *Camatkāra* is of the essence of *prakāśa* and *ānanda,* sheer compact consciousness and bliss—which is the very soul of all the mantras (*sarvamantra-jīvita-bhūtā*), which is perfect (*pūrṇā*), the highest *vimarśa (parābhaṭṭārikā-rūpā*).[192] This lordship

190. *Samvit-devatā-cakram*—Macrocosmically, the *samvit-devatās* are the *khecarī-cakra, gocarī-cakra, dik-carī-cakra,* and *bhūcarī-cakra* described earlier. Microcosmically, this consists of limited knowership, internal and external senses, and limited objective knowledge.

191. *Kālāgnyādeḥ carama-kalā-paryantasya*—From Rudra, known as *kālāgni-bhuvaneśa* in Nivṛttikalā—the lowest phase of manifestation—up to the highest phase known as *śāntā-kalā. Kalā* here means phase of manifestation. See the Chart of Manifestation, p. 97.

192. *Parā-bhaṭṭārikā* here refers to the highest *vimarśa.* There are three kinds of

accrues to the greatest yogin referred to in this context. *Īti Śivam* is to be construed as "all this is [really] the form of Śiva;" this is the conclusion. This being so, then the essence of whatever is cognized (*prameya*) is cognition (*pramāṇa*). Of this again, the inwardly turned experients (*pramātās*), full of self-consciousness, are the essential truth.

Of these [experients], *sadāśiva-īśvaraship* is the essence in which the sense of identification with the limiting adjuncts of body, etc., has dissolved and whose body is the whole universe. And the highest reality of this [*sadāśiva-īśvaraship*] is the blissful great Lord Himself, who is full of *camatkāra*[193] or *vimarśa* (the bliss of perfect self-consciousness) of the entire universe, brought about by one-ness of being[194] (*eka-sadbhāva*) with *prakāśa* (the substratum of all manifestation).[195]

Nothing can manifest unless it shares [lit. enters] the light [the source and substratum of all manifestation] of the Highest Reality. And the Highest Lord is full of the flow of bliss because of His being free from all desire, because of His being fully perfect, because of His being the essence of absolute freedom, and because of His having attained the state of full *jagadānanda*.[196] He made the entire world—consisting of indicator or word (*vācaka*) and indicated or object

---

vimarśa: para, apara, and *parāpara*. *Para* is the *vimarśa* of Śiva in which there is *abheda* or complete non-difference between "I" and "this, "knower" and "known;" *apara* is the *vimarśa* of *aṇu,* or the empirical individual, in which there is *bheda* or difference between "I" and "this," knower and known; *parāpara* is the *vimarśa* or *śakti* in which there is *bhedābheda*—the difference between "I" and "this" is posited and forever transcended.

193. *Camatkāra* is the wonderful joy of creativity. Here it means *aham-vimarśa*—the bliss of perfect Self-consciousness, the bliss of the consciousness of the entire manifestation as "I." This *aham-vimarśa* is the result of the feeling of oneness of being with *prakāśa* (consciousness-existence). Regarding *prakāśa* and *vimarśa,* see fn. 20–21. The ultimate is *prakāśa-vimarśa-maya*. It is both the universe, in its manifested and unmanifested state, and also its permanent substratum.

194. *Eka-sad-bhāva* means oneness of being with (*prakāśa*).

195. Kṣemarāja gives here the ascending stages of reality. The first is *samvedya* or *prameya,* the known. The second is *samvedana* or *pramāṇa,* knowledge. The third is the *pramātā,* the experient who has self-consciousness. The fourth and deeper stage of reality is that of Sadāśiva, whose consciousness is not identified with the limiting adjuncts of body, etc., but whose body is the whole universe. The highest stage of reality is Maheśvara, whose consciousness of Self includes the entire manifestation and is identical with his *prakāśa*.

196. See end note 20.

(*vācya*)—his own by reflection [lit. seizing mentally] on the entire assemblage of *non-māyīya* words[197] from "a" to "kṣa."

Therefore the extended universe, beginning with [the letter] "a" which is the nature of the highest "*akula*"[198] up to the letter "ha," indicative of the unfolding or expansion of *Śakti*—"*kṣa*" indicating only the end of the expansion—that [universe] flashing forth or vibrating, by virtue of the combination of "a" and "ha" and being accepted inwardly in the manner of *pratyāhāra,*[199] rests in the Highest Reality in the form of *bindu,*[200] indicative of the consciousness of non-differentiation. Thus this natural *vimarśa* or inward experience is of the nature of the congregation of words.

As has been said (by Utpaladeva in *Ajaḍa-pramātṛ-siddhi,* v. 22-23):

> Resting all objective experience[201] within oneself is what is meant by I-feeling. This "resting" [within oneself] is called Sovereignty of Will, primary doership, and lordship because of the cancellation of all relational consciousness and dependence on anything outside oneself.

This I-feeling is the stage of great power, for all mantras arise from and come to rest in it; by its power all activities with an object are performed.

It has been said in the excellent *Spanda* (beginning with *Spandakārikā,* Niṣyanda II, vv. 1-2) "All mantras approaching this power" and closing with "All these [mantras] are endowed with the nature of the characteristic mark of Śiva."

The *Śiva Sūtras* also state: "By unification with the great lake,[202] one acquires the experience of mantra power."

Here [in this sūtra] the penetration into the perfect Self, which is of the nature of great mantra-power, is becoming one with it by the immersion of the body, *prāṇa,* etc. [into it], by steadiness in the

197. See end note 21.

198. *Akula: kulam śaktiriti proktam, akulam Śiva ucyate (Svacchanda tantra)—kula* is Śakti and *akula* is Śiva. *Kula,* (total) or the entire manifestation, is *Śakti*. One who is not lost in this total (manifestation) is *akula,* or Śiva. The letter "a," from the point of view of *mātṛkā-cakra,* is of the nature of Śiva.

199. See end note 22.

200. See end note 23.

201. *Prakāśa* here does not mean "the divine light," but *ghaṭasukhādi-vedya-prakśasya*—all objective experience like jar, pleasure, etc.

202. *Mahāhrada*—the great or deep lake—refers to the Supreme Spiritual

achievement of that stage (of perfect Self), and by immersing in its essence the [experience of] body, blue, etc. So that then whatever appears—the body, pleasure [inner experience], blue [experience of outer objects], etc., or whatever is known for certain [by *buddhi*], or remembered, or thought out [by *manas*]—becomes the play of *citi-śakti* that flashes forth as the background [of all experience]. It has been rightly said, "without its flashing, there is no flashing of anything [whatever]." Only while flashing in this manner, she, by *māyā-śakti,* appearing as of this or that nature owing to her assuming [considering herself] the nature [lit. color] of manifested body, blue, etc., is considered by the *māyā*-subjects [*jīvas* or empirical selves] as knowledge, ideation, resolution, etc. In reality, however, this *citi-śakti* is one and the same. As has been said (in *Īśvarapratyabhijñā,* Jñānādhikāra, VII Āhn. v.1):

> That consciousness which is colored [identified] with the succession of different objects (*tat-tat-padāmrthakrama*) is nothing other than the great Lord, the highest knower, and of the nature of successionless,[203] infinite consciousness.

So [also] it has been said (in *Īśvarapratyabhijñā,* Jñānādhikāra, V Āhn. v. 18):

> Owing to the *māyā śakti* of the Lord, she herself, having to do with different knowables, is called knowledge, ideation, resolution and by other names.

Thus it is one and the same *citi-śakti* that appears in various ways under all conditions. If by means of entry into and firm grip of her she is attained [as described in Sūtra 18], then, by entering into her, and by the means previously described (successive unfolding and unfolding of the senses) because of everything being of the nature of everything else, even in the reabsorption, etc. of everything, whatever group of natural consciousness-deities exists (the non-*māyiyā* group of inner and external senses, which is ever projecting and ever withdrawing over all this) the highest yogin acquires lordship and *parabhairava*-ship [becomes the highest *bhairava*].

As has been said:

---

awareness. It has been so called because it is clear, uncovered by anything, infinite, and profound.

203. Maheśvara would be limited by time, if there is succession in His consciousness. His consciousness is *akrama* (timeless), *ananta* (spaceless).

When one is rooted in the one place—in the *Spandatattva* consisting of the perfect I-consciousness—then controlling the *udbhava* (emanation) and *laya* (absorption) of it [of the *puryaṣṭaka* or *Sūkṣmaśarīra*—the subtle body and thereby also of the universe, by means of *unmīlana* and *nimīlana samāveśa*], one acquires the status of a [real] enjoyer, and then becomes the lord of *cakra* [of the group of the sense-deities].

(*Spandakārikā,* Niṣyanda III, 19)

Here "the one place" [is explained in the following, *Spandakārikā,* Niṣyanda III.12]

Everything should be deposited into the one place [into the *cit-śakti*].

Ekatra or "one place" should be interpreted as the state of the general vibration of *cit,* being of the nature of *unmeṣa.*

Then the word *tasya*[204] in the verse cited above is to be understood to mean *puryaṣṭaka* (subtle body), inasmuch as the previous sūtra [in *Spanda Kārikā* III. 17] begins with "held or bound by *puryaṣṭaka* (subtle body)." It is not to be interpreted as "in one place, i.e. gross or subtle body," as Kallaṭācārya,[205] the author of *Vivaraṇa,* has done.

And it has been lauded by me [in the following verse]:

He who has become an independent ruler[206] [who is no longer under the control of the senses] of the *citicakra* and the great lord, being served by the group of sense-deities,[207] is a rare being that excels all.

The word *iti* in this sūtra connotes conclusion. The word *Śiva* here means that whatever is the body of the above text [whatever has been said in the text] is Śiva, because it is a means to the attainment

204. *Tasya* (of it) as interpreted by the text refers to *puryaṣṭaka* or the subtle body; a better interpretation, as given by Swāmī Lakṣamaṇa Joo, is that it refers to *śakti-cakra* or the group of *śaktis,* for it is the *Śakti-cakra* that is responsible for *laya* (absorption) and *udbhava* (emanation).

205. Kallaṭācārya was the pupil of Vasugupta and wrote a *vṛtti* on the *Spandasūtras.* He flourished in the latter half of the ninth century.

206. *Cakravartī* has a double meaning here: (1) ruler of the *cakra*—circle or group of sense deities, and (2) universal sovereign.

207. When the senses are divinized, they become *saṁvit-devatā-cakra,* or *karaṇeśvarīs.*

of Śiva. It is Śiva also because it has come from Śiva, because it is not different from the true nature of Śiva, and because it is indeed Śiva.

Man, bound in all the phases of waking, dream, and dreamless sleep, by the body, *prāṇa,* pleasure, etc., does not recognize his own *citi* (consciousness), which is of the nature of the great power and full of perfect bliss.

But he who, owing to this instruction, beholds, in the ocean of the nectar of [spiritual] awareness, the universe as a mass of its foam [of the ocean of the nectar of awareness] on all sides, is said to be Śiva Himself in disguise.

This instruction in the truth has been given for those who have accrued the descent of Śakti wrought by Śiva but who, for want of the discipline of serious study, are unfit for keen arguments and are thus incapable of understanding the *Īśvara-pratyabhijñā* [the *Pratyabhijñā* philosophy by Utpaladeva].

The *Pratyabhijñāhṛdaya* (The Doctrine of Recognition) is concluded.

This work, by the glorious teacher Rājānaka Kṣemarāja, is dependent on the lotus feet of the glorious Abhinavagupta, the best among the great venerable Śaiva teachers.

May there be welfare (for all)!

Chart 1. Details of Sutra 3

Tattva 1	*Presiding Deity* 2	*Experient* 3	*Corresponding field of experience* 4
1. Śiva	Śiva	Śiva Pramātā	All existence is mere Prakāśa or Śiva.
2. Sadāśiva. (Icchā or Will is predominant	Sadāśiva-bhaṭṭāraka	Mantra-maheśvara. The experience of "I" or Śiva is clear, but there is also a dim experience of the Universe.	Indistinct experience of the universe; not yet distinct from the Self experience.
3. Iśvara tattva (jñāna or knowledge is predominant)	Iśvara-bhaṭṭāraka	Mantreśvara who, like Iśvara, has a distinct experience of both 'I' and the Universe but the Universe is only an aspect of the Self.	Experience of Self and the universe both distinct and equal, but the universe is still an aspect of the Self.
4. Śuddhavidyātattva or Sadvidyā tattva (Kriyā or action is predominant)	Ananta-bhaṭṭāraka	Mantra who has an experience of both 'I' and the universe as separate, but the universe is closely related to the Self.	Experience of difference from everything and yet everything appears closely related to the Self.
5. Mahāmāyā tattva		Vijñānākala has knowledge but is dévoid of agency. He is free from Māyiya and Kārma mala but is still subject to Ānava malas.	All the pralayākalas and Sakalas.
6. Māyātattva		Pralayākala or Pralayakavelī or Sūnyapramātā. He is free from Kārma mala but is still subject to Āṇava and Māyiya malas.	Mere void.
7. Remaining tattvas up to the Earth.		Sakala, from the *devas* up to the plant and minerals. This is subject to all the three malas: Āṇava, Māyīya and Kārma mala.	Experience of all things as differing from one another and from the Self.

Chart 2. Kalās and Bhuvanas According to Abhinavagupta

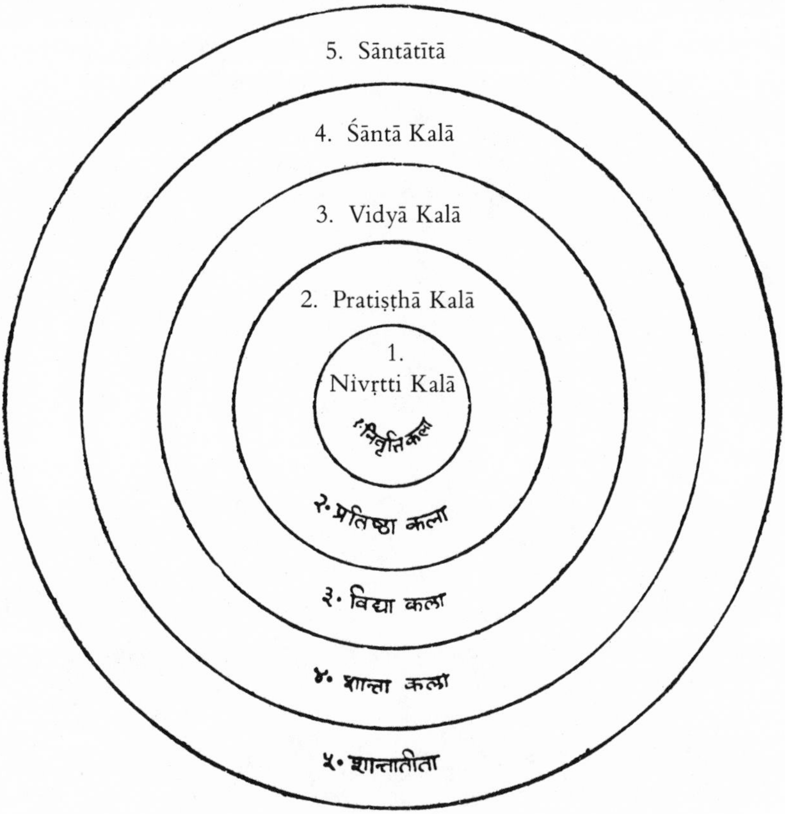

The whole manifestation is divided into five *Kalās* or phases. The lowest is:

1. NIVṚTTI-KALĀ, the first Kalā, is formed mainly of *pṛthvī tattva* and has 16 *bhuvanas* or planes of existence. The lowest of these is called *Kālāgni rudra-bhuvana*. It is this *bhuvana* that *Kṣemarāja* refers to in *Kālāgnyādeḥ*.

2. PRATIṢṬHĀ KALĀ. This is the second *Kalā* counting from the lowest. It consists of 23 *tattvas,* from *jala-tattva* to *prakṛti tattva,* and contains *56 bhuvanas.*

3. VIDYĀ KALĀ. This third *Kalā* contains seven *tattvas,* from *puruṣa tattva* to *māyā tattva,* and 28 *bhuvanas.*

4. ŚĀNTĀ KALĀ. This fourth *Kalā* contains three *tattvas—Śuddha Vidyā, Īśvara,* and *Sadāśiva*—and 18 *bhuvanas.*

5. ŚĀNTĀTĪTĀ KALĀ. This fifth *Kalā* is comprised of only *Śiva* and *Śakti tattvas* and has no *bhuvana.*

Parama Śiva transcends all *Kalās.* The total *bhuvanas* (16 + 56 + 28 + 18) is 118.

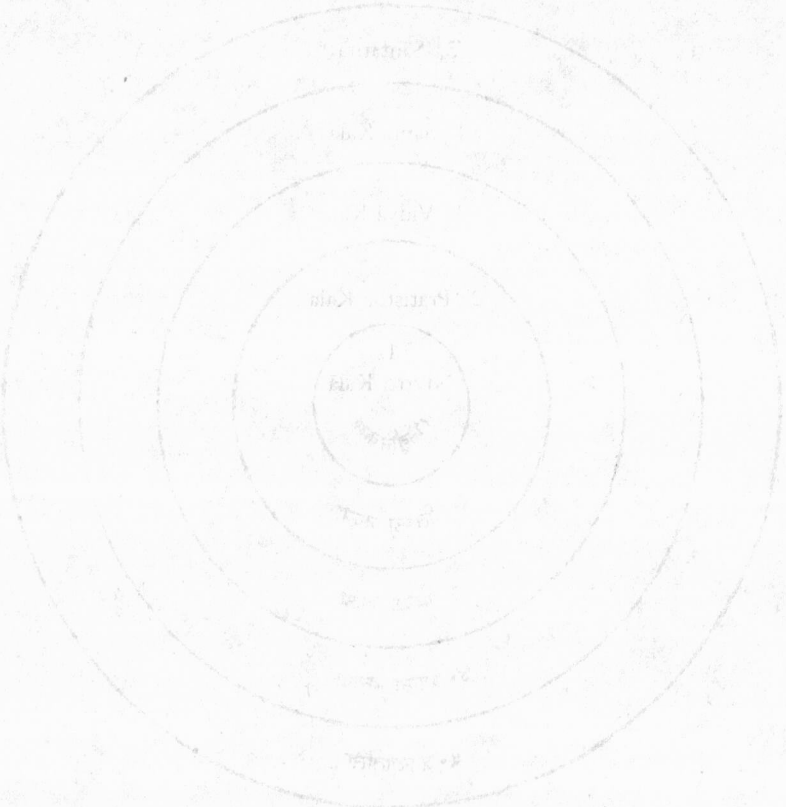

END NOTES

1. *Recognition.* This doctrine teaches that the individual self (*nara* or *jīva*) is identical with the Universal Self (Śiva). He has forgotten his Real Self, due to the limitations of his psychophysical mechanism. The Śaiva doctrine of Kashmir is called *Pratyabhijñā-darśana,* or The Doctrine of Recognition, because it brings home to the individual this truth: once he recognizes his Real Self, he will be free from his ego—the product of his identification with his psycho-physical mechanism. Thus he will realize that his Real Self is identical with the Universal Self. *Īśvara-pratyabhijñā-vimarśinī* by Abhinavagupta gives the following exposition of *Pratyabhijñā:*

प्रतीपमात्माभिमुख्येन ज्ञानं प्रकाशः प्रत्यभिज्ञा । प्रतीपम् इति—स्वात्मावभासो हि न अननुभूतपूर्वोऽविच्छिन्नप्रकाशत्वात् तस्य, स तु तच्छक्तयैवविच्छिन्न इव विकल्पित इव लक्ष्यते इति वक्ष्यते । प्रत्यभिज्ञा च–भातभासमानरूपानुसंधानात्मिका, स एवायं चैत्र-इति प्रतिसन्धानेन अभिमुखीभूते वस्तुनि ज्ञानम्; लोकेऽपि एतत्पुत्र एवंगुण एवंरूपक इत्येवं वा, अन्ततोऽपि सामान्यात्मना वा ज्ञातस्य पुनरभिमुखीभावावसरे प्रतिसंधितप्राणितमेव ज्ञानं प्रत्यभिज्ञा—इति व्यवह्रियते । इहापि प्रसिद्धपुराणसिद्धान्तागमानुमानादिविहितपूर्णशक्तिस्वभाव ईश्वरे, सति स्वात्मन्यभिमुखीभूते तत्प्रतिसन्धानेन ज्ञानम् उदेति, नूनं स एव ईश्वरोऽहम्—इति" (p. १९-२०)

> "Prati" means *pratipam*—though known, now appearing as forgotten through delusion. "Abhi" means facing, close at hand. "Jna" means illumination or knowledge. So Pratyabhijñā means re-cognition of the real Self. "Pratīpam" implies that it is not that the consciousness of Self has not been a fact of experience before—for the Self is a light that can never be extinguished—but that, as will be explained, through its own Power, it appears to be extinguished or limited. Recognition (Pratyabhijñā) is the unification of what appeared before with what appears now, as in the judgement "This is the same Caitra." It is a cognition by recollection, referring to what is directly present.

In ordinary life also, recognition is the unification of experiences at the time of a subsequent appearance of one who was known before. This can be either in general or specific terms, such as "the son of so and so, of such and such qualities and description," or like "so and so has been recognized by the king."

Here also, with the knowledge of the Lord, as one who has perfect power, acquired through the well-known Purāṇas, Siddhānta Āgama, inference, etc. and the immediate experience of one's Self, *re-cognition* arises. Through the unification of the two, one experiences "Certainly, I am that very Lord."

This system is also known as Trika darśana—the system of the triad: (1) Nara, the bound soul (2) Śakti, the divine power, and (3) Śiva, the lord who releases the bound soul. This is a mystic philosophy, describing all three of these conditions.

It is also called *Spandaśāstra,* or the system of vibration, because it is to the vibrating energy or Śakti of Śiva that the world-process owes its existence.

2. *Śiva.* This word is derived from the root *śi* (to lie), and from the root *śvi* (to cut asunder). Both meanings are implied in Śiva: (1) the one "in whom all things (all objects and subjects) lie or rest," and (2) the one who cuts asunder (*śyati pāpam iti Śivaḥ*) all sins. Śiva is thus both the fundamental ground of all reality and the supreme Benevolence or Good who, by His grace, saves all. He is the supreme or Absolute, both from the metaphysical and soteriological point of view.

In addition to Pratyabhijñā, Trika, and Spanda, this system is also known as Śaiva-darśana or Bhairava-darśana—the system positing Śiva as the all-of-reality-and-good. As this system is non-dual, it is sometimes called Kashmirian Śaiva philosophy to distinguish it from the dual Śaiva philosophy of the South.

3. *Pañcakṛtya* or the five acts brought about by Śiva are:

(1) *Sṛṣṭi*—letting go; casting out of oneself. The usual translation, "creation," is misleading because it implies that the creator acts upon an external material, and thus brings about the world-process. *Sṛṣṭi* is derived from the root *sṛj,* which means "to let go," "to pour forth," "to cast out." This implies that the world process is already implicitly contained in Śiva; he merely lets it go or casts it out of himself. According to Śaivism, the world is not a creation, but an emanation; it is a theophany. (2) *Sthiti*—maintenance (of the world-process). (3) *Saṁhāra* or *Samhṛti*—withdrawal or reabsorption. It does not mean destruction. There is no destruction of the world; it is only reabsorbed by Śiva for a time. Destruction is only a metaphorical and secondary sense of *saṁhāra.* (4) *Vilaya* or *pidhāna*—concealment of the real nature of the Self. (5) *Anugraha*—grace. These five *kṛtyas* imply that Śiva lets go the universe out of himself, imparts existence to it, and finally withdraws it into himself only to let it appear again. This cycle is called a *kalpa.* There is no end to the world-process; the cosmic process is repeated from eternity to eternity.

Anugraha is the act of grace by which Śiva brings about the liberation of man. The first four *kṛtyas* are cosmological, the last is soteriological. The five *kṛtyas* are not an artificial mixture of two standpoints—one cosmological and the other soteriological. Rather *anugraha* is the *raison d'etre* of the first four *kṛtyas;* it is that for the sake of which the first four *kṛtyas* come into play. It expresses the abounding love of Śiva.

4. *Sadāśivādeḥ bhūmyantasya*—from Sadāśiva down to the earth. According to this system, there are thirty-six *tattvas* or principles. These are divisible into: (1) the *Śuddha adhvā,* the pure or the supramundane way or course and (2) the *Aśuddha adhvā* or the impure, the mundane way or course. *Śuddha adhvā* is that which is above *Māyā,* in which there is no difference between the knower and the known. *Aśuddha adhvā* is that in which difference begins right up to the earth. The thirty-six *tattvas* are given below in descending order from Śiva, the Supreme principle:

Above Manifestation

1. *Śiva,* the Highest Principle or universal consciousness. In this, *cit* or consciousness is predominant.

2. *Śakti* is Śiva's inseparable conscious energy. In this, *ānanda* or bliss is predominant.

These two *tattvas* are the source of all manifestation, and so they are above manifestation.

Supramudane Manifestation or Śuddha adhvā

3. *Sadāśiva,* the ever benevolent. In this *tattva, ahantā* or I-consciousness and *icchā* or Will are predominant. Idaṁtā or this-consciousness (world-consciousness) is not so prominent. It is also called *sādākhya tattva,* for in this state there is the first notion of "being" (*sat ākhyā yataḥ*). It is the incipient world-experience. The world is indistinct at this stage. The consciousness of this state is *Aham idam*—"I am this." There is no distinction between "I" (the Divine Experient) and "this" (the universe). This is a state of perfect identity.

4. *Īśvara,* the Lord. In this, both I-consciousness and world-consciousness are equally prominent, and *jñāna* or knowledge is predominant. The consciousness of this state is *Idam aham*—"This is I," the universe is I. The universe has come distinctly into consciousness but is still identical with the Divine Self. This is a state of *abheda,* or non-difference between the "I," or Self and "this," or the universe.

5. *Vidyā, Śuddhavidyā,* or *Sadvidyā* is pure, unlimited knowledge. Here the consciousness is *Aham idam ca*—"I am I and also this (universe)." This state is one of *bhedābheda*—the universe is a distinct object to consciousness, yet its distinction is overcome in Self-consciousness. It appears only as an aspect of the Self. This is a state of "identity in difference." *Kriyā* or action is predominant here.

The first five—from *Śiva* to *Sadvidyā*—are called *Śuddha adhvā,* because the object is perceived as a part of the subject to this state; there is no veiling of the Self so far. These five *tattvas* represent the universal aspect of consciousness.

Mundane Manifestation or Aśuddha adhvā

6. Māyā, the universally formative or limiting principle. Sometimes this is not included in the *kañcukas,* as it is a principle that gives rise to them. Māyā veils the real Self and brings about the consciousness of difference and plurality.

The Five Coverings (Kañcukas) of Māyā

7. *Kalā,* limitation with respect to authorship or efficacy.

8. *Vidyā,* limitation with respect to knowledge.

9. *Rāga,* limitation of fullness, giving rise to desires for various objects (I could enjoy this, I could own that, etc.)

10. *Kāla,* limitation of eternity, giving rise to division of past, present, and future.

11. *Niyati,* limitation of freedom, giving rise to limitation of space and cause.

12. *Puruṣa,* when the Divine, by his Māyā, veils His real Self and accepts the status of a limited experient, he is known as Puruṣa, At this stage, the *Sarvakartṛtva* or omnipotence of the Divine is reduced to *kalā* or limited authorship: His *sarvajñatva* or omniscience is reduced to *vidyā* or limited knowledge; His *pūrṇatva* or all-fulfillment is reduced to *rāga,* or desire; His *nityatva* or eternity is reduced to *kāla,* or time-division; His *vyāpakatva* or all-pervasiveness is reduced to cause and effect relationship. The principles from *Kalā* to *Niyati* are generally known as the five *kañcukas* or coverings, veils of Māyā put on by the divine.

13. *Prakṛti,* the root or matrix of objectivity from Buddhi down to earth.

14. *Buddhi,* the ascertaining intelligence.

15. *Ahaṁkāra,* the ego-making principle.

16. *Manas,* the conceptive consciousness.

17-21. The five *jñānamendriyas* or organs of perception (audition, touch, vision, taste, and smell).

22-26. The five organs of action (*karmendriyas*)

27-31. The five *tanmātras*—the undifferentiated origins of the five perceptions.

32-36. The five *mahābhūtas;* the gross elements—*ākāśa* (ether), *vāyu* (air), *agni* (fire), *āpas* (water), and *bhūmi* (earth).

5. *Vimarśa.* The root *mṛś* means to touch; *vimṛś* means to touch mentally. It is a highly technical term of this system. Paramaśiva, the ultimate reality, is not only *prakāśa* or luminous consciousness, but also *vimarśa*—conscious of its consciousness. *Vimarśa* is Self-consciousness or pure I-consciousness of the highest Reality. It is this *vimarśa* or self-consciousness of reality that brings about the emergence of the universe (*sṛṣṭi*), its manifestation (*sthiti,*) and its withdrawal (*saṁhāra*) into it again as identical with its joy of pure I-consciousness. *Vimarśa* assumes three mo-

ments: going out of itself (*sṛṣṭi*), maintaining its continued existence (*sthiti*), and then returning to itself (*saṁhāra*).

> Iha khalu parameśvaraḥ prakāśātmā; prakāśaśca vimarśa-svabhāvaḥ; vimarśo nāma viśvākāreṇa, viśvaprakāśanena, viśvasaṁharaṇena ca akṛtrimāham iti visphuraṇam.
>
> *Parāprāveśika*, pp. 1-2, Kashmir Sanskrit Series

The entire universe is already contained in the highest consciousness or the highest Self, just as the variegated plumage of the peacock is contained in the plasma of its egg (*mayūrāṇḍarasa-nyāyena*). *Vimarśa* is the positing of this Self, which leads to manifestation.

6. *Sadāśiva tattva* may be said to be the first principle of manifestation. Out of the *Śiva-śakti* state emerges *Sadāśiva tattva,* where consciousness is of the form, "I am this." "This" (*idantā*) here refers to the total universe. "I" (*ahantā*) refers to the Divine Experient. It is the absolute or universal I. The first consciousness of the absolute in manifestation is, "I am this." The "this" (*idantā*) or the entire universe is already implicitly contained in the absolute consciousness, but when it begins to posit the "I" as the "this," the "this" becomes the first glimmer of the universe to be. In this stage of consciousness, the "this" aspect is in germinal form; it is dominated by the "I" aspect (*ahantācchādita-asphuṭa-idantāmayam*), where the *viśva* or universe is both different and non-different (*parāpara rūpam*) from Sadāśiva. In this stage, *Icchā* or Will is predominant. In the consciousness "*I am* this," existence or being is clearly posited; hence this principle is also known as *sādākhya-tattva*. The system now starts giving a hierarchy of individual experients. Corresponding to the universal experient or Sadāśiva is the individual (mystic) experient, Mantramaheśvara, who has realized *Sadāśiva tattva* and whose experience is, therefore, of the form—"I am this." The whole universe is identified with his Self. See end note 4 for a discussion of the thirty-six *tattvas*.

7. *Vikalpa* means difference of perception; an idea as different from other ideas; differentiation. *Vikalpanam* (*viśeṣeṇa vividhena kalpanam*) means ideating a "this" as different from "that;" the differentiation-making activity of the mind. *Vikalpa* is the nature of the individual mind (*citta*) which differentiates between one thing and another. Compare the *vivṛti* of Yogarāja in verse 11 of *Paramārthasāra* of Abhinavagupta: *Vikalpo hi anyāpoha-lakṣaṇo'dvayam ghaṭāghaṭa-rūpam ākṣipan, aghaṭāt vyavacchinnam ghaṭam niścinoti* (p. 33): *vikalpa* is of the nature of differentiating one thing from another. For instance, dividing an experience into jar and non-jar, it marks out the jar from the non-jar, and thus ascertains it as a jar. In the *Yoga Sūtra* of Patañjali (Samādhi-Pāda, 9), *vikalpa* means a mere fancy, which has no foundation in reality. That is not the meaning here.

The objector is driving at this: The nature of the individual mind is differentiation-making, knowing "this" as different from "that," whereas Śiva or the Universal Consciousness is free of all *vikalpas* or differentiating ideas. How then can you call the individual experient non-different from Śiva, so long as the differentiation-making mind of the individual lasts?

8. *Mala* means dust, dirt, impurity, taint; dross. Dross is the best English equivalent. *Mala* is what conceals and limits the pure gold of divine consciousness. It is of three forms: *āṇava mala, māyiya mala,* and *kārma mala.* In this system, *mala* means those cosmic and individualistic limiting conditions that hamper the free expression of the spirit.

Āṇava mala is the *mūla-mala,* the primal limiting condition, which reduces the universal consciousness to an *aṇu,* a small, limited entity. It is a cosmic limiting condition over which the individual has no control. Due to it, the *jīva* (individual soul) considers himself *apūrṇa,* imperfect, a separate entity, cut off from the universal consciousness. The greatness of Śiva in this condition is concealed, and the individual forgets his real nature. The *āṇava mala* is brought about in two ways. Bodha or knowledge loses its *svātantrya* or unimpeded power, and *svātantrya* or *śakti* loses its *bodha* or inherent knowledge.

Māyiyamala is the limiting condition brought about by *māyā* that gives to the soul its gross and subtle body. It is also cosmic. It is *bhinna-vedya-prathā*—that which brings about the consciousness of difference, owing to the differing, limiting adjuncts of the bodies.

Kārma-mala is the *vāsanās* or impressions of actions done by the *jñānendriyas* and *karmendriyas* under the influence of *antaḥkaraṇa.* It is the force of these *vāsanās* that carries the *jīva* from one life to another.

It may be noted that Vijñānākala has only *āṇava mala;* Pralayākala has two—*āṇava* and *māyiya mala;* and Sakala has all three—*āṇaca, māyiya,* and *kārma mala.*

9. *Śabda-brahman.* The philosophy of Vyākaraṇa considers the Absolute or Highest Reality as *"Śabda-brahman." Śabda* (word) is to them consciousness itself, whereas thought and word are the same and are not yet distinguished. Brahman is the external word from which emanates everything. According to the Trika system, the universe of objects, and so also of thoughts and words, is always potentially in Parama Śiva. This is the stage of the Parāvāk—the highest word, which is yet unmanifest. The next stage is that of Paśyantī, which is the divine view of the universe in its undifferentiated form, far beyond human experience. Kṣemarāja means to say that the grammarians go only as far as Paśyantī, which is confined to the stage of Sadāśiva but not up to Parāvāk, which refers to the stage of Parama Śiva. After Paśyanti, comes Madhyamā, which marks the next stage of the manifestation of the universe from undifferentiated mass to differentiated particulars. Madhyamā (lit. the middle one) is thus a link between Paśyantī, the vision of the undifferentiated universe, and Vaikharī, the stage of differentiated particulars, the stage of empirical thought and speech. It is word in a subtle form in the mind, or *antaḥkaraṇa.* In Vaikharī, the "word" appears separately from "thought" and "object."

10. *Turīya* or the fourth state of consciousness. In Saṁskṛta, *catur* means "four." When the *īyat* suffix is added to *catur, ca* is dropped and the "t" of *īyat* suffix is dropped, and thus the word becomes *turīya,* which means "fourth." Every man's consciousness is in three states: *jāgrat* (wak-

ing), *svapna* (dreaming), *suṣuptī* (deep sleep). These states are mutually exclusive. When a man is in one state, he does not have access to the others. *Turīya* is the witnessing consciousness of these three states. The ego, limited by body, *prāṇa,* and *manas,* has no experience of *turīya,* although it is always present as the background of all three states. Only when *avidyā* (the primal ignorance) is removed does man have the experience of *turīya* consciousness. Microcosmically, the fourth state holds together the other three. Macrocosmically, the fourth state holds together the three *kṛtyas* (*sṛṣṭi, sthiti,* and *saṁhāra*). *Sṛṣṭi-sthiti-saṁhāra-melana-rūpā iyam turīyā:* Just as a string holds together various flowers in a garland, so it holds together the other three forms of experiences and runs through them all. It is *integral awareness.* But it is other than the three states of waking, dream, and sleep. Hence it is called the fourth. When an individual consciously experiences *turīyā,* the sense of difference disappears.

Turīyā has been described as *pūrṇā* (full), from the point of view of *saṁhāra* or withdrawal, because in that condition she has withdrawn all that had emanated from her; *kṛśa* or emaciated, from the point of view of *udvamana* or emanation, because in that condition she is letting go the entities that she had held in her. So Turīyā may be said to be *ubhaya-rūpā*—both full and emaciated. In the highest sense, however, she is *anubhayātmā,* beyond the conditions of fullness and emaciation.

11. *Paśu and Pati Stages.* The idea is that so long as the soul is in the *paśu* (bound) stage, the *Śakti-cakras* (the *śaktis* with their differentiation-making hosts) cause *sṛṣṭi* and *sthiti* to appear—the emanation and maintenance of *bheda* or difference only, and *saṁhāra* or complete disappearance of *abheda* or non-difference or oneness. At this stage, consciousness of difference is created and maintained, and consciousness of oneness is completely withdrawn. At the *pati* stage, when bondage of the soul dissolves, the reverse of the previous condition happens. Here the *śaktis* bring about *sṛṣṭi* and *sthiti,* emanation and maintenance of *abheda,* non-difference or oneness of all, and *saṁhāra* or complete withdrawal of *bheda* or difference. The *pati* stage is of two kinds: (1) *anādisiddha,* eternally present as in the case of Śiva and (2) *Yogi-daśā,*—that which appears at the stage of yogin. *Pati-daśā* here means the latter.

It should be borne in mind that at the *pati* stage, the *cakras* (the differentiation-making hosts) of the *śaktis* dissolve, and the *śaktis* begin to function in their pure state. In the *paśu* stage, these are called *khecarī cakra, gocarī cakra, dikcarī cakra* and *bhūcarī cakra,* but in the *pati* stage, these are called simply *cidgaganacarī* or *khecarī, gocarī, dikcarī,* and *bhūcarī* respectively.

12. *Bhairava-mudrā* has been defined thus:

अन्तर्लक्ष्यो बहिर्दृष्टिर्निमेषोन्मेषवर्जितः ।
इयं सा भैरवीमुद्रा सर्वतन्त्रेषु गोपिता ॥

This is kind of psychophysical condition brought about by the following practice:

> Attention should be turned inwards; the gaze should be turned outwards, without the blinking of the eyes. This is the *mudrā* pertaining to Bhairava, kept secret in all the Tantras.

13. *Khechari. Khecharī, gocarī, dikcarī* and *bhūcari* are only subspecies of Vāmeśvarī śakti. *Khecarī* is connected with the *pramātā,* the empirical subject, the limited experient; *gocarī* is connected with his *antaḥkaraṇa,* the inner psychic apparatus; *dikcarī* is connected with the *bahiṣkaraṇa,* the outer sense; *bhūcarī* is connected with the *bhāvas,* existents or outer objects. These *śakti-cakras* indicate the processes of the objectification of the universal consciousness. By *khecarī cakra,* one is reduced from the position of an all-knowing consciousness to that of a limited experient; by *gocarī cakra,* he becomes endowed with an inner psychic apparatus; by *dikcarī cakra,* he is endowed with outer senses; by *bhūcarī cakra,* he becomes confined to *bhāvas* or external objects.

Khecarī is one that moves in *kha* or *ākāśa*. *Kha* or *ākāśa* is here a symbol of consciousness. The *śakti* is called *khecarī* because her sphere is *kha,* or consciousness. *Gocarī* is so called because her sphere is the inner psychic apparatus. The *saṁskṛta* word *go* indicates movement, and thus the terms light-rays, cow, senses are known as "go," because they are all connected with movement. The *antaḥkaraṇa* is the seat of the senses and sets them in motion; it is the dynamic apparatus of the spirit par excellence. Hence it is said to be the sphere of *gocarī*. *Dikcarī* is literally the *śakti* that moves in *dik* or space. The outer senses have to do with the consciousness of space. Hence the outer senses are said to be the sphere of *dikcarī*. The word *bhū* in *bhūcarī* means "existence" (world). Hence existent objects are the sphere of *bhūcarī śakti*. The empirical individual experient, his psycho-physical powers, and his objects of experience have all been described here as expressions of various *śakti-cakras.*

14. *Prāṇa, apāna, samāna śaktis. There are five prāṇas—prāṇa, apāna, samāna, udāna,* and *vyāna*. These are, however, *vāyus* or vital airs. *Prāṇas* are the *vāyus* that carry out the functions of vegetative life. They are distinct from the body. Like vitalism, Indian philosophy maintains that life is something different from mere matter. Life is maintained by various *prāṇas.* Breath is the most palpable and concrete expression of *prāṇa*. The five *prāṇas* are divided according to various functions: Roughly, *prāṇa* is the vital *vāyu* that goes out, *apāna* is the vital *vāyu* that goes in downward toward the anus. *Samāna* is the vital *vāyu* that is said to be located on the interior of the body. It helps in assimilation, etc., hence it is known as *samāna*. *Vyāna* means "going in all directions." It is everywhere in the body. *Udāna* means "going upward." Here the word *śakti* has been used, not *vāyu*. The various *vāyus* are the functions of the various *śaktis* of the same name. By means of *prāṇa, apāna,* and *samāna śaktis,* one becomes a bound soul (*paśu*); by means of *udāna* and *vyāna śaktis,* one is freed; one becomes a *pati.*

15. *Turya* literally means the fourth (see fn. 139). Normally man's waking consciousness functions only in three states: walking (*jāgrat,*)

dreaming (*svapna,*) and dreamless sleep (*suṣupti.*) When *udāna śakti* becomes active in the *madhya-dhāma* or *suṣumnā,* one develops the consciousness of *turya* or the fourth state, in which one has unity-consciousness and the sense of difference disappears. This consciousness is full of bliss.

In the waking condition, the body, *prāṇa, manas,* and senses are active. In the dreaming condition, only *prāṇa* and *manas* are active. In the state of deep sleep, even the *manas* stops functioning, and *ātman* or pure consciousness is in association with mere void. In the *turya* or fourth state, the *ātman* is detached from these limitations and remains pure consciousness and bliss (*cidānandaghana*). Our waking, dream, and deep sleep states are exclusive of each other; when we are in one state, we are not aware of the other two states. But *turya* is *integral awareness*—it is always aware or conscious of all the three states; it is not cut off from any of them. When *turya* awareness is established, the habit of *manas*—of knowing things in parts or fragments, of departmentalized awareness—is reduced. *Turya* is a consciousness that is aware of all the three states: walking, dream, and deep sleep. It is not under the influence of *māyā,* which brings about a sense of difference. Though piercing all the three states, the *turya* is unaffected by them, for it is completely free from any impressions of subject-object duality, being pure consciousness and bliss. See Yogarāja's commentary on Verse 35 of the *Paramārthasāra:*

> *Turīyam grāhya-grāhaka-kṣobha-pralayasaṁskāra-parikṣayāt jñānaghanaprakā-śanandamūrti;*
> *Ataḥ tadantaḥsthamapi tābhyo 'vasthā-bhyaḥ cinmayatayā samuttīrṇatvāt "paraṁ" anyat-iti.* (p. 80)

16. *Madhya.* From the point of view of Śambhu or Śiva, *madhya* is the universal consciousness that is the innermost or central reality of all existence; it is the pure I-consciousness of Śiva. From the point of view of Śakti, it is *jñāna-krīyā*—the spiritual urge that expresses itself in knowlege and action. From the point of view of *aṇu* or the individual, it is the *madhya-nāḍī* that lies between *iḍā* and *piṅgalā nāḍīs.* The word *nāḍī* is derived from the root *naḍ* (*bhranś*)—to fall, drop. That through which something drops or flows is *nāḍī.* The *nāḍīs* are subtle channels of *prāṇic* energy. *Madhya* or *madhyamā nāḍī* is so called because it is centrally situated. It is also called *suṣumnā.* The derivation of the word *suṣumnā* is somewhat uncertain. According to Śabdakalpadruma, *su ṣu ityavyaktaśbdam mnāyatī*—that which repeats the indistinct sound *su ṣu* may be its derivation.

Suṣumnā is situated on the interior of the cerebro-spinal axis or Merudaṇḍa. It extends from the Mūlādhāra to the Sahasrāra. Within the "fiery red" Tāmasika, Suṣumnā is the lustrous Rājasika Vajrā or Vajriṇī Nāḍī; within the Vajriṇī is the pale Sāttvika Citrā or Citriṇī. The interior of the Citriṇī is called Brahma-nāḍī. Suṣumnā is said to be fire-like (*vahnisvarūpa*); Vajriṇī is said to be sun-like (*sūryasvarūpā*); Citriṇī is said to be moon-like (*candrasvarūpā*). The opening at the end of the *Citriṇī nāḍī* is called Brahmadvāra. It is through this that Kuṇḍalinī rises.

Iḍā and Piṅgalā *nāḍī* are outside *suṣumnā* and run parallel over it. Iḍā is on the left and Piṅgalā on the right. They are curved like a bow. These three (Iḍā, Piṅgalā, and Suṣumnā) join at the Ājñā cakra, which is known as Triveṇī or the confluence of the three.

Some have taken *nāḍīs* and *cakras* to mean nerve and ganglia. They are not physical constituents. They are constituents of the *prāṇṃaya-kośa,* the vital sheath in the *sūkṣma śarīra* (the subtle body). Their impact in the physical body is felt through the nerves and the ganglia. The *cakras* are the seats of *śakti.*

17. *Vahni-viṣa. Vahni* refers to *adhaḥ-kuṇḍalinī* and *viṣa* to *ūrdhva-kuṇḍalinī.* The entrance into the *adhaḥ-kuṇḍalinī* is *saṅkoca* or *vahni;* rising into *ūrdhva-kuṇḍalinī* is *vikāsa* or *viṣa. Vahni* is symbolic of *prāṇa vāyu* and *viṣa* of *apāna vāyu.* When *prāṇa* enters the *ṣuṣumnā* and goes down into *adhaḥ-kuṇḍalinī* or *mūlādhāra,* then this condition is known as *vahni.* Entering into the full portion of the root and half of the middle of *adhaḥ-kuṇḍalinī* is known as *vahni* or *saṅkoca. Vahni* is derived from the root *vah*—to carry. Since *prāṇa* is carried down to the *mūlādhāra* in this state, it is called *vahni.* In Sanskrit, *vahni* means "fire." In this sense also, the root meaning of *vah* (to carry) is implied. Fire is called *vahni* because it carries the oblations to the *devas* (gods). The *āveśa,* or entering into the remaining half of the *madhya,* or middle and full portion of the *agra* or tip of the *adhaḥ-kuṇḍalinī* right up to the lowest spot of *ūrdhva-kuṇḍalinī,* is known as *viṣa.*

The word *viṣa* does not mean poison here. It is derived from the root *viṣ,* "to pervade." *Viṣa,* therefore, refers to *prasara* or *vikāsa.* Poison is also called *viṣa* because it pervades the whole body.

What is meant to be conveyed is that when the *prāṇa* and *apāna* enter the *suṣumnā,* the *citta* or individual consciousness should be stopped or suspended between the *vahni* and *viṣa;* in other words, between the *adhaḥ-kuṇḍalinī* and the *ūrdhva-kuṇḍalinī.*

Vāyupūrṇa (full of *vāyu*) means that the *citta* should be restrained in such a way that *vāyu* may pass out neither through the nostrils nor through the male organ and the anus. *Citta* and *vāyu* are interconnected. Restraint of one brings about restraint of the other.

18. *Development of Madhya.* Perfection is accomplished by the development of "madhya," which, in the case of *aṇu* or the individual *jīva,* means the development of *prāṇa-śaktī* in the *suṣumnā.* One way to develop *madhya* is through the *saṅkoca* and *vikāsa* of the *śakti.* The literal translation of *saṅkoca* and *vikāsa* hardly do justice to the yogic practice indicated by these. *Saṅkoca* connotes the following discipline: Even while the mind is going forth towards external objects through the senses, even while the senses are actively functioning in grasping form, color, sound, smell, etc., attention is *withdrawn* from them and *turned towards* the inner reality, which is the source and background of all activity.

Vikāsa means *concentration* on the inner reality even while the sense organs are quite open, as in the practice of *bhairavī mudrā. Saṅkoca* implies *withdrawal of attention* from external objects; *vikāsa* implies *concentration of attention on the inner consciousness and not allowing it to go out at all,* even when the eyes, ears, etc., are open to their respective objects. It means remaining steady within, like a golden pillar, even while the senses are directed towards their objects.

Saṅkoca and *vikāsa* have to be further developed by the technique of *prasara-viśrānti,* at the level of *ūrdhva-kuṇḍalinī. Prasara* is, here, practically synonymous with *vikāsa* and *viśrānti* with *saṅkoca.* The yogin develops the *prāṇa-śakti* in the *suṣumnā* and, by restraining it between the eye-brows, he attains to *ūrdhva-kuṇḍalinī* level. Here he practices *prasaraviśrānti.*

This practice of *saṅkoca* and *vikāsa* has to be developed in *adhaḥ-kuṇḍalinī* also. Entering completely into the root and half of the middle of *adhaḥ-kuṇḍalinī* is known as *saṅkoca* or *vahni,* and entering into the remaining half and wholly into the tip of the *adhaḥ-kuṇḍalinī,* right up to the position where the *ūrdhva-kuṇḍalinī* ends, is known as *vikāsa, viṣa,* or *unmīlana samādhi.*

19. *Samāveśa.* For the meaning of *samāveśa*, see Abhinavagupta:

आवेशश्चास्वतंत्रस्य स्वतद्रूपनिमज्जनात् ।
परतद्रूपता शम्भोराद्याच्छक्त्यविभागिनः ॥

—*Tantrāloka* I, 173

Āveśa or *Samāveśa* means the merging and identity of the helpless, limited self with the supreme Śiva, who is at one with the primal Śakti. *Samāveśa* means subordinating one's limited nature and acquiring the nature of the Supreme.

20. *Jagadānanda* is a technical word of this system and means the bliss of the Self appearing as the universe. The universe in this system is not a fall from the bliss of the Divine; it is rather the bliss of the Divine made visible. Compare the following verses of Abhinavagupta:

यत्र कोऽपि व्यवच्छेदो नास्ति यद्विश्वतः स्फुरत् ।
यदनाहतसंवित्ति परमामृतबृंहितम् ॥
यत्रास्ति भावनादीनां न मुख्या कापि संगतिः ।
तदेव जगदानन्दमस्मभ्यं शंभुरूचिवान् ।

—*Tantrāloka,* v. 50-51

That in which there is no division or limitation, for it flashes forth all round; in which the consciousness is intact—in which consciousness alone expresses itself, whether as knower, means of knowledge, or as known; that which increases and expands by the nectar of divine joy, of absolute sovereignty in which there is no need for imagination or meditation. Śambhu told me that that was *jagadānanda.*

The commentator says:

जगता निजानन्दाद्यात्मना विश्वेन रूपेणानन्दो यत्र यतश्चेति जगदानन्दशब्दवाच्यम् ।

That is *jagadānanda* where the universe appears as a visible form of the bliss of the Self. Śambhu, referred to in the above verse, was the chief guru of Abhinavagupta in the Trika system.

21. *Non-Māyaya Words.* According to Tantra, there is a correspondence between the *parā-śakti,* the ultimate divine creative power which brings about the sum total of all objects, and the *parāvāk* which is the ultimate divine word, the source of the sum total of words. By means of mantras, which consist of words or letters, one can establish contact with the various *śaktis.* Every word is a *vācaka* or indicator, and every object is *vācya* or the indicated. The *vācya* or object is nothing but the intent of the divine word made visible.

The divine words or letters are, however, *amāyīya*—out of the scope of *māyā.* Words are of two kinds: *māyiya* (pertaining to *māyā*) and *amāyīya* (not pertaining to *māyā*). *Māyīya* words are those upon which meaning is imposed by convention; they are *vikalpas* or fancied constructions. *Amāyīya* words are *nirvikalpaka,* this whose meaning is just the *real,* not dependant on fancy imposition or convention; they are *cinmaya.*

22. *The word pratyāhāra* has been used here in the technical sense of Sanskrit grammar, which means "the comprehension of several letters or affixes into one syllable, effected by combining the first letter of a sūtra with its final indicatory letter." Thus the *pratyāhāra* "ac" means a, i, u, ṛ, ḷ, e, o, for it combines the first letter "a" and the final indicatory letter "c" of the following sūtras— अइउण्, ऋलक्, एओङ्, ऐऔच्.

So here the *pratyāhāra* of "a," the first letter, and "ha," the final letter, would be "aha," which suggests "aham," meaning "I" or Self. "Aha" includes all the letters of the Sanskrit language, and since each letter is indicative of an object, "aha" suggests the sum total of all objects—the universe. The entire universe lies in the highest Reality, or Maheśvara, in an undifferentiated state.

23. *Bindu* means a drop, a dot. In the calm of the highest Reality (*anuttara*), there arises a metaphysical point of stress. This is known as *bindu.* In this the universe to be lies gathered up into a point. The *bindu* is known as *ghanībhūtā śakti*—the creative forces compressed into a point. It is as yet undifferentiated into objects. It is the *cidghana* or massive consciousness in which lie, potentially in an undifferentiated mass, all the worlds and beings to be manifested. Therefore, the text says that "a" and "ha" joined into "aha," and thus *together* summing up the entire manifestation, lie undifferentiated into a point in the highest Reality. A point is indicative of non-differentiation. From the point of view of language, the *bindu* in Sanskrit is indicated by *anusvāra*—the nasal sound marked by a dot on a letter. *Bindu* is thus the *anusvāra,* and this completes "aha" into "aham" (अहं).

This *anusvāra,* after having joined "a" and "ha" in oneness, shows that all manifestation—though appearing emanated and different—is actually residing in Śiva, and is not different from him. "A" represents Śiva; "ha" represents Śakti; the *anusvāra* represents the fact that though Śiva is manifested right up to the earth through Śakti, he is not divided thereby; he remains undivided (*avibhāga-vedanātmaka-bindu-rūpatayā*).

GLOSSARY OF TECHNICAL TERMS

A symbol of Śiva.

Ābhāsana appearance; esoteric meaning is *sṛṣṭi* or emanation.

Adhaḥ-kuṇḍalinī the field of Kuṇḍalinī from Lambikā to one-three-fourths of its folds in the mūlādhāra.

Adho-vaktra Meḍhra-Kanda, situated at the root of the rectum.

Ādikoṭi the first edge or point; the heart from which the measure of breath is determined.

Ahaṁ-bhāva I-feeling; I-consciousness.

Ahantā "I"-consciousness; I-ness.

Akhyāti ignorance.

Akula Śiva.

Alaṁgrāsa bringing experienced object completely to sameness with the consciousness of the Self, when no impression of *saṁsāra* as separate from consciousness is allowed to remain.

Amāyīya beyond the scope of Māyā; *Amāyiya Śabdas* are the words whose meaning does not depend on convention or supposition; the word and the object are one.

Anacka-lit., sounding the consonants without the vowels; esoteric meaning is to concentrate on any mantra back to its unuttered source.

Ānanda bliss, the nature of Śakti.

Anantabhaṭṭāraka the presiding deity of the Mantra experients.

Anāśrita-Śiva the state of Śiva in which there is no objective content yet, in which the universe is negated from Him.

Āṇava Mala mala pertaining to aṇu, i.e. the innate ignorance of the jīva; primary limiting condition which reduces universal consciousness to a jīva, depriving consciousness of Śakti and Śakti of consciousness, thus bringing about a sense of imperfection.

Antakoṭi the last edge or point; it is *dvādaśānta* a measure of twelve fingers.

Antarmukhībhāva introversion of consciousness.

Anugraha grace.

Anuttara the Highest, the Supreme, the Absolute.

Apāna the vital *vāyu* that goes in downwards towards the anus.

Apara lower or lowest.

Apavarga liberation.

Ārhata Jaina.

Artha object; end; sense-object; meaning; notion; aim.

Asat non-being.

Āśyānatā shrunken, dried up state; congealment; solidification.

Ātmasātkṛ assimilate to the Self.

Ātma-viśrānti resting in the Self.

Avyakta unmanifest.

Bahirmukhatā extroversion of consciousness.

Bahirmukhībhāva externalization; extroverion.

Baindavī Kalā *Baindavī*—pertaining to Bindu or the Knower; *Kaḷā*—will-power. *Baindavī Kalā* is that freedom of Parama Śiva by which the knower always remains the knower and is never reduced to the known.

Bala *Cid-bala,* power of the true Self or Universal Consciousness.

Bandha bondage; yogic practice in which certain organs of the body are contracted and locked.

Bhairava Parama Śiva; the Highest Reality. This is an anacrostic word, "bha" indicating *bharaṇa,* maintenance of the world; "ra," *ravaṇa* or withdrawal of the world; and "va" *vamana,* or projection of the world.

Bhāva existence—both internal and external; object.

Bhoga experience, sometimes used in the narrow sense of enjoyment.

Bhoktā experient.

Bhūcarī subspecies of Vāmeśvari, connected with the *bhāvas* or existent objects. *Bhū* means existence; hence existent objects are the sphere of *bhūcari.*

Bhūmikā role.

Bhuvana becoming; place of existence; world; place of being, abode.

Bījāvasthāpana setting of the seed; esoteric meaning, *vilaya*—concealment of true nature.

Bindu written also as Vindu, a point; a metaphysical point; *ghanībhutā śakti,* the compact mass of Śakti gathered into an undifferentiated point ready to create; also *paraḥ pramātā* the highest Self or Consciousness; the *anusvāra* or nasal sound indicated by a dot on a letter indicating the fact that Śiva, in spite of the manifestation of the universe, is undivided.

Brahmanāḍī suṣumnā or the central prāṇic nāḍī.

Brahmarandhra the sahasrāra cakra.

Brahmavāda in this system, *Śāṅkara Vedānta.*

Buddhi Sometimes the higher mind; the super-personal mind; the ascertaining intelligence, intuitive aspect of consciousness by which the essential Self awakens to truth.

Camatkāra bliss of the pure I-consciousness; delight of artistic experience.

Caramakalā the highest phase of manifestation known as Śāntyatīta or Śāntātītakalā.

Cārvāka the materialist.

Cārvāka Darśana materialistic philosophy.

Cetana self; Paramaśiva; soul, conscious individual.

Cetya knowable; object of consciousness.

Cheda cessation of prāṇa and apāna by the sounding of *anacka* sounds.

Cidānanda lit., consciousness and bliss, the nature of ultimate reality; the bliss of universal consciousness.

Cintā thought; idea.

Cit the Absolute; foundational consciousness; the unchanging principle of all changes.

Citi the consciousness-power of the Absolute that brings about the world-process.

Citi-Cakra Saṁvit-cakra; the senses.

Citta the individual mind, the limitation of Citi or Universal Consciousness manifested in the individual mind, consisting mainly of Sattva, the mind of the Māyā-pramātā.

Darśana seeing; system of philosophy.

Deśa space.

Dikcarī subspecies of Vāmeśvari, connected with the *bahiṣkaraṇa* or outer senses. *Dik* means "space." Outer senses have to do with space; hence they are the sphere of *dikcari.*

Gocarī subspecies of Vāmeśvari, connected with the *antaḥkaraṇa* of the experient. *Go* means "sense;" *antaḥkaraṇa* is the seat of the senses; hence *gocarī* is connected with *antaḥkaraṇa*.

Grāhaka knower; subject.

Grāhya known; object.

Ha symbol of Śakti.

Haṭhapāka persistent process of assimilating experience to the consciousness of the experient.

Hetu cause.

Hetumat effect.

Hṛdaya heart; central consciousness (in yoga).

Icchā Will, the Śakti of Sadāśiva.

Idantā "This"-consciousness.

Īśvarabhaṭṭāraka the presiding deity of the Mantreśvaras residing in Īśvaratattva.

Īśvara-Tattva the fourth tattva of the system, counting from Śiva. In this tattva, the consciousness of "I" and "This" is equally prominent. The consciousness of Sadā-Śiva is "I am this." The consciousness of Īśvara is "This am I." Jñāna is predominant in this tattva.

Jagadānanda the bliss of the Self or the Divine appearing as the universe; the bliss of the Divine made visible.

Jagat the world process.

Jāgrat the waking condition.

Jīva the individual; the individual soul; the empirical self.

Jīvanmukti liberation while one is alive.

Jñāna knowledge, the Śakti of Īśvara.

Kalā limited agency; creativity; phase of manifestation; part letter or word (in *ha-kalāparyantam*).

Kāla time; Śkti or power that determines succession.

Kālāgni the lowest bhuvana or plane of existence in Nivṛtti Kalā.

Kañcuka covering.

Kāraṇa cause.

Karaṇeśvaryaḥ Khecharī, Gocarī, Dikcarī, and Bhūcarī cakra.

Kārmamala *mala* due to *vāsanas* or impressions left behind on the mind due to karma or action.

Kārya effect.

Khecarī subspecies of Vāmeśvari Śakti, connected with the *pramātā*, the empirical self. Khecarī is one that moves in *"kha"* or *"ākāśa,"* symbol of consciousness.

Khyāti jñāna; knowledge; wisdom.

Kriyā action, the Śakti of Śuddha-vidyā.

Kula Śakti.

Kulāmnāya the Śākta system or doctrine.

Madhya the central Consciousness—Saṁvit; the pure I-consciousness; the suṣumnā, or central prāṇic nāḍī.

Madhyadhāma Suṣumnā, the central nāḍī in the *prāṇamaya-kośa,* also known as *brahmanāḍī.*

Madhyamā *Śabda* in its subtle form as existing in the mind or *antaḥkaraṇa* prior to its gross manifestation.

Mādhyamika follower of the Madhyamaka system of Buddhist philosophy.

Madhyaśkti Saṁvit-Śakti, the central Consciousness-power.

Mahāmantra the great mantra, i.e. of pure consciousness.

Mahārtha the greatest end; the highest value; the pure I-consciousness; the *krama* discipline.

Maheśvara the highest lord, Parama-Śiva; the Absolute.

Māheśvarya the power of Maheśvara.

Mala dross; ignorance which hampers the free expression of the spirit.

Mantreśvara the experient who has realized Īśvara tattva.

Mantra the experient who has realized the Śuddha vidyā-tattva; sacred words or formula to be reflected upon and chanted.

Mantra-Maheśvara the experient who has realized Sadā-Śiva tattva.

Māyā from *ma,* "to measure;" the limiting principle of the Divine; a tattva below Śuddha vidyā, the principle of veiling the Infinite and projecting the finite; the source of the five kañcukas; the finitizing power of Parama Śiva.

Māyāpramātā the empirical self, governed by Māyā.

Māyīya Mala *mala* due to Māyā, which gives to the soul its gross and subtle body, and brings about sense of difference.

Meya (prameya) object.

Mīmāṁsaka the follower of the Mīmāṁsā system of philosophy.

Mokṣa liberation.

Mudrā *mud* (joy), *ra* (to give). It is called *mudrā* because it gives the bliss of spiritual consciousness, or because it seals up *(mudraṇāt)* the universe into the being of the turīya consciousness; also, yogic control of certain organs that help in concentration.

Mudrā-Krama or *Kramamudrā* the condition in which the mind, by force of *samāveśa,* swings alternately between the internal (Self or Śiva) and the external (the world that now appears as the form of Śiva).

Mukti liberation.

Naiyāyika the follower of Nyāya philosophy; logician; dialectician.

Nibhālana perception; mental practice.

Nimeṣa lit., closing of the eye; dissolution of the world.

Nimīlana-Samādhi the inward meditative condition in which the individual consciousness gets absorbed into the Universal Consciousness.

Nityatva eternity.

Niyati limitation of cause-effect relation; spatial limitation.

Pancakṛtya the five-fold act of *sṛṣṭi, sthiti, saṁhāra, vilaya* and *anugraha* or the five-fold act of *ābhāsana, rakti, vimarśana, bījāvasthāpana,* and *vilāpana.*

Pāñcarātra the philosophy of Vaiṣṇavism; the follower of such philosophy.

Pāñcarātrika followers of the Pāñcarātra system.

Para highest.

Parāmarśa seizing mentally; experience; comprehension; remembrance.

Parama Śiva the Highest Reality; the Absolute.

Parāpara intermediate stage; both identical and different; unity in diversity.

Para-Pramātā the highest Experient; Parama-Śiva.

Parā-Śakti highest Śakti of the Divine; Citi.

Parāvāk the unmanifest Śakti or vibratory movement of the Divine; Logos; cosmic ideation.

Paricchinna limited.

Pariṇāma transformation.

Paramārtha highest reality; essential truth; the highest goal.

Pāśa bondage.

Paśu one who is bound; the individual soul.

Paśyantī the divine view of the universe in undifferentiated form; Vāk Śakti going forth as "seeing," manifesting, ready to create, in which there is no differentiation between *vācya* (object) and *vācaka* (word).

Pati lord; Śiva.

Patidaśā the status of the highest experient; the state of liberation.

Prakāśśa lit., light; the principle of Self-revelation; consciousness; the principle by which everything else is known.

Prakṛti the source of objectivity from Buddhi down to earth.

Pralayākala or *Pralayakevalin* resting in Māyā tattva, not cognizant of anything.

Pramāṇa-means of knowing; proof.

Pramātā the knower, the subject, the experient.

Prameya object of knowledge; known; object.

Prāṇa generic name for the vital Śakti; specifically it is the vital *vāyu* in expiration; vital energy; life energy.

Prāṇāyāma breath-control.

Prasara lit., expansion, manifestation of Śiva in the form of the universe through His Śakti.

Prath to expand; unfold; appear; shine.

Prathā the mode of appearance; the way.

Pratyabhijñā recognition.

Pratyāhāra comprehension of several letters or affixes into one syllable effected by combining the first letter of a sūtra with its final indicatory letter. In yoga, withdrawal of the senses from their objects.

Prithivī the earth tattva.

Pūrṇāhantā the perfect I-consciousness; non-relational I-consciousness.

Pūrṇatva perfection.

Puryaṣṭaka lit., "the city of the group of eight;" the five *tanmātras, buddhi, ahaṁkāra,* and *manas;* the *sūkṣmaśarīra* consisting of the above eight.

Rāga the *kañcukas* of Māyā responsible for limitation by desire.

Rajas the principle of motion, activity and disharmony—a constituent of Prakṛti.

Rakti relish; enjoyment; esoteric meaning is *sthiti,* maintenance.

Śabda word.

Śabda-Brahama Ultimate reality in the form of vibration, of which the human word is a gross representation. In this state, thought and word are one.

Sadāśiva the third tattva, counting from Śiva. At this stage, the "I" experience is more prominent than the "this" experience. This tattva is also known as Sādākhya, inasmuch as *sat* or being is posited at this stage. Icchā or Will is predominant in this tattva.

Sahaja natural (from the point of view of the Universal Consciousness).

Sakala All the jīvas, from gods down to the mineral, who rest in Māyā tattva. They have no knowlege of the real Self and their consciousness is only that of diversity.

Śakti-pāta descent of the divine Śakti; grace.

Śakti-prasara Śakti-vikāsa; emergence from samādhi and retaining that experience.

Śakti-Saṅkoca withdrawal of attention from sense-activity and turning it towards the inner reality.

Śakti-Vikāsa concentration of attention on the inner consciousness even when the senses are open to their respective objects.

Śakti-Viśrānti Merging back into samādhi and resting in that condition.

Samādhi collectedness of mind; mental absorption.

Samāna the vital Vāyu that helps in assimilation of food, etc. and brings about equilibrium between prāṇa and apāna.

Samāpatti Sometimes a synonym of samādhi; consummation, attainment of psychic at-one-ment.

Samarasa one having the same feeling or consciousness.

Sāmarasya identity of consciousness; unison of Śiva and Śakti.

Samāveśa being possessed by the divine; absorption of the individual consciousness in the divine.

Saṁhāra withdrawal; reabsorption.

Saṁsāra transmigratory existence; world process.

Saṁsārin a transmigratory being.

Saṁsṛti transmigratory existence; the world process.

Saṁvit consciousness; supreme consciousness.

Saṁvit-Devatā from the macrocosmic point of view; *samvitdevatās* are khecarī, gocarī, dikcari, and bhūcari. From the microcosmic point of view, this consists of the internal and external senses.

Sāṅkhya the system of philosophy that believes in two fundamental realities, such as Puruṣa and Prakṛti; the follower of such a system.

Saṅkoca contraction; limitation.

Sarvajñatva omniscience.

Sarvakartṛtva omnipotence.

Śāsana Śastra; philosophical text.

Ṣaṣṭha-vaktra lit, the sixth organ; *meḍhra-kanda,* near the root of the rectum.

Sat existence which is consciousness.

Sattva the principle of being, light and harmony—a constituent of Prakṛti.

Saugata follower of Buddha.

Śiva the name of the divine in general; good.

Śiva-tattva the first of the thirty-six tattvas. Main characteristic is *cit*.

Sṛṣṭi letting go; emanation; manifestation.

Sthiti maintenance.

Śuddha-vidyā (sometimes abbreviated as vidyā) the fifth tattva, counting from Śiva. In this tattva, the consciousness of both "I" and "This" is equally prominent. Though the universe is seen differently, identity runs through it as a thread. There is identity in diversity at this stage. Kriyā is predominant in this tattva. The consciousness of this stage is "I am I and also this."

Śuddhādhvā the pure path; extramundane existence; mainfestation of the first five tattvas: Śiva, Śakti, Sadāśiva, Īśvara, and Śuddha-vidyā.

Śūnya void; the state in which no object is experienced.

Śūnya-pramātā having the experience of only void; *pralayākala*.

Suṣupti the condition of dreamless sleep.

Svapna the dream condition.

Svarūpāpatti attaining one's real nature or true Self.

Svatantra of absolute will; of unimpeded will.

Svātantrya the absolute Will of the Supreme.

Svātmasātkṛ to assimilate to oneself; to integrate to oneself.

Svecchā Śiva's or Śakti's own will, synonymous with *svātantrya*.

Svarūpa one's own form; real nature; essence.

Tamas the principle of inertia, and delusion—a constituent of Prakṛti.

Tāntrika follower of Tantra; pertaining to Tantra.

Tanutā becoming gradually less; reduction; a state of subtleness.

Tarka-Śāstra logic and dialectics.

Tattva thatness; the very being of a thing; principle.

Trika the system or philosophy of the triad: (1) Śiva, (2) Śakti, and (3) Nara—the bound soul. Or (1) para—the highest, having to do with identity; (2) parāpara—identity in difference, and (3) apara—difference and sense of difference.

Turīya the fourth state of consciousness, beyond the state of waking, dreaming and deep sleep, which strings together all the states; integral awareness; the metaphysical Self as distinct from the psychological or empirical self; the Sāksī or witnessing Consciousness.

Turya lit., the fourth, same as above.

Turyātīta the state of consciousness transcending the Turiya state; the state in which the distinctions of the three states are annulled; that pure blissful consciousness in which there is no sense of difference, in which the entire universe appears as the Self.

Udāna the vital Vāyu that goes upward; the Śakti that moves up in the suṣumnā at spiritual awakening.

Udvamantī lit., vomiting; externalizing; manifesting.

Unmeṣa lit., opening of the eye; the start of the world process; in Śaiva yoga, the unfolding of the the spiritual consciousness, which comes about by concentrating on the inner consciousness that is the background of ideations or rise of ideas.

Unmīlana unfolding; manifestation.

Unmi[ana Samādhi that state of the mind in which, even when the eyes are open, the external world appears as Universal Consciousness or Śiva.

Upādāna material cause.

Upādhi limiting adjunct or condition.

Ūrdhva-Kuṇḍalinī the risen up kuṇḍalinī when the prāṇa and apāna enter the suṣumnā.

Vācaka word or indicator.

Vācya object or the indicated; referent.

Vāha the prāṇa flowing in the iḍā nāḍī on the left and apāna flowing in the piṅgalā nāḍī on the right are together known as Vāha (lit., flow).

Vahni a technical word of Śaiva-Yoga, meaning "entering completely" into the root and half of the middle of *adhaḥ kuṇḍalinī* (from the root *vah,* to carry).

Vaikharī Śakti as gross physical word.

Vaiṣṇava the follower of Viṣṇu; follower of Vaiṣṇava philosophy.

Vāmeśvarī the divine Śakti that emits (*vam,* "to emit") or sends forth the universe out of the Absolute, and produces the reverse (*vāma*) consciousness of difference (whereas there is non-difference in the divine).

Vibhūti splendor; power.

Vidyā limited knowledge.

Vigraha individual form or shape; body.

Vigrahī the embodied.

Vijñānākala the experient below Śuddha Vidyā but above Māyā; has pure awareness but no agency. He is free of kārma and *māyīyamala* but not yet free of *āṇavamala*.

Vikalpa difference of perception; diversity; distinction; option; an idea as different from other ideas; ideation; fancy; imagination.

Vikalpa-kṣaya the dissolution of all *vikalpas*.

Vikalpanam the differentiation-making activity of the mind.

Vikāsa unfoldment; development.

Vilāpana dissolution; esoteric meaning is *anugraha*—grace.

Vilaya concealment.

Vimarśa lit., experience; technically, the Self-consciousness of the Supreme, full of jñāna and kriyā, which brings about the world-process.

Vimarśana intuitive awareness; esoteric meaning is *saṁhāra*, absorption.

Viṣa a technical word of Śaiva Yoga, meaning "entering into the remaining half and wholly into the top of *adhaḥ-kuṇḍalinī*, right up to the position where *ūrdhva-kuṇḍalinī* ends (from the root *viṣ*, to pervade).

Viśva the universe; the all.

Viśvamaya immanent.

Viśvātmaka immanent.

Viśvottīṛna transcendent.

Vyāmohitatā delusion.

Vyāna the vital Vāyu that is everywhere or the pervasive prāṇa.

Vyāna the vital Vāyu that is everywhere or the all-pervasive prāṇa.

Vyāpakatva all-pervasiveness.

Vyutthāna lit., "rising;" coming to normal consciousness after contemplation.

SANSKRIT INDEX

Ābhāsana 68
Abhāva 60
Abhihitaprāyam 52
Abhinavagupta 95
Ācchādita 50
Adhaḥ kuṇḍalini 85
Adho vaktra 81
Āgamas 54, 61, 74
Ahantā 50
Aiśvarya-śakti 73
Ajaḍa-pramātṛ-siddhi 92
Ajñāna 73
Akhyāti 54, 59
Akhyātimaya 53
Akula 92
Alaṁgrāsa 68
Anacka 85
Ānanda 59, 90
Anantabhaṭṭāraka 51
Anāśrita-śiva 53, 56
Āṇava-mala 64
Āṇavopāya 73
Antaḥ-karaṇa 72
Antaḥ-svarūpayā 89
Aṇu 59, 64
Anugraha 66
Anugrahītṛtā 67
Anurūpa 50
Ārhatas 61
Āveśa 48
Apāna 73, 85
Aparijñāne 69
Asphuṭa 50
Āśyānatārūpa 53
Atharvaupaniṣads 83
Atmā 58, 61, 62, 63
Ātman 65
Avacchinna 73
Āveśa 88
Avikalpa 70, 71, 82
Avyakta 61

Baindavī Kalā 47
Bala 78
Bandha 82
Bhagavān viśvaśariraḥ 53
Bhairava 54, 93
Bhairava-mudrā 71, 84
Bhāvanā 87
Bhāvas 53
Bheda 50
Bheda-abhomāna 72
Bheda-niścaya 72
Bheda-vikalpana 72
Bhoga 47
Bhūcarī 72, 73
Bhūmikā 63
Bhuvanas 53
Bindu 92
Brahmā 77
Brahman 48, 49, 81
Brahma-nāḍī 81
Brahmarandhra 81
Brahmavādins 60, 65
Brāhmī 70
Buddhi 60, 61, 63, 72, 80, 93

Caitanyam 58
Cakra 90, 94
Camakāra 68
Camatkāra 72, 90, 91
Cārvākas 60

Cetana 55, 56, 75
Cetya 55
Cheda 85
Cidaikya-akhyātimaya 53
Cideva bhagavatī 46
Cid-gagana-carī 72
Cidvat sūtra 74
Cit 46, 48, 54, 56, 58, 59, 76, 79, 80, 81, 82, 88, 90, 94
Citi 45, 46, 48, 49, 52, 55, 56, 58, 75, 76, 77, 78, 89
Citicakra 94
Citi-śkti 71, 76, 89, 93, 94
Citta 55, 56, 57, 58, 75, 82, 85
Cittam 58

Dakārikā 92
Dāmodara 72
Darśana 63
Dikcarī 72, 73
Drāvaṇāt 89
Dvādaśānta 86

Eka-sadbhāva 91
Ekatra 94

Gocarī 72, 73
Grāhaka 50, 52
Grāhya 50, 52
Guṇas 61
Guru 69

Haṭhapāka 68
Hetu 46, 47, 48
Hṛdaya 86

Icchā 59
Idantā 50
Indra 77
Īśa 56
Īśvarādvaya 65
Īśvara-pratyabhijñā 43, 57, 66, 71, 83, 93, 95
Īśvara tattva 50
Iti Śivam 91
Ityāmnātāh 67

Jagadānanda 91
Jagat 46
Jīva 54, 55, 56, 64
Jīvas 81, 93
Jīvanmukti 79
Jñāna 56, 57, 59
Jñānagarbha 83, 84

Kakṣyāstotra 84
Kalā 59, 64, 65, 72, 90
Kāla 59, 65
Kālāgni 90
Kalās 73
Kallaṭa 84
Kallaṭācārya 94
Kañcukas 64
Karma 59
Kārma-mala 64
Kartṛtā 51
Kaṭhavallī 83
Khecarī 72, 73
Koṭi 82
Krama 89
Kramā mudrā 88, 89, 90
Krama-mudrayā 89
Kramasūtras 78, 88
Kriyā 56, 57, 59
Kṛtyas 65
Kṣemarāja 42, 95
Kula 62

Madhya 80, 81, 82, 87
Madhyamā 70
Madhyama-nāḍī 80, 81
Madhya śakti 84
Madhyadhāma 73
Mādhyamikas 60
Mahārthadṛṣṭyā 67
Maheśatā 71
Mala 59, 64
Manas 72, 87, 93
Mantramaheśvara 50, 52
Mantras 51, 69, 78, 90, 92
Mantreśvara 50
Māyā 46, 51, 56, 57, 59, 63, 76, 80
Māyā-pramātṛ 57, 58
Māyā-pramātā 76
Māyā-pramātuḥ 70
Māyā-Śakti 54, 93
Māyīya-mala 64
Mātrā 77
Meḍhrakanda 85
Mīmāṁsa 60
Mokṣa 47, 63
Muda 89
Mudrā 82, 89
Mudrā-krama 88

Mudrayati 89
Mukti 58

Nāḍis 80, 85
Nānā 50
Netra Tantra 63
Nibhālana 86
Nilīnākṣaḥ 86
Nimīlana-samādhi 88
Nimīlana samāveśa 94
Nityodita 89
Niyati 59, 65
Nyāyā 60

Palāśa 81
Pañca 59
Pañcakṛtya 81
Pāñcarātras 60, 61
Parā 70
Parābhaṭṭārikā-rūpā 90
Paramaśiva 52
Parā-para 50
Paricita 51
Parijñāna 73
Paśyanti 61, 70
Paśu 56, 57, 70, 71, 73, 81, 86
Pati 71, 74
Prakāśa 52, 56, 90, 91
Prakāśābhedena 52
Prakāśamānatayā sphurati 52
Prakāśa-parāmarśa-pradhānatve 56
Prakṛti 46, 60
Pralayākalas 51, 51
Pralayakevalins 51
Pramāṇa 47, 48
Pramātā 48, 91
Pramātṛ 56
Pramātārs 50
Pramātāras 53
Pramātṛ 47
Prameya 47, 51, 91
Prāṇa 48, 58, 59, 60, 66, 73, 74, 78, 79, 80, 84, 85, 86, 92, 95
Prāṇa-śakti 80, 81, 85
Prāṇas 70
Prāṇāyāma 82
Prasara 77, 85
Pratyabhijñā 56, 57, 74, 79, 83, 95
Pratyabhijñāhṛdaya 95
Pratyabhijñākārikā 66
Pratyabhijñā-ṭikā 63
Pratyāhāra 92
Praveśa 89
Pūrṇa 73, 90
Puruṣa 61
Pūrvāvasthā 51
Puryaṣṭaka 59, 73, 94

Rāga 59, 65
Rajas 56, 57

Sādhaka 88, 89
Sadāśiva 45, 49, 50, 52, 56, 61, 78
Sakala 51, 52, 59
Samādhi 56, 68, 87, 88, 89, 90
Saṁhṛti 89
Sākṣāt vyavasthitaḥ 54
Samāpatti 87
Samāna śaktis 73
Samāveśa 42, 79, 83, 87, 88, 89
Samāviṣṭa 89
Saṁhāra 45, 47, 63, 66, 68, 77
Saṁhartṛtā 66
Saṅkoca 82, 83, 84, 85
Saṁsāra 42, 58, 59, 66,68, 71
Sāsarasya 47
Saṁsārin 64, 65, 69, 73, 74
Saṁskāras 58, 68, 77
Samvid 82
Saṁvit 80, 81
Ṣaṁvit-santati 63
Ṣana-samaye 68
Sāṅkhyas 61
Saṇkoca 77
Ṣaṅkocinī 55
Śāntā kalā 90
Sapta 59
Sarga 77
Sarvamantra-jīvita-bhūtā 90
Sarvavīrabhaṭṭāraka 69
Sattva 56, 57
Siddhi 45, 47, 48
Siddhānta 53
Smarānanda 85
Spanda 83, 86, 92
Spandakārikā 55, 80, 83, 86, 92, 94
Spandasandoha 67
Spandaśāstra 55, 80
Spandatattva 94
Sphurattā 73
Sphuṭa 50
Sraṣṭṛtā 66
Sṛiyate 68
Sṛṣṭi 45, 66, 89

Sthāpakatā 66
Sthiti 45, 63, 66, 68, 89
Sugata 60
Sūkṣmaśarīra 94
Svabhittau 49
Svacchanda 66
Svacchanda Tantra 62, 66
Svatantrā 47, 48
Svātantrya 75
Svecchayā 49

Śabda-brahman 61
Śākta 71
Śakti 43, 45, 56, 62, 63, 64, 65, 69, 72, 75, 82, 83, 84, 89, 92, 95
Śaktis 65, 70, 71, 73, 74
Śāktopāya 71
Śāmbhava 71
Śāmbhavopāya 71
Śaṃkara 42
Śaṁsārin 71
Śiva 41, 52, 54, 55, 56, 57, 58, 59, 63, 65, 66, 69, 70, 74, 75, 78, 84, 90, 91, 92, 94, 95
Śivabhaṭṭāraka 46, 52
Śiva-stotrāvali 77
Śivasūtras 58, 92
Śāṅkara Vedānta 48
Śāstras 69
Śuddha-bodhātmānaḥ 51
Śuddha vidhyā 51
Śūnya 51, 59

Tadabhedasāram 51
Tamas 56, 57
Tāntrikas 61
Tat 50, 57, 63, 69
Tathābhūtam 51
Tathāvidha eva 50
Tattva-garbha-stotra 57
Tattvas 53, 59, 75
Trika 62
Trikasāra 47
Triśiromata 53
Turīyā 63, 89
Turya 74, 83
Turyātīta 74, 83

Udāna-śakti 73
Udbhava 94
Udeṣyat 63
Unmeṣa 86, 94
Unmīlana 49, 94
Upādhis 60
Ūrdhva-kuṇḍalinī 84
Utpaladeva 57, 92, 95

Vācaka 91
Vācya 92
Vahni 85
Vaiśeśika 60
Vaiṣṇavas 62
Vākśakti 70
Vālas 85
Vamana 89
Vāmeśa 73
Vāmeśvarī 71, 73
Vastu-vṛtta-anusasmreṇa 58
Vāsudeva 60
Vasugupta 55
Vaṭa 53
Vāyu 85
Veda 60
Vedānta 60, 61
Vidyā 51, 59, 62, 65
Vidyāpramātā 56
Vijñānabhairava 48, 85, 86, 87
Vijñānabhaṭṭāraka 48, 85
Vijñākala 51, 56, 61
Vikalpa 55, 57, 70, 82, 83
Vikālpa śākti 71
Vikāsa 82, 84, 85
Vilaya 66, 68
Vilayakāritā 66
Vimarśa 45, 48, 56, 68, 90, 91, 92
Vimarśna-samaye 68
Vimuktakas 72
Viṣa 85
Viśva 45, 48, 50
Viṣṇu 77
Vivaraṇa 94
Vyākaraṇa 61
Vyānaśakti 74
Vyāmohitatvam 69
Vyutthāna 79, 88

Yogin 68, 87, 88, 915

ENGLISH INDEX

"A" 70
Absolute 45
  limitation of 64-65
Absorption 66, 83-84, 94
  in *adhaḥ kuṇḍalinī* 85
Act, fivefold 41, 65-69, 75, 82
Action 59
Adoration 41
Agency, sense of 51
Assimilating, objects of experience 77, 89
Awareness, sense of pure 51

Birth 69
Bliss 41, 42, 59, 63, 71, 74, 87, 90, 91
  highest 89
  of *cit* 79, 81
  of sexual union 85
  perfect 95
Body 48, 53, 66, 70, 73, 74, 75, 78, 79, 80, 82, 95
  and Self 60
  as God 53, 74
  as universe 52, 54, 91
  emergence and immergence of 78
  gross 94
  identification with 78, 91
  immersion of 92-93
  subtle 94
Bondage 47, 55, 73, 83
Breath
  vital 80, 85

Cause 46
  material 48-49
Causality, universal 43
Cavities, of nose 84
Center 80-81, 87
Channels, of *vāyu* 85
Cognition 91
Concealment 66
  of real nature 68
Concentration 85
Consciousness 42, 46-47, 48, 71, 73, 74, 76, 81, 84, 86, 89, 90, 93, 95
  collectedness of 68
  divine 45, 46
  external and internal 88
  firmness of 79
  fire of 68
  fourth level of 63, 89
  individual 56-58, 82
  light of 46, 52, 54, 58, 70, 74
  multiple forms of 58
  nature of 57, 59, 67
  objects of 55-56
  powers of 57, 78
  ultimate 47
  unity of 52, 71
  universal 55, 80, 81, 88-89
  withdrawal of 83
Consciousness-power 46, 71
Contemplation 56, 68, 79, 82
Contraction 84
  as consciousness 54
  of consciousness 56
Cycle 89

Death 69
Deeds. *See* acts.
Deep sleep state 73, 95
Deities 70-71, 72, 90, 94
Delight 68
Delusion 69, 71, 73
Descent, of Śakti 43
Devotee 67
Devotion 68
Dialectics 42
Differences 70, 72, 76
  perception of 72
Differentiation 50, 68
Disciplines, yogic 82, 88
Dissolution 67
  of *vikalpa* 82
Divinity 43
Doctrine
  secret 42
  of Brahman 48-49
Doership 92
  limited 72
  of Lord 73
  universal 72
Doubts 69
Dream state 73, 95
Dualism 48, 64

Earth 54
Emanation 63, 66, 70-71, 89-90, 94
Emancipation 48
Existence
  continued 45
  objective 73
Expansion
  condition of 84
  of *Śaktī* 92
Experient 45, 51-52, 53, 70, 76, 77, 91
  and *Śiva* 54
  and *vikalpa* 55
  false identification of 62
  groups, consciousness of 50
  of impure path 58
  universal 54
  See also subject
Extrinsic course 66
Extroversion 75

Feelings 47
Fire, of *citi* 76
Form 46

Freedom 57, 76, 91
Free will 45, 47, 48, 58

Goddesses 73
Grace 66, 68, 83
Guru 69

Happiness 83, 86
Heart 72, 82, 85, 86
  lotus of 85-86

"I" consciousness, perfect 70, 89-90, 94
"I" feeling 92
Ideation 93
Identity, with *cit* 88
Ignorance 69, 80
Immortality 83
Impressions, past 58, 68, 77, 79
Individual, migrating 74

Joy 87, 89

"Ksa" 70
Knower, the 47-48
  highest 93
  real 82
Knowledge 47-48, 54, 59, 93
  empirical, and *Śiva* 63
  objects of 50-52
  subjects of 52
Known, the 47

Letters 69
Liberation 47, 55, 58, 60, 63, 73, 74, 79, 81
Liberty 59
Light 52
  divine 73
Limitation 56-57, 58, 64-65, 74, 75
Logic 42
Lord 50, 53, 66-67, 74, 93
  essential nature of 73
  Highest 42, 91
  of *cakra*
  with a body 74

Maintenance 63, 66, 68, 70-71, 89
  goddess 68
Manifestation 45, 91
  glory of
  of universe 46, 47
  of *Śiva* 53

Manifesting 67-68
Manifoldness 68
Mantras. *See* Sanskrit index.
Meditation, on Self 87
Mental agitation 83
Mind 85, 86, 87

Nectar, of spiritual awareness 95
Nescience 54
Non-being 60
Non-difference 71, 92
  ascertainment of 72
Non-duality 64
Non-manifest 61

Objects 47, 72, 75, 83-84, 93
  consciousness of 48
  of knowledge 50-51, 68, 76-77
  reabsorption of 63
  sense 78, 89
One-pointedness 83, 86
Organ
  inner and outer 72
  sense 84
  sixth 85

Path, pure 56
Peace, inner 63, 73
Pentads, seven 59
Perfection 47, 68, 75, 91
Philosophy
  Pratyabhijñā 95
  systems of 59-60
Pleasure 95
  of eating and drinking 87
Poison, of *saṁsāra* 42
Power 45, 49, 68, 74, 75, 77, 92, 95
Powers, and objects 84
Principle(s)
  of Sadāśiva 50
  of Īśvara 50
  thirty-five 59, 75
  thirty-six 59, 75
Processess. *See* acts.
Psychic apparatus 72

Reabsorption 63, 68, 89-90, 93
Reality
  Highest 41, 57, 92
  innermost 80
Recognition, doctrine of 41, 42, 95
Reflection, on words 92
Relishing 67-68
Restraining, of *prāṇa* 84

Sacred texts 62, 69
Seed 67
Self (limited) 65, 67
Self 43, 58, 61, 63, 68, 83
  and body 60
  consciousness 90
  cosmos as 71
  highest 89
  identification of 72
  merging in 48, 90
  perfect 92-93
  Real 41, 72
Sense-activities 83
Sense-objects. *See* objects.
Senses 86
  control of 94
  divine 77
  inner 93
  opening of 83-84
  outer 72-73, 93
Service 69
Sight, goddess of 68
Soul, bound 70, 73
Sounds 69, 85
Space 46, 58, 66
Speech, power of 70
State, pure 83
Subject 47, 53, 73, 75
  as *Śiva* 54
  consciousness of 48
  empirical 70, 72
  knowledge of 50
  limited 56
  nature of 55
  See also experient

Taste 87
This, consciousness of 50
Time 46, 58, 66
Transmigration 58, 64-65, 69, 71, 73
Truth 55, 75

Unity-consciousness 73, 79
Universe 54, 55, 74, 76, 77, 94
  and Atman 62
  and free will 49
  and light 49
  apprehension of 50
  as Self 78-80

body as 91
cause of 48
creation of 46
defined 47
differention of 51
emanation and reabsorption 90
extended 92
foundation of 84
manifestation of 46, 47, 76
projection of
siddhi of 45
Upaniṣads 60, 61

Value, Highest 41
Vibration, of *cit* 94
Void 51, 53, 56, 58, 72

Waking state 73, 95
Water 54
Will 49, 59, 84
Absolute 62
of *citi* 78
sovereignty of 92
Withdrawal 71
See reabsorption.
World
as play of divine 80
germinal form of 68
process 89

Yoga 78, 88
Yogin 88-89, 91, 93

APPENDIX

ओं नमो मङ्गलमूर्तये ।

अथ

प्रत्यभिज्ञाहृदयम् ।

नमः शिवाय सततं पञ्चकृत्यविधायिने ।
चिदानन्दघनस्वात्मपरमार्थावभासिने ॥ १ ॥
शांकरोपनिषत्सारप्रत्यभिज्ञामहोदधेः ।
क्षेमेणोद्ध्रियते सारः संसारविषशान्तये ॥ २ ॥

इह ये सुकुमारमतयोऽकृततीक्ष्णतर्कशास्त्रपरिश्रमाः शक्तिपातोन्मिषित-पारमेश्वरसमावेशाभिलाषिणः कतिचित् भक्तिभाजः तेषाम् ईश्वरप्रत्यभिज्ञो-पदेशतत्त्वं मनाक् उन्मील्यते ।

तत्र स्वात्मदेवताया एव सर्वत्र कारणत्वं सुखोपायप्राप्यत्वं महाफलत्वं च अभिव्यङ्क्तुमाह—

चितिः स्वतन्त्रा विश्वसिद्धिहेतुः ॥ १ ॥

'विश्वस्य' – सदाशिवादेः भूम्यन्तस्य 'सिद्धौ'–निष्पत्तौ, प्रकाशने, स्थित्यात्मनि, परप्रमातृविश्रान्त्यात्मनि च संहारे, पराशक्तिरूपा 'चितिः' भगवती 'स्वतन्त्रा' – अनुत्तरविमर्शमयी शिवभट्टारकाभिन्ना 'हेतुः' – कारणम् । अस्यां हि प्रसरन्त्यां जगत् उन्मिषति व्यवतिष्ठते च, निवृत्तप्रसरायां च निमिषति;–इति स्वानुभव एव अत्र साक्षी । अन्यस्य तु मायाप्रकृत्यादेः चित्प्रकाशभिन्नस्य अप्रकाशमानत्वेन असत्त्वात् न क्वचिदपि हेतुत्वम्; प्रकाशमानत्वे तु प्रकाशैकात्म्यात् प्रकाशरूपा चितिरेव हेतुः; न त्वसौ कश्चित् । अत एव देशकालाकारा एतत्सृष्टा एतदनुप्राणिताश्च नैतत्स्वरूपं भेत्तुमलम्; – इति व्यापक-नित्योदित-परिपूर्णरूपा इयम्-इत्यर्थलभ्यमेव एतत् ।

ननु जगदपि चितो भिन्नं नैव किञ्चित्; अभेदे च कथं हेतुहेतुमद्भावः? उच्यते । चिदेव भगवती स्वच्छस्वतन्त्ररूपा तत्तदनन्तजगदात्मना स्फुरति,– इत्येतावत्परमार्थोऽयं कार्यकारणभावः । यतश्च इयमेव प्रमातृ-प्रमाण-प्रमेयमयस्य विश्वस्य सिद्धौ–प्रकाशने हेतुः, ततोऽस्याः स्वतन्त्रापरिच्छिन्नस्वप्रकाशरूपायाः सिद्धौ अभिनवार्थप्रकाशनरूपं न प्रमाणवराकमुपयुक्तम् उपपन्नं वा । तदुक्तं त्रिकसारे—

'स्वपदा स्वशिरश्छायां यद्वल्लङ्घितुमीहते ।
पादोद्देशे शिरो न स्यात्तथेयं बैन्दवी कला ॥'

इति ।

यतश्च इयं विश्वस्य सिद्धौ पराद्वयसामरस्यापादनात्मनि च संहारे हेतुः, तत एव स्वतन्त्रा । प्रत्यभिज्ञातस्वातन्त्र्या सती, भोगमोक्षस्वरूपाणां विश्व-सिद्धीनां हेतुः ।—इति आवृत्त्या व्याख्येयम् ।

अपि च 'विश्वं'—नील—सुख—देह—प्राणादि; तस्य या 'सिद्धिः'—प्रमाणो-पारोहक्रमेण विमर्शमयप्रमात्रावेशः, सैव 'हेतुः'—परिज्ञाने उपायो यस्याः । अनेन च सुखोपायत्वमुक्तम् । यदुक्तं श्रीविज्ञानभट्टारके—

'ग्राह्यग्राहकसंवित्तिः सामान्या सर्वदेहिनाम् ।
योगिनां तु विशेषोऽयं संबन्धे सावधानता ॥'

इति ।

'चितिः'—इति एकवचनं देशकालाद्यनवच्छिन्नताम् अभिदधत् समस्तभेद-वादानाम् अवास्तवतां व्यनक्ति । 'स्वतन्त्र'-शब्दो ब्रह्मवादवैलक्षण्यम् आचक्षाणः चितो माहेश्वर्यसारतां ब्रूते । 'विश्व'—इत्यादिपदम् अशेषशक्तित्वं, सर्वकारणत्वं, सुखोपायत्वं महाफलं च आह ॥ १ ॥

ननु विश्वस्य यदि चितिः हेतुः, तत् अस्या उपादानाद्यपेक्षायां भेदवादा-परित्यागः स्यात्—इत्याशङ्क्य आह—

स्वेच्छया स्वभित्तौ विश्वमुन्मीलयति ॥ २ ॥

'स्वेच्छया', न तु ब्रह्मादिवत् अन्येच्छया, तयैव च, न तु उपादानाद्यपेक्षया,—एवं हि प्रागुक्तस्वातन्त्र्यहान्या चित्त्वमेव न घटेत—'स्वभित्तौ', न तु अन्यत्र क्वापि, प्राक् निर्णीतं 'विश्वं' दर्पणे नगरवत् अभिन्नमपि भिन्नमिव 'उन्मीलयति' । उन्मीलनं च अवस्थितस्यैव प्रकटीकरणम् ।—इत्यनेन जगतः प्रकाशैकात्म्येन अवस्थानम् उक्तम् ॥ २ ॥

अथ विश्वस्य स्वरूपं विभागेन प्रतिपादयितुमाह—

तन्नाना अनुरूपग्राह्यग्राहकभेदात् ॥ ३ ॥

'तत्' विश्वं 'नाना' —अनेकप्रकारम्। कथं ? 'अनुरूपाणां'— परस्परौचित्यावस्थितीनां 'ग्राह्याणां ग्राहकाणां' च 'भेदात्' —वैचित्र्यात्। तथा च सदाशिवतत्त्वे अहन्ताच्छादित-अस्फुटेदन्तामयं यादृशं परापररूपं विश्वं ग्राह्यं, तादृगेव श्रीसदाशिवभट्टारकाधिष्ठितो मन्त्रमहेश्वराख्यः प्रमातृवर्गः परमेश्वरेच्छावकल्पिततथावस्थानः। ईश्वरतत्त्वे स्फुटेदन्ताहन्तासामानाधिकरण्यात्म यादृक् विश्वं ग्राह्यं, तथाविध एव ईश्वरभट्टारकाधिष्ठितो मन्त्रेश्वरवर्गः। विद्यापदे श्रीमदनन्तभट्टारकाधिष्ठिता बहुशाखावान्तरभेदभिन्ना यथाभूता मन्त्राः प्रमातारः, तथाभूतमेव भेदैकसारं विश्वमपि प्रमेयम्। मायोर्ध्वे यादृशा विज्ञानाकलाः कर्तृताशून्यशुद्धबोधात्मानः, तादृगेव तदभेदसारं सकल-प्रलयाकलात्मक-पूर्वावस्थापरिचितम् एषां प्रमेयम्। मायायां शून्यप्रमातॄणां प्रलयकेवलिनां स्वोचितं प्रलीनकल्पं प्रमेयम्। क्षितिपर्यन्तावस्थितानां तु सकलानां सर्वतो भिन्नानां परिमितानां तथाभूतमेव प्रमेयम्। तदुत्तीर्णशिवभट्टारकस्य प्रकाशैकवपुषः प्रकाशैकरूपा एव भावाः। श्रीमत्परमशिवस्य पुनः विश्वोत्तीर्ण-विश्वात्मक-परमानन्दमय-प्रकाशैकघनस्य एवंविधमेव शिवादि-धरण्यन्तम् अखिलम् अभेदेनैव स्फुरति; न तु वस्तुतः अन्यत् किंचित् ग्राह्यं ग्राहकं वा; अपि तु श्रीपरमशिवभट्टारक एव इत्थं नानावैचित्र्यसहस्रैः स्फुरति।—इत्यभिहितप्रायम्॥ ३॥

यथा च भगवान् विश्वशरीरः, तथा

चितिसंकोचात्मा चेतनोऽपि संकुचितविश्वमयः॥ ४॥

श्रीपरमशिवः स्वात्मैक्येन स्थितं विश्वं सदाशिवाद्युचितेन रूपेण अवबिभासयिषुः पूर्वं चिदैक्याख्यातिमयानाश्रितशिवपर्यायशून्यातिशून्यात्मतया प्रकाशाभेदेन प्रकाशमानतया स्फुरति; ततः चिद्रसाश्यानतारूपाशेषतत्त्वभुवनभावतत्तत्प्रमात्राद्यात्मतयापि प्रथते। यथा च एवं भगवान् विश्वशरीरः, तथा 'चितिसंकोचात्मा' संकुचितचिद्रूपः; 'चेतनो' ग्राहकोऽपि वटधानिकावत् संकुचिताशेषविश्वरूपः। तथा च सिद्धान्तवचनम्

'विग्रहो विग्रही चैव सर्वविग्रहविग्रही।'

इति। त्रिशिरोमतेऽपि

सर्वदेवमयः कायस्तं चेदानीं शृणु प्रिये।
पृथिवी कठिनत्वेन द्रवत्वेऽम्भः प्रकीर्तितम्॥'

इत्युपक्रम्य

'त्रिशिरोभैरवः साक्षाद्व्याप्य विश्वं व्यवस्थितः ॥'

इत्यन्तेन ग्रन्थेन ग्राहकस्य संकुचितविश्वमयत्वमेव व्याहरति ।

अयं च अत्राशयः—ग्राहकोऽपि अयं प्रकाशैकात्म्येन उक्तागमयुक्त्या च विश्वशरीरशिवैकरूप एव, केवलं तन्मायाशक्त्या अनभिव्यक्तस्वरूपत्वात् संकुचित इव आभाति; संकोचोऽपि विचार्यमाणः चिदैकात्म्येन प्रथमानत्वात् चिन्मय एव, अन्यथा तु न किंचित् ।—इति सर्वो ग्राहको विश्वशरीरः शिवभट्टारक एव । तदुक्तं मयैव

'अख्यातिर्यदि न ख्याति ख्यातिरेवावशिष्यते ।
ख्याति चेत् ख्यातिरूपत्वात् ख्यातिरेवावशिष्यते ॥'

इति । अनेनैव आशयेन श्रीस्पन्दशास्त्रेषु

'यस्मात्सर्वमयो जीवः ……।'
'तेन शब्दार्थचिन्तासु न सावस्था न यः शिवः ॥'

इत्यादिना शिवजीवयोरभेद एव उक्तः । एतत्तत्त्वपरिज्ञानमेव मुक्तिः, एतत्तत्त्वापरिज्ञानमेव च बन्धः; —इति भविष्यति एव एतत् ॥ ४ ॥

ननु ग्राहकोऽयं विकल्पमयः, विकल्पनं च चित्तहेतुकं; सति च चित्ते, कथमस्य शिवात्मकत्वम् ?—इति शङ्कित्वा चित्तमेव निर्णेतुमाह—

चितिरेव चेतनपदादवरूढा चेत्यसंकोचिनी चित्तम् ॥ ५ ॥

न चित्तं नाम अन्यत् किंचित्, अपि तु सैव भगवती तत् । तथा हि सा स्वं स्वरूपं गोपयित्वा यदा संकोचं गृह्णाति, तदा द्वयी गतिः; कदाचित् उल्लसितमपि संकोचं गुणीकृत्य चित्प्राधान्येन स्फुरति, कदाचित् संकोचप्रधानतया । चित्प्राधान्यपक्षे सहजे, प्रकाशमात्रप्रधानत्वे विज्ञानाकलता; प्रकाशपरामर्शप्रधानत्वे तु विद्याप्रमातृता । तत्रापि क्रमेण संकोचस्य तनुतायाम्, ईश-सदाशिवानाश्रितरूपता । समाधिप्रयत्नोपार्जिते तु चित्प्रधानत्वे शुद्धाध्वप्रमातृता क्रमात्क्रमं प्रकर्षवती । संकोचप्राधान्ये तु शून्यादिप्रमातृता । एवमवस्थिते सति, 'चितिरेव'

संकुचितग्राहकरूपा 'चेतनपदात् अवरूढा'–अर्थग्रहणोन्मुखी सती 'चेत्येन'–नील-सुखादिना 'संकोचिनी' उभयसंकोचसंकुचितैव चित्तम् । तथा च—

'स्वाङ्गरूपेषु भावेषु पत्युर्ज्ञानं क्रिया च या ।
मायातृतीये ते एव पशोः सत्वं रजस्तमः ॥'

इत्यादिना स्वातन्त्र्यात्मा चितिशक्तिरेव ज्ञानक्रिया-मायाशक्तिरूपा पशु-दशायां संकोचप्रकर्षात् सत्त्व-रजस्तमः-स्वभावचित्तात्मतया स्फुरति; इति श्रीप्रत्यभिज्ञायामुक्तम् । अत एव श्रीतत्त्वगर्भस्तोत्रे विकल्पदशायामपि तात्त्विक-स्वरूपसद्भावात् तदनुसरणाभिप्रायेण उक्तम्—

'अत एव तु ये केचित्परमार्थानुसारिणः ।
तेषां तत्र स्वरूपस्य स्वज्योतिष्ट्वं न लुप्यते ॥'

इति ॥ ५ ॥

चित्तमेव तु मायाप्रमातुः स्वरूपम्–इत्याह—

तन्मयो मायाप्रमाता ॥ ६ ॥

देहप्राणपदं तावत् चित्तप्रधानमेव; शून्यभूमिरपि चित्तसंस्कारवत्येव; अन्यथा ततो व्युत्थितस्य स्वकर्तव्यानुधावनाभावः स्यात्;–इति चित्तमय एव मायीयः प्रमाता । अमुनैव आशयेन शिवसूत्रेषु वस्तुवृत्तानुसारेण

'चैतन्यमात्मा' (१—१)

इत्यभिधाय, मायाप्रमातृलक्षणावसरे पुनः

'चित्तमात्मा' (३—१)

इत्युक्तम् ॥ ६ ॥

अस्यैव सम्यक् स्वरूपज्ञानात् यतो मुक्तिः, असम्यक् तु संसारः, ततः तिलश एतत्स्वरूपं निर्भङ्क्तुमाह—

स चैको द्विरूपस्त्रिमयश्चतुरात्मा
सप्तपञ्चकस्वभावः ॥ ७ ॥

निर्णीतदृशा चिदात्मा शिवभट्टारक एव 'एक' आत्मा, न तु अन्यः कश्चित्; प्रकाशस्य देशकालादिभिः भेदायोगात्; जडस्य तु ग्राहकत्वानुपपत्तेः। प्रकाश एव यतः स्वातन्त्र्यात् गृहीतप्राणादिसंकोचः संकुचितार्थग्राहकतामश्नुते, ततः असौ प्रकाशरूपत्वसंकोचावभासवत्त्वाभ्यां 'द्विरूपः'। आणव-मायीय-कार्ममला-वृतत्वात् 'त्रिमयः'। शून्य-प्राण-पुर्यष्टकशरीरस्वभावत्वात् 'चतुरात्मा' सप्त-पञ्चकानि'–शिवादिपृथिव्यन्तानि पञ्चत्रिंशत्तत्त्वानि 'तत्स्वभावः'। तथा शिवादि सकलान्त-प्रमातृसप्तकस्वरूपः; चिदानन्देच्छा-ज्ञान-क्रियाशक्तिरूपत्वेऽपि अख्यातिवशात् कला-विद्या-राग-काल-नियतिकञ्चुकवलितत्वात् पञ्चकस्वरूपः। एवं च शिवैकरूपत्वेन, पञ्चत्रिंशत्तत्त्वमयत्वेन, प्रमातृसप्तकस्वभावत्वेन चिदादि-शक्तिपञ्चकात्मकत्वेन च अयं प्रत्यभिज्ञायमानो मुक्तिदः; अन्यथा तु संसारहेतुः ॥७॥

एवं च

तद्भूमिकाः सर्वदर्शनस्थितयः ॥ ८ ॥

'सर्वेषां' चार्वाकादिदर्शनानां 'स्थितयः'–सिद्धान्ताः 'तस्य' एतस्य आत्मनो नटस्येव स्वेच्छावगृहीताः कृत्रिमा 'भूमिकाः'। तथा च

'चैतन्यविशिष्टं शरीरमात्मा।'

इति चार्वाकाः

नैयायिकादयो ज्ञानादिगुणगणाश्रयं बुद्धितत्त्वप्रायमेव आत्मानं संसृतौ मन्यन्ते, अपवर्गे तु तदुच्छेदे शून्यप्रायम्।

अहंप्रतीतिप्रत्येयः सुखदुःखाद्युपाधिभिः तिरस्कृतः आत्मा—इति मन्वाना मीमांसका अपि बुद्धावेव निविष्टाः।

ज्ञानसंतान एव तत्त्वम्—इति सौगता बुद्धिवृत्तिषु एव पर्यवसिताः।

प्राण एव आत्मा—इति केचित् श्रुत्यन्तविदः।

असदेव इदमासीत्—इत्यभावब्रह्मवादिनः शून्यभुवमवगाह्य स्थिताः।

माध्यमिका अपि एवमेव।

परा प्रकृतिः भगवान् वासुदेवः तद्विस्फुलिङ्गप्राया एव जीवा–

इति पाञ्चरात्राः परस्या प्रकृतेः परिणामाभ्युपगमात् अव्यक्ते एव अभिनिविष्टाः ।

सांख्यादयस्तु विज्ञानाकलप्रायां भूमिमवलम्बन्ते ।

सदेव इदमग्र आसीत्—इति ईश्वरतत्त्वपदमाश्रिता अपरे श्रुत्यन्तविदः ।

शब्दब्रह्ममयं पश्यन्तीरूपम् आत्मतत्त्वम्—इति वैयाकरणाः श्रीसदाशिवपदमध्यासिताः । एवमन्यदपि अनुमन्तव्यम् । एतच्च आगमेषु

'बुद्धितत्त्वे स्थिता बौद्धा गुणेष्वेवार्हताः स्थिताः ।
स्थिता वेदविदः पुंसि अव्यक्ते पाञ्चरात्रिकाः ॥'

इत्यादिना निरूपितम् ।
विश्वोत्तीर्णमात्मतत्त्वम्—इति तान्त्रिकाः ।
विश्वमयम् इति—कुलाद्याम्नायनिविष्टाः ।
विश्वोत्तीर्णं विश्वमयं च—इति त्रिकादि दर्शनविदः ।

एवम् एकस्यैव चिदात्मनो भगवतः स्वातन्त्र्यावभासिताः सर्वा इमा भूमिकाः स्वातन्त्र्यप्रच्छादनोन्मीलनतारतम्यभेदिताः । अत एक एव एतावद्व्याप्तिक आत्मा । मितदृष्टयस्तु अंशांशिकासु तदिच्छयैव अभिमानं ग्राहिताः येन देहादिषु भूमिषु पूर्वपूर्वप्रमातृव्याप्तिसारताप्रथायामपि उक्तरूपां महाव्याप्तिं परशक्तिपातं विना न लभन्ते । यथोक्तम्—

'वैष्णवाद्यास्तु ये केचिद्विद्यारागेण रञ्जिताः ।
न विदन्ति परं देवं सर्वज्ञं ज्ञानशालिनम् ॥'

इति । तथा

'भ्रमयत्येव तान्माया ह्यमोक्षे मोक्षलिप्सया ।'

इति ।

'त आत्मोपासकाः शैवं न गच्छन्ति परं पदम् ॥'

इति च ।

अपि च 'सर्वेषां दर्शनानां'—समस्तानां नीलसुखादिज्ञानानां याः 'स्थितयः' —अन्तर्मुखरूपा विश्रान्तयः ताः 'तद्भूमिकाः' —चिदानन्दघनस्वात्मस्वरूपाभिव्यक्त्युपु-

भायाः । तथा हि यदा यदा बहिर्मुखं रूपं स्वरूपे विश्राम्यति, तदा तदा बाह्यवस्तूपसंहारः; अन्तः प्रशान्तपदावस्थितिः; तत्तदुदेष्यत्संवित्संतत्यासूत्रणम्; —इति सृष्टि-स्थिति-संहारमेलनरूपा इयं तुरीया संविद्भट्टारिका तत्तत्सृष्ट्यादिभेदान् उद्वमन्ती संहरन्ती च, सदा पूर्णा च, कृशा च, उभयरूपा च अनुभयात्मा च, अक्रममेव स्फुरन्ती स्थिता । उक्तं च श्रीप्रत्यभिज्ञाटीकायाम्—

'तावदर्थावलेहेन उत्तिष्ठति, पूर्णा च भवति'

इति । एषा च भट्टारिका क्रमात्क्रमम् अधिकमनुशील्यमाना स्वात्मसात्करोत्येव भक्तजनम् ॥८॥

यदि एवंभूतस्य आत्मनो विभूतिः, तत् कथम् अयं मलावृतः अणुः कलादिवलितः संसारी अभिधीयते ?—इत्याह—

चिद्वत्तच्छक्तिसंकोचात् मलावृतः संसारी ॥ ९ ॥

यदा 'चिदात्मा' परमेश्वरः स्वस्वातन्त्र्यात् अभेदव्याप्तिं निमज्य भेदव्याप्तिम् अवलम्बते, तदा 'तदीया इच्छादिशक्तयः' असंकुचिता अपि 'संकोचवत्यो' भान्ति; तदानीमेव च अयं 'मलावृतः संसारी' भवति । तथा च अप्रतिहतस्वातन्त्र्यरूपा इच्छाशक्तिः संकुचिता सती अपूर्णंमन्यतारूपम् आणवं मलम्; ज्ञानशक्तिः क्रमेण संकोचात् भेदे सर्वज्ञत्वस्य किंचिज्ज्ञत्वाप्तेः अन्तःकरण-बुद्धीन्द्रियतापत्तिपूर्वम् अत्यन्तं संकोचग्रहणेन भिन्नवेद्यप्रथारूपं मायीयं मलम्; क्रियाशक्तिः क्रमेण भेदे सर्वकर्तृत्वस्य किंचित्कर्तृत्वाप्तेः कर्मेन्द्रियरूप-संकोचग्रहणपूर्वम् अत्यन्तं परिमिततां प्राप्ता शुभाशुभानुष्ठानमयं कार्मं मलम् । तथा सर्वकर्तृत्व-सर्वज्ञत्व-पूर्णत्व-नित्यत्व-व्यापकत्वशक्तयः संकोचं गृह्णाना यथाक्रमं कला-विद्या-राग-काल-नियतिरूपतया भान्ति । तथाविधश्च अयं शक्तिदरिद्रः संसारी उच्यते; स्वशक्तिविकासे तु शिव एव ॥९॥

ननु संसार्यवस्थायाम् अस्य किंचित् शिवतोचितम् अभिज्ञानमस्ति येन शिव एव तथावस्थितः ?—इत्युद्घोष्यते । अस्ति इत्याह—

तथापि तद्वत् पञ्च कृत्यानि करोति ॥१०॥

इह ईश्वराद्वयदर्शनस्य ब्रह्मवादिभ्यः अयमेव विशेषः, यत्

'सृष्टिसंहारकर्तारं विलयस्थितिकारकम् ।
अनुग्रहकरं देवं प्रणतार्तिविनाशनम् ॥'

इति श्रीमत्स्वच्छन्दादिशासनोक्तनीत्या सदा पञ्चविधकृत्यकारित्वं चिदात्मनो भगवतः । यथा च भगवान् शुद्धेतराध्वस्फारणक्रमेण स्वरूपविकासरूपाणि सृष्ट्यादीनि करोति, 'तथा' संकुचितचिच्छक्तितया संसारभूमिकायामपि 'पञ्चकृत्यानि' विधत्ते । तथा हि

'तदेवं व्यवहारेऽपि प्रभुर्देहादिमाविशन् ।
भान्तमेवान्तरर्थौघमिच्छया भासयेद्बहिः ॥'

इति प्रत्यभिज्ञाकारिकोक्तार्थदृष्ट्या देहप्राणादिपदम् आविशन् चिद्रूपो महेश्वरो बहिर्मुखीभावावसरे नीलादिकमर्थं नियतदेशकालादितया यदा आभासयति, तदा नियतदेशकालाद्याभासांशे अस्य स्रष्टृता; अन्यदेशकालाद्याभासांशे अस्य संहर्तृता; नीलाद्याभासांशे स्थापकता; भेदेन आभासांशे विलयकारिता; प्रकाशैक्येन प्रकाशने अनुग्रहीतृता । यथा च सदा पञ्चविधकृत्यकारित्वं भगवतः, तथा मया वितत्य स्पन्दसंदोहे निर्णीतम् ।

एवमिदं पञ्चविधकृत्यकारित्वम् आत्मीयं सदा दृढप्रतिपत्त्या परिशील्यमानं माहेश्वर्यम् उन्मीलयत्येव भक्तिभाजाम् । अत एव ये सदा एतत् परिशीलयन्ति, ते स्वरूपविकासमयं विश्वं जानाना जीवन्मुक्ता इत्याम्नाताः । ये तु न तथा, ते सर्वतो विभिन्नं मेयजातं पश्यन्तो बद्धात्मानः ॥१०॥

न च अयमेव प्रकारः पञ्चविधकृत्यकारित्वे, यावत् अन्योऽपि कश्चित् रहस्यरूपोऽस्ति । इत्याह—

आभासन-रक्ति-विमर्शन-बीजावस्थापन-
विलापनतस्तानि ॥ ११ ॥

'पञ्चविधकृत्यानि करोति' इति पूर्वतः संबध्यते । श्रीमन्महार्थदृष्ट्या दृगादिदेवीप्रसरणक्रमेण यत् यत् आभाति, तत् तत् सृज्यते; तथा सृष्टे पदे तत्र यदा प्रशान्तनिमेषं कंचित् कालं रज्यति, तदा स्थितिदेव्या तत् स्थाप्यते; चमत्कारापरपर्यायविमर्शनसमये सं ह्रियते । यथोक्तं श्रीरामेण

'समाधिवज्रेणाप्यन्यैरभेद्यो भेदभूधरः ।
परामृष्टश्च नष्टश्च त्वद्भक्तिबलशालिभिः ॥

इति । यदा तु संह्रियमाणमपि एतत् अन्तः विचित्राशङ्कादिसंस्कारम् आधत्ते, तदा तत् पुनः उद्भविष्यत्संसारबीजभावमापन्नं विलयपदम् अध्यारोपितम् । यदा पुनः तत् तथा अन्तः स्थापितम् अन्यत् वा अनुभूयमानमेव हठपाकक्रमेण अलंग्रासक्युत्या चिदग्निसाद्भावम् आपद्यते, तदा पूर्णतापादनेन अनुगृह्यते एव । ईदृशं च पञ्चविधकृत्यकारित्वं सर्वस्य सदा संनिहितमपि सद्गुरूपदेशं विना न प्रकाशते, इति सद्गुरुसपर्यैव एतत्प्रथार्थम् अनुसर्तव्या ॥११॥

यस्य पुनः सद्गुरूपदेशं विना एतत्परिज्ञानं नास्ति, तस्य अवच्छादितस्वस्वरूपाभिः निजाभिः शक्तिभिः व्यामोहितत्वं भवति । इत्याह

तदपरिज्ञाने स्वशक्तिभिर्व्यामोहितता
संसारित्वम् ॥ १२ ॥

'तस्य' एतस्य सदा संभवतः पञ्चविधकृत्यकारित्वस्य 'अपरिज्ञाने'—शक्तिपातहेतुकस्वबलोन्मीलनाभावात् अप्रकाशने 'स्वाभिः शक्तिभिः व्यामोहितत्वं'-विविधलौकिकशास्त्रीयशङ्काशङ्कुकीलितत्वं यत्, इदमेव 'संसारित्वम्' । तदुक्तं श्रीसर्ववीरभट्टारके

'अज्ञानाच्छङ्कते लोकस्ततः सृष्टिश्च संहृतिः ॥

इति ।

'मन्त्रा वर्णात्मकाः सर्वे सर्वे वर्णाः शिवात्मकाः ॥

इति च । तथा हि—चित्प्रकाशात् अव्यतिरिक्ता नित्योदितमहामन्त्ररूपा पूर्णाहंविमर्शमयी या इयं परा वाक्शक्तिः आदि-क्षान्त-रूपाशेषशक्तिचक्रगर्भिणी सा तावत् पश्यन्तीमध्यमादिक्रमेण ग्राहकभूमिकां भासयति । तत्र च परारूपत्वेन स्वरूपम् अप्रथयन्ती मायाप्रमातुः अस्फुटासाधारणार्थावभासरूपां प्रतिक्षण नवनवां विकल्पक्रियामुल्लासयति, शुद्धामपि च अविकल्पभूमिं तदाच्छादितामेव दर्शयति । तत्र च ब्राह्म्यादिदेवताधिष्ठितककारादिविचित्रशक्तिभिः व्यामोहितो देहप्राणादिमेव परिमितम् अवशम् आत्मानं मन्यते मूढजनः । ब्राह्म्यादिदेव्यः पशुदशायां भेदविषये सृष्टिस्थिती, अभेदविषये च संहारं प्रथयन्त्यः, परिमितविकल्पपात्रतामेव संपादयन्ति; पतिदशायां तु भेदे संहारम् अभेदे च

सर्गस्थिती प्रकटयन्त्यः, क्रमात्क्रमं विकल्पनिर्ह्रासनेन श्रीमद्भैरवमुद्रानुप्रवेशमयीं महतीम् अविकल्पभूमिमेव उन्मीलयन्ति ।

'सर्वो ममायं विभव इत्येवं परिजानतः ।
विश्वात्मनो विकल्पानां प्रसरेऽपि महेशता ॥'

इत्यादिरूपां चिदानन्दावेशमग्नां शुद्धविकल्पशक्तिम् उल्लासयन्ति ततः उक्तनीत्या स्वशक्तिव्यामोहिततैव संसारित्वम् ।

किंच चितिशक्तिरेव भगवती विश्ववमनात् संसारवामाचारत्वाच्च वामेश्वर्याख्या सती, खेचरी-गोचरी-दिक्चरी-भूचरीरूपैः अशेषैः प्रमातृ-अन्तःकरणबहिष्करण-भावस्वभावैः परिस्फुरन्ती, पशुभूमिकायां शून्यपदविश्रान्ता किंचित्कर्तृत्वाद्यात्मक-कलादिशक्त्यात्मना खेचरीचक्रेण गोपितपारमार्थिक-चिद्गगनचरीत्वस्वरूपेण चकास्ति; भेदनिश्चयाभिमान-विकल्पनप्रधानान्तः-करणदेवीरूपेण गोचरीचक्रेण गोपिताभेदनिश्चयाद्यात्मकपारमार्थिकस्वरूपेण प्रकाशते; भेदालोचनादिप्रधानबहिष्करणदेवतात्मना च दिक्चरीचक्रेण गोपिताभेदप्रथात्मकपारमार्थिकस्वरूपेण स्फुरति; सर्वतो व्यवच्छिन्नाभास-स्वभावप्रमेयात्मना च भूचरीचक्रेण गोपितसार्वात्म्यस्वरूपेण पशुहृदयव्यामोहिना भाति । पतिभूमिकायां तु सर्वकर्तृत्वादिशक्त्यात्मकचिद्गगनचरीत्वेन, अभेदनिश्चयाद्यात्मना गोचरीत्वेन, अभेदालोचनाद्यात्मना दिक्चरीत्वेन, स्वाङ्गकल्पाद्वयप्रथासारप्रमेयात्मना च भूचरीत्वेन पतिहृदयविकासिना स्फुरति । तथा च उक्तं सहजचमत्कारपरिजनिताकृतकादरेण भट्टदामोदरेण विमुक्तकेषु-

'पूर्णाविच्छिन्नमात्रान्तर्बहिष्करणभावगाः ।
वामेशाद्याः परिज्ञानाज्ञानात्स्युर्मुक्तिबन्धदाः ॥'

इति एवं च निजशक्तिव्यामोहिततैव संसारित्वम् ।

अपि च चिदात्मनः परमेश्वरस्य स्वा अनपायिनी एकैव स्फुरत्तासार-कर्तृतात्मा ऐश्वर्यशक्तिः । सा यदा स्वरूपं गोपयित्वा पाशवे पदे प्राणापान-समान-शक्तिदशाभिः जाग्रत्स्वप्न-सुषुप्तभूमिभिः देहप्राण-पुर्यष्टककला-भिश्च व्यामोहयति, तदा तद्व्यामोहितता संसारित्वम्; यदा तु मध्यधामोल्लासाम्

उदानशक्तिं, विश्वव्याप्तिसारां च व्यानशक्तिं, तुर्यदशारूपां तुर्यातीतदशारूपां च चिदानन्दघनाम् उन्मीलयति तदा देहाद्यवस्थायामपि पतिदशात्मा जीवन्मुक्तिर्भवति । एवं त्रिधा स्वशक्तिव्यामोहितता व्याख्याता । 'चिद्वत्' इति (६) सूत्रे चित्प्रकाशो गृहीतसंकोचः संसारी इत्युक्तम्, इह तु स्वशक्तिव्यामोहितत्वेन अस्य संसारित्वं भवति,—इति भङ्ग्यन्तरेण उक्तम् । एवं संकुचितशक्तिः प्राणादिमानपि यदा स्वशक्तिव्यामोहितो न भवति तदा अयम्

'…………शरीरी परमेश्वरः ।'

इत्याम्नायस्थित्या शिवभट्टारक एव,—इति भङ्ग्या निरूपितं भवति । यदागमः

'मनुष्यदेहमास्थाय छन्नास्ते परमेश्वराः ।

इति । उक्तं च प्रत्यभिज्ञाटीकायाम्

'शरीरमेव घटाद्यपि वा ये षट्त्रिंशत्तत्त्वमयं शिवरूपतया पश्यन्ति तेऽपि सिध्यन्ति'

इति ॥ १२ ॥

उक्तसूत्रार्थप्रातिपक्ष्येण तत्त्वदृष्टिं दर्शयितुमाह

तत्परिज्ञाने चित्तमेव अन्तर्मुखीभावेन चेतनपदाध्यारोहात् चितिः ॥१३॥

पूर्वसूत्रव्याख्याप्रसङ्गेन प्रमेयदृष्ट्या वितत्य व्याख्यातप्रायमेतत् सूत्रम्; शब्दसंगत्या तु अधुना व्याख्यायते । 'तस्य' आत्मीयस्य पञ्चकृत्यकारित्वस्य 'परिज्ञाने' सति अपरिज्ञानलक्षणकारणापगमात् स्वशक्तिव्यामोहिततानिवृत्तौ स्वातन्त्र्यलाभात् प्राक् व्याख्यातं यत् 'चित्तं' तदेव संकोचिनीं बहिर्मुखतां जहत्, 'अन्तर्मुखीभावेन चेतनपदाध्यारोहात्'—ग्राहकभूमिकाक्रमणक्रमेण संकोचकलाया अपि विगलनेन स्वरूपापत्त्या 'चितिर्' भवति; स्वां चिन्मयीं परां भूमिमाविशति इत्यर्थः ॥ १३ ॥

ननु यदि पारमार्थिकं चिच्छक्तिपदं सकलभेदकवलनस्वभावं, तत् अस्य

मायापदेऽपि तथारूपेण भवितव्यं यथा जलदाच्छादितस्यापि भानोः भावावभासकत्वम् । इत्याशङ्क्य आह—

चितिवह्निरवरोहपदे छन्नोऽपि मात्रया
मेयेन्धनं प्लुष्यति ॥ १४ ॥

'चितिरेव' विश्वग्रसनशीलत्वात् 'वह्निः'; असौ एव 'अवरोहपदे'—मायाप्रमातृतायां 'छन्नोऽपि'—स्वातन्त्र्यात् आच्छादितस्वभावोऽपि, भूरिभूतिच्छन्नाग्निवत् 'मात्रया'—अंशेन, नीलपीतादिप्रमेयेन्धनं 'प्लुष्यति'—स्वात्मसात्करोति । मात्रापदस्य इदम् आकूतम्—यत् कवलयन् अपि सार्वात्म्येन न ग्रसते, अपि तु अंशेन; संस्कारात्मना उत्थापयति । ग्रासकत्वं च सर्वप्रमातॄणां स्वानुभवत एव सिद्धम् । यदुक्तं श्रीमदुत्पलदेवपादैः निजस्तोत्रेषु

'वर्तन्ते जन्तवोऽशेषा अपि ब्रह्मेन्द्रविष्णवः ।
ग्रसमानास्ततो वन्दे देव विश्वं भवन्मयम् ॥

इति ॥ १४ ॥

यदा पुनः करणेश्वरीप्रसरसंकोचं संपाद्य सर्गसंहारक्रमपरिशीलनयुक्तिम् आविशति तदा

बललाभे विश्वमात्मसात्करोति ॥ १५ ॥

चितिरेव देहप्राणाद्याच्छादननिमज्जनेन स्वरूपम् उन्मग्नत्वेन स्फारयन्ती बलम्; यथोक्तं

'तदाक्रम्य बलं मन्त्राः ··· ··· ।

इति । एवं च 'बललाभे'—उन्मग्नस्वरूपाश्रयणे क्षित्यादि-सदाशिवान्तं 'विश्वम् आत्मसात् करोति'—स्वस्वरूपाभेदेन निर्भासयति । तदुक्तं पूर्वगुरुभिः स्वभाषामयेषु क्रमसूत्रेषु

'यथा वह्निरुद्बोधितो दाह्यं दहति, तथा विषयपाशान् भक्षयेत्'

इति ।

'न चैवं वक्तव्यम्—विश्वात्मसात्काररूपा समावेशभूः कादाचित्की। कथम् उपादेया इयं स्यात् इति; यतो देहाद्युन्मज्जननिमज्जनवशेन इदम् अस्याः कादाचित्कत्वम् इव आभाति। वस्तुतस्तु चितिस्वातन्त्र्याव-भासितदेहाद्युन्मज्जनात् एव कादाचित्कत्वम्। एषा तु सदैव प्रकाशमाना; अन्यथा तत् देहादि अपि न प्रकाशेत। अत एव देहादिप्रमातृताभिमाननिमज्जनाय अभ्यासः, न तु सदा प्रथमानतासारप्रमातृता-प्राप्त्यर्थम्,

इति श्रीप्रत्यभिज्ञाकाराः ॥ १५ ॥

एवं च

चिदानन्दलाभे देहादिषु चेत्यमानेष्वपि चिदैकात्म्य-प्रतिपत्तिदार्ढ्यं जीवन्मुक्तिः ॥ १६ ॥

विश्वात्मसात्कारात्मनि समावेशरूपे 'चिदानन्दे लब्धे' व्युत्थानदशायां बलकल्पतया देहप्राणनीलसुखादिषु आभासमानेषु अपि, यत्समावेशसंस्कारबलात् प्रतिपादयिष्यमाणयुक्तिक्रमोपबृंहितात् 'चिदैकात्म्यप्रतिपत्तिदार्ढ्यम्'—अविचला, चिदेकत्वप्रथा, सैव 'जीवन्मुक्तिः'—जीवतः प्राणान् अपि धारयतो मुक्तिः; प्रत्यभिज्ञातनिजस्वरूपविद्रावितशेषपाशराशित्वात्। यथोक्तं स्पन्दशास्त्रे

'इति वा यस्य संवित्तिः क्रीडात्वेनाखिलं जगत्।
स पश्यन्सततं युक्तो जीवन्मुक्तो न संशयः॥'

इति ॥ १६ ॥

अथ कथं चिदानन्दलाभो भवति? इत्याह—

मध्यविकासाच्चिदानन्दलाभः ॥ १७ ॥

सर्वान्तरतमत्वेन वर्तमानत्वात् तद्भित्तिलग्नतां विना च कस्यचित् अपि स्वरूपानुपपत्तेः संविदेव भगवती 'मध्यम्'। सा तु मायादशायां तथाभूतापि स्वरूपं गूहयित्वा

'प्राक् संवित्प्राणे परिणता'

इति नीत्या प्राणशक्तिभूमिं स्वीकृत्य, अवरोहक्रमेण बुद्धिदेहादि-भवम् अधिशयाना, नाडीसहस्रसरणिम् अनुसृता । तत्रापि च पलाश-पर्णमध्यशाखान्यायेन आब्रह्मरन्ध्रात् अधोवक्त्रपर्यन्तं प्राणशक्तिब्रह्माश्रय-मध्यमनाडीरूपतया प्राधान्येन स्थिता; तत एव सर्ववृत्तीनाम् उदयात्, तत्रैव च विश्रामात् । एवंभूतापि एषा पशूनां निमीलितस्वरूपैव स्थिता । यदा तु उक्तयुक्तिक्रमेण सर्वान्तरतमत्वे मध्यभूता संविद्भगवती विकसति, यदि वा वक्ष्यमाणक्रमेण मध्यभूता ब्रह्मनाडी विकसति, तदा 'तद्विकासात् चिदानन्दस्य' उक्तरूपस्य 'लाभः'—प्राप्तिर्भवति । ततश्च प्रागुक्ता जीवन्मुक्तिः ॥ १७ ॥

मध्यविकासे युक्तिमाह

विकल्पक्षय-शक्तिसंकोचविकास-वाहच्छेदाद्यन्तकोटि-
निभालनादय इहोपायाः ॥ १८ ॥

'इह मध्यशक्तिविकासे 'विकल्पक्षयादय उपायाः' । प्रागुपदिष्ट-पञ्चविधकृत्यकारित्वाद्यनुसरणेन सर्वमध्यभूतायाः संविदो विकासो जायते—इति अभिहितप्रायम् । उपायान्तरम् अपि तु उच्यते;—प्राणायाम-मुद्राबन्धादिसमस्तयन्त्रणातन्त्रत्रोटनेन सुखोपायमेव, हृदये निहित-चित्तः, उक्तयुक्त्या स्वस्थितिप्रतिबन्धकं विकल्पम् अकिंचिच्चिन्तकत्वेन प्रशमयन्, अविकल्पपरामर्शेन देहाद्यकलुषस्वचित्प्रमातृतानिभालनप्रवणः, अचिरादेव उन्मिषद्विकासां तुर्यतुर्यातीतसमावेशदशाम् आसादयति । यथोक्तम्—

'विकल्पहानेनैकाग्र्यात्क्रमेणेश्वरतापदम् ।'

इति श्रीप्रत्यभिज्ञायाम् । श्रीस्पन्देऽपि

'यदा क्षोभः प्रलीयेत तदा स्यात्परमं पदम् ॥'

इति । श्रीज्ञागर्भेऽपि

'विहाय सकलाः क्रिया जननि मानसीः सर्वतो
विमुक्तकरणक्रियानुसृतिपारतन्त्र्योज्ज्वलम् ।
स्थितैस्त्वदनुभावतः सपदि वेद्यते सा परा
दशा नृभिरतन्द्रितासमसुखामृतस्यन्दिनी ॥'

इति । अयं च उपायो मूर्धन्यत्वात् प्रत्यभिज्ञायां प्रतिपादितत्वात् आदौ उक्तः । शक्तिसंकोचादयस्तु यद्यपि प्रत्यभिज्ञायां न प्रतिपादिताः, तथापि आम्नायिकत्वात् अस्माभिः प्रसङ्गात् प्रदर्श्यन्ते; बहुषु हि प्रदर्शितेषुकश्चित् केनचित् प्रवेक्ष्यति इति ।

'शक्तेः संकोच'—इन्द्रियद्वारेण प्रसरन्त्या एव आकुञ्चनक्रमेण उन्मुखीकरणम् । यथोक्तम् आथर्वणिकोपनिषत्सु कठवल्ल्यां चतुर्थवल्लीप्रथम-मन्त्रे ।

'पराञ्चि खानि व्यतृणत्स्वयंभू-
स्तस्मात्पराङ् पश्यति नान्तरात्मन् ।
कश्चिद्धीरः प्रत्यगात्मानमैक्षद्
आवृत्तचक्षुरमृतत्वमश्नन् ॥'

इति । प्रसृताया अपि वा कूर्माङ्गसंकोचवत् त्राससमये हृत्प्रवेशवच्च सर्वतो निवर्तनम् । यथोक्तम्

'तदपोद्धृते नित्योदितस्थितिः ।'

इति ।

'शक्तेर्विकासः, अन्तर्निगूढाया अक्रममेव सकलकरणचक्र-विस्फारणेन

'अन्तर्लक्ष्यो बहिर्दृष्टिर्निमेषोन्मेषवर्जितः ।'

इति । भैरवीयमुद्रानुप्रवेशयुक्त्या बहिः प्रसरणम् । यथोक्तं कक्ष्यास्तोत्रे

'सर्वाः शक्तीश्चेतसा दर्शनाद्याः
स्वे स्वे वेद्ये यौगपद्येन विष्वक् ।

क्षिप्त्वा मध्ये हाटकस्तम्भभूत-
स्तिष्ठन्विश्वाधार एकोऽवभासि ॥'

इति । श्रीभट्टकल्लटेनापि उक्तम्

'रूपादिषु परिणामात् तत्सिद्धिः ।'

इति शक्तेश्च संकोचविकासौ, नासापुटस्पन्दनक्रमोन्मिषत्सूक्ष्मप्राणशक्त्या भ्रूभेदनेन क्रमासादितोर्ध्वकुण्डलिनीपदे प्रसरविश्रान्ति-दशापरिशीलनम्; अधःकुण्डलिन्यां च षष्ठवक्त्ररूपायां प्रगुणीकृत्य शक्तिं, तन्मूल-तदग्र-तन्मध्यभूमिस्पर्शावेशः । यथोक्तं विज्ञानभट्टारके

'वह्नेर्विषस्य मध्ये तु चित्तं सुखमयं क्षिपेत् ।
केवलं वायुपूर्णं वा स्मरानन्देन युज्यते ॥'

इति । अत्र वह्निः अनुप्रवेशक्रमेण संकोचभूः, विषस्थानम् प्रसरयुक्त्या विकासपदम्, 'विष्लृ व्याप्तौ' इति अर्थानुगमात् ।

'बाह्योः'—वामदक्षिणगतयोः प्राणापानयोः 'छेदो'—हृदय-विश्रान्ति-पुरःसरम् अन्तः ककारहकारादिप्रायानच्कवर्णोच्चारेण विच्छेदनम् । यथोक्तं ज्ञानगर्भे

'अनच्कककृतायतिप्रसृतपार्श्वनाडीद्वय-
च्छिदो विधृतचेतसो हृदयपङ्कजस्योदरे ।
उदेति तव दारितान्धतमसः स विद्याङ्कुरो
य एष परमेशतां जनयितुं पशोरप्यलम् ॥

इति ।

'आदिकोटिः' हृदयम्, 'अन्तकोटिः' द्वादशान्तः; तयोः प्राणोल्लास-विश्रान्त्यवसरे 'निभालनं'—चित्तनिवेशनेन परिशीलनम् । यथोक्तं विज्ञानभैरवे

'हृद्याकाशे निलीनाक्षः पद्मसंपुटमध्यगः ।
अनन्यचेताः सुभगे परं सौभाग्यमाप्नुयात् ॥'

इति । तथा

'यथा तथा यत्र तत्र द्वादशान्ते मनः क्षिपेत् ।
प्रतिक्षणं क्षीणवृत्तेर्वैलक्षण्यं दिनैर्भवेत् ॥'

इति । आविपदात् उन्मेषदशानिषेवणम् । यथोक्तम्

'उन्मेषः स तु विज्ञेयः स्वयं तमुपलक्षयेत् ॥'

इति स्पन्दे । तथा रमणीयविषयचर्वणादयश्च संगृहीताः । यथोक्तं श्रीविज्ञानभैरवे एव

'जग्धिपानकृतोल्लासरसानन्दविजृम्भणात् ।
भावयेद्भरितावस्थां महानन्दमयो भवेत् ॥
गीतादिविषयास्वादासमसौख्यैकतात्मनः ।
योगिनस्तन्मयत्वेन मनोरूढेस्तदात्मता ।
यत्र यत्र मनस्तुष्टिर्मनस्तत्रैव धारयेत् ।
तत्र तत्र परानन्दस्वरूपं संप्रकाशते ॥'

इति । एवंमन्यदपि आनन्दपूर्णस्वात्मभावनादिकम् अनुमन्तव्यम् । इत्येवमादयः अत्र मध्यविकासे उपायाः ॥ १८ ॥

मध्यविकासाच्चिदानन्दलाभः, स एव च परमयोगिनः समावेशसमापत्त्याविपर्यायः समाधिः, तस्य नित्योदितत्वे युक्तिमाह—

समाधिसंस्कारवति व्युत्थाने भूयो भूयश्चिदैक्यामर्शान्नित्योदितसमाधिलाभः ॥ १९ ॥

आसादितसमावेशो योगिवरो व्युत्थाने अपि समाधिरससंस्कारेण क्षीव इव सानन्दं घूर्णमानो, भावराशिं शरदभ्रलवम् इव चिद्गगन एव लीयमानं पश्यन्, भूयो भूयः अन्तर्मुखताम् एव समवलम्बमानो, निमीलनसमाधिक्रमेण चिदैक्यमेव विमृशन् व्युत्थानाभिमतावसरे अपि समाध्येकरस एव भवति । यथोक्तं क्रमसूत्रेषु

'क्रममुद्रया अन्तःस्वरूपया बहिर्मुखः समाविष्टो
भवति साधकः । तत्रादौ बाह्यात् अन्तः प्रवेशः,

आभ्यन्तरात् बाह्यस्वरूपे प्रवेशः आवेशवशात्
जायते;—इति सबाह्याभ्यन्तरोऽयं मुद्राक्रमः'

इति । अत्रायमर्थः सृष्टि-स्थिति-संहृतिसंविच्चक्रात्मकं क्रमं मुद्रयति, स्वाधिष्ठितम् आत्मसात् करोति येयं तुरीया चितिशक्तिः, तया 'क्रममुद्रया'; 'अन्तरिति'—पूर्णाहन्तास्वरूपया; 'बहिर्मुख'—इति, विषयेषु व्यापृतः अपि; 'समाविष्टः'—साक्षात्कृतपरशक्तिस्फारः 'साधकः'—परमयोगी भवति । तत्र च 'बाह्याद्' ग्रस्यमानात् विषयग्रामात् 'अन्तः' परस्यां चितिभूमौ, प्रसनक्रमेणैव 'प्रवेशः'—समावेशो भवति । 'आभ्यन्तरात्' चितिशक्तिस्वरूपात् च साक्षात्कृतात् 'आवेशवशात्'—समावेशसामर्थ्यात् एव 'बाह्यस्वरूपे'—इदन्तानिर्भासे विषयग्रामे, वमनयुक्त्या 'प्रवेशः'—चिद्रसाश्यानताप्रथनात्मा समावेशो जायते;—इति 'सबाह्याभ्यन्तरः अयं' नित्योदितसमावेशात्मा 'मुदो'—हर्षस्य वितरणात्, परमानंदस्वरूपत्वात्, पाशद्रावणात्, विश्वस्य अन्तः तुरीयसत्तायां मुद्रणात् च मुद्रात्मा, क्रमः अपि सृष्ट्यादिक्रमाभासकत्वात् तत्क्रमाभासरूपत्वात् च 'क्रम' इति अभिधीयते इति ॥ १९ ॥

इदानीम् अस्य समाधिलाभस्य फलमाह

तदा प्रकाशानन्दसारमहामन्त्रवीर्यात्मकपूर्णाहन्तावेशात्सदा
सर्वसर्गसंहारकारिनिजसंविद्देवताचक्रेश्वरताप्राप्ति-
र्भवतीति शिवम् ॥ २० ॥

नित्योदिते समाधौ लब्धे सति, 'प्रकाशानन्दसारा'—चिदाह्लादैकघना 'महती मन्त्रवीर्यात्मिका'—सर्वमन्त्रजीवितभूता 'पूर्णा' पराभट्टारिकारूपा या इयम् 'अहन्ता'—अकृत्रिमः स्वात्मचमत्कारः, तत्र 'आवेशात्' 'सदा' कालाग्न्यादेः चरमकलापर्यन्तस्य विश्वस्य यौ 'सर्गसंहारौ'—विचित्रौ सृष्टिप्रलयौ 'तत्कारि' यत् 'निजं संविद्देवताचक्रं' 'तदैश्वर्यस्य' 'प्राप्तिः'—आसादनं 'भवति' प्राकरणिकस्य परमयोगिन इत्यर्थः; 'इति' एतत् सर्वं शिवस्वरूपमेव इति उपसंहारः—इति संगतिः । तत्र यावत् इदं किंचित् संवेद्यते, तस्य संवेदनमेव स्वरूपं; तस्यापि अन्तर्मुखविमर्शमयाः प्रमातारः तत्त्वम्; तेषामपि विगलितदेहाद्युपाधिसंकोचाभिमाना अशेषशरीरा सदाशिवेश्वरतैव सारम्; अस्या अपि प्रकाशैकसद्भावापादिताशेषविश्वचमत्कारमयः श्रीमान् महेश्वर

एव परमार्थः;—नहि पारमार्थिक-प्रकाशावेशं विना कस्यापि प्रकाशमानता घटते—स च परमेश्वरः स्वातन्त्र्यसारत्वात् आदि-क्षान्तामायीयशब्दराशि-परामर्शमयत्वेनैव एतत्स्वीकृतसमस्तवाच्य-वाचकमयाशेषजगदानन्दसद्भावा-पादनात् परं परिपूर्णत्वात् सर्वाकाङ्क्षाशून्यतया आनन्दप्रसरनिर्भरः; अत एव अनुत्तराकुलस्वरूपात् अकारात् आरभ्य शक्तिस्फाररूपहकलापर्यन्तं यत् विश्वं प्रसृतं, क्षकारस्य प्रसरशमनरूपत्वात्; तत् अकार-हकाराभ्यामेव संपुटीकारयुक्त्या प्रत्याहारन्यायेन अन्तः स्वीकृतं सत् अविभागवेदनात्मक-बिन्दुरूपतया स्फुरितम् अनुत्तर एव विश्राम्यति;—इति शब्दराशिस्वरूप एव अयम् अकृतको विमर्शः। यथोक्तं

'प्रकाशस्यात्मविश्रान्तिरहंभावो हि कीर्तितः।
उक्ता च सैव विश्रान्तिःसर्वापेक्षानिरोधतः॥
स्वातन्त्र्यमथ कर्तृत्वं मुख्यमीश्वरतापि च।'

इति। एषैव च अहन्ता सर्वमन्त्राणाम् उदयविश्रान्तिस्थानत्वात् एतद्बलेनैव च तत्तदर्थक्रियाकारित्वात् महती वीर्यभूमिः। तदुक्तम्

'तदाक्रम्य बलं मन्त्राः ··· ···।'

इत्यादि

··· ··· त एते शिवधर्मिणः॥'

इत्यन्तम् श्रीस्पन्दे। शिवसूत्रेषु अपि

'महाह्रदानुसंधानान्मन्त्रवीर्यानुभवः।' (१२२ सू०)

इति। तदत्र महामन्त्रवीर्यात्मिकायां पूर्णाहन्तायाम् 'आवेशो'—देहप्राणादि-निमज्जनात् तत्पदावाप्त्यवष्टम्भेन देहादीनां नीलादीनामपि तद्रसाप्लावनेन तन्मयीकरणम्। तथा हि—देहसुखनीलादि यत् किंचित् प्रथते, अध्यवसीयते, स्मर्यते, संकल्प्यते वा, तत्र सर्वत्रैव भगवती चितिशक्तिमयी प्रथा भित्तिभूतैव स्फुरति;—तदस्फुरणे कस्यापि अस्फुरणात् इति उक्तत्वात्। केवलं तथा स्फुरन्त्यपि सा तन्मायाशक्त्या अवभासितदेहनीलाद्युपरागदत्ताभिमानवशात् भिन्न-भिन्नस्वभावा इव भान्ती ज्ञानसंकल्पाध्यवसायादिरूपतया मायाप्रमातृभिः अभिमन्यते; वस्तुतस्तु एकैव असौ चितिशक्तिः। यथोक्तम्—

''या चैषा प्रतिभा तत्तत्पदार्थक्रमरूषिता ।
अक्रमानन्तचिद्रूपः प्रमाता स महेश्वरः ।।'

इति । तथा

'मायाशक्त्या विभोः सैव भिन्नसंवेद्यगोचरा ।
कथिता ज्ञानसंकल्पाध्यवसायादिनामभिः ।।'

इति। एवम् एषा सर्वदशासु एकैव चितिशक्तिः विजृम्भमाणा यदि तदनुप्रवेश-तदवष्टम्भयुक्त्या समासाद्यते, तत् तदावेशात् पूर्वोक्तयुक्त्या करणोन्मीलननिमीलनक्रमेण सर्वस्य सर्वमयत्वात् तत्तत्संहारादौ अपि 'सदा सर्वसर्गसंहारकारि' यत् 'सहजसंवित्तिदेवताचक्रम्'—अमायीयान्तर्बहिष्करण-मरीचिपुञ्जः, तत्र 'ईश्वरता'—साम्राज्यं परभैरवात्मता, तत्प्राप्तिः भवति परमयोगिनः । यथोक्तम्—

'यदा त्वेकत्र संरूढस्तदा तस्य लयोद्भवौ ।
नियच्छन्भोक्तृतामेति ततश्चक्रेश्वरो भवेत् ।।

इति । अत्र एकत्र इति

'एकत्रारोपयेत्सर्वम्··· ···।'

इति चित्सामान्यस्पन्दभूः उन्मेषात्मा व्याख्यातव्या । तस्य इति अनेन

'पुर्यष्टकेन संरुद्ध··· ···।'

इति उपक्रान्तं पुर्यष्टकम् एव परामृष्टव्यम्; न तु यथा विवरणकृतः 'एकत्र सूक्ष्मे स्थूले शरीरे वा' इति व्याकृतवन्तः । स्तुतं च मया

'स्वतन्त्रश्चितिचक्राणां चक्रवर्ती महेश्वरः ।
संवित्तिदेवताचक्रजुष्टः कोऽपि जयत्यसौ ।।

इति । इतिशब्द उपसंहारे, यत् एतावत् उक्तप्रकरणशरीरं तत् सर्वं 'शिवम्—शिवप्राप्तिहेतुत्वात् शिवात् प्रसृतत्वात् शिवस्वरूपाभिन्नत्वात् च शिवमयमेव

इति शिवम् ॥

देहप्राणसुखादिभिः प्रतिकलं संरुध्यमानो जनः
पूर्णानन्दघनामिमां न चिनुते माहेश्वरीं स्वां चितिम् ।
मध्येबोधसुधाब्धि विश्वमभितस्तत्फेनपिण्डोपमं
यः पश्येदुपदेशतस्तु कथितः साक्षात्स एकः शिवः ॥

येषां वृत्तः शांकरः शक्तिपातो
येऽनभ्यासात्तीक्ष्णयुक्तिष्वयोग्याः ।
शक्ता ज्ञातुं नेश्वरप्रत्यभिज्ञा-
मुक्तस्तेषामेष तत्वोपदेशः ॥

समाप्तमिदं प्रत्यभिज्ञाहृदयम् ॥

कृतिस्तत्रभवन्महामाहेश्वराचार्यवर्यश्रीमदभिनवगुप्तपादपद्मोपजीविनः श्रीमतो राजानकक्षेमराजाचार्यस्य ॥

शुभमस्तु ॥